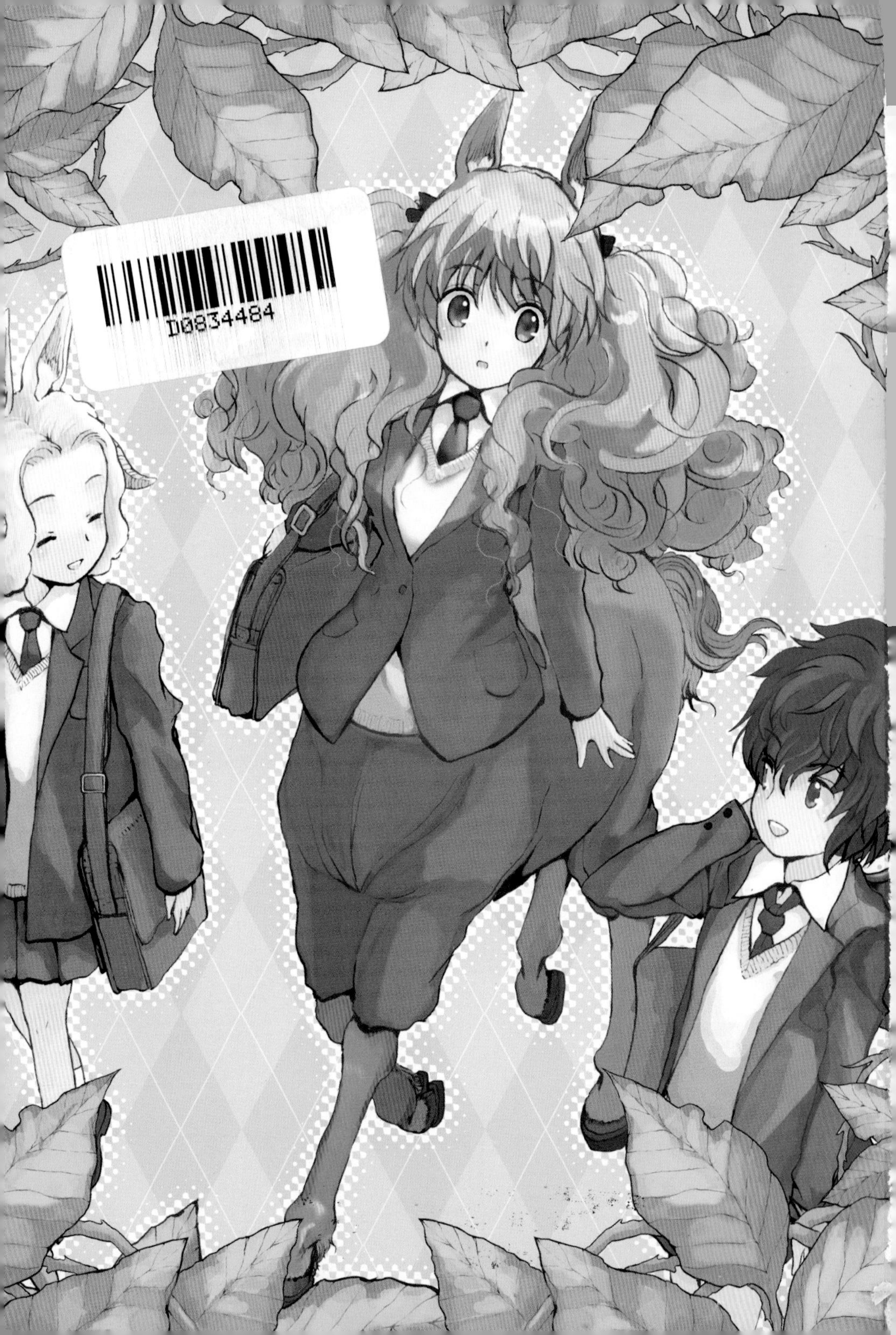

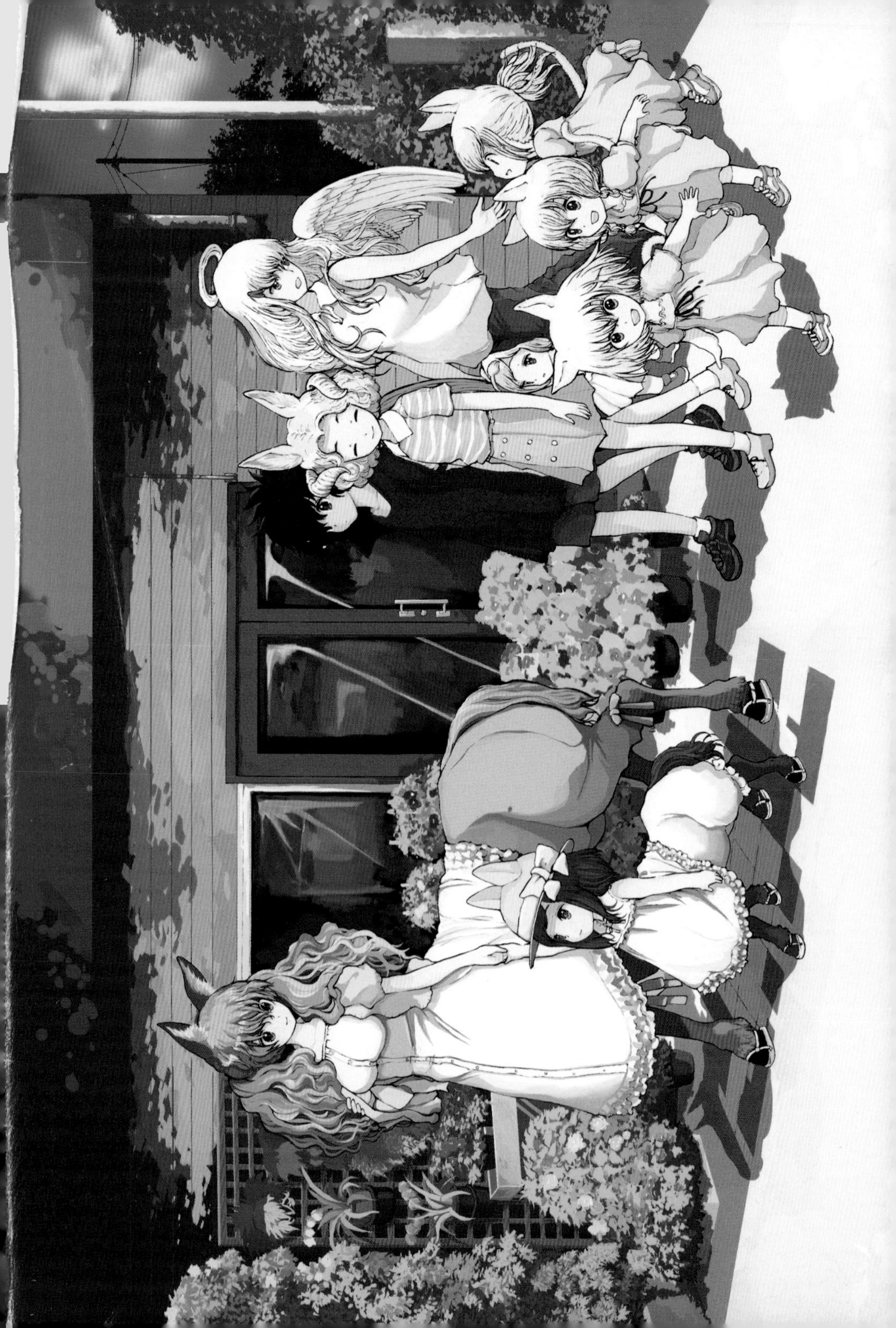

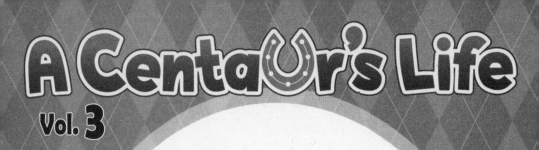

A Centaur's Life

Vol. 3

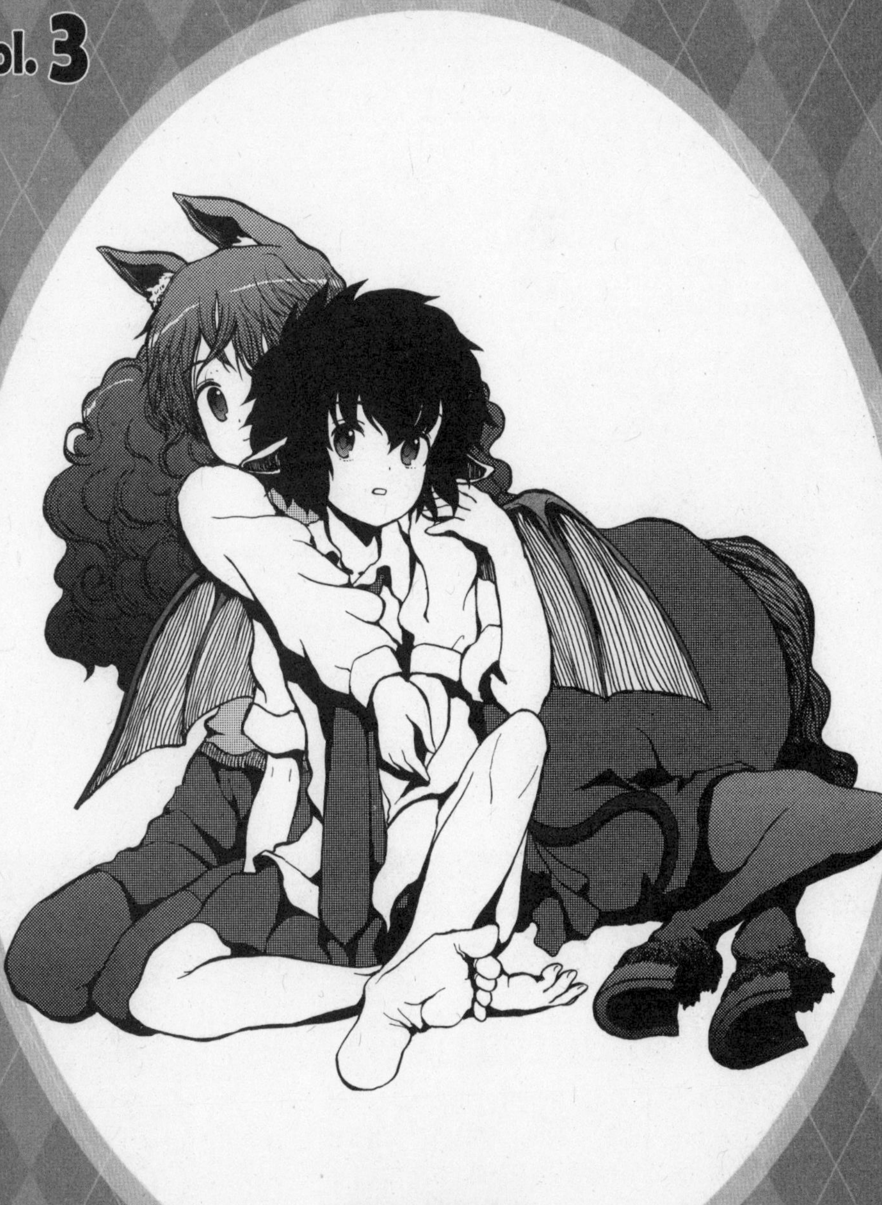

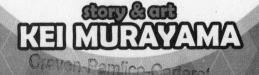

story & art
KEI MURAYAMA

SEVEN SEAS ENTERTAINMENT PRESENTS

A Centaur's Life

story and art by KEI MURAYAMA

VOLUME 3

TRANSLATION
Angela Liu

ADAPTATION
Holly Kolodziejczak

LETTERING AND LAYOUT
Jennifer Skarupa

LOGO DESIGN
Courtney Williams

COVER DESIGN
Nicky Lim

PROOFREADER
Lee Otter
Conner Crooks

MANAGING EDITOR
Adam Arnold

PUBLISHER
Jason DeAngelis

CENTAUR NO NAYAMI VOLUME 3
© KEI MURAYAMA 2012
Originally published in Japan in 2012 by TOKUMA SHOTEN PUBLISHING
CO., LTD., Tokyo. English translation rights arranged with TOKUMA SHOTEN
PUBLISHING CO., LTD., Tokyo, through TOHAN CORPORATION, Tokyo.

Seven Seas books may be purchased in bulk for educational, business, or
promotional use. For information on bulk purchases, please contact Macmillan
Corporate & Premium Sales Department at 1-800-221-7945 (ext 5442)
or write specialmarkets@macmillan.com.

Seven Seas and the Seven Seas logo are trademarks of
Seven Seas Entertainment, LLC. All rights reserved.

ISBN: 978-1-626920-33-0

Printed in Canada

First Printing: June 2014

10 9 8 7 6 5 4 3 2 1

FOLLOW US ONLINE: *www.gomanga.com*

READING DIRECTIONS

This book reads from *right to left*, Japanese style. If
this is your first time reading manga, you start
reading from the top right panel on each page and
take it from there. If you get lost, just follow the
numbered diagram here. It may seem backwards at
first, but you□ll get the hang of it! Have fun!!

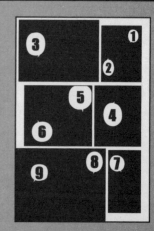

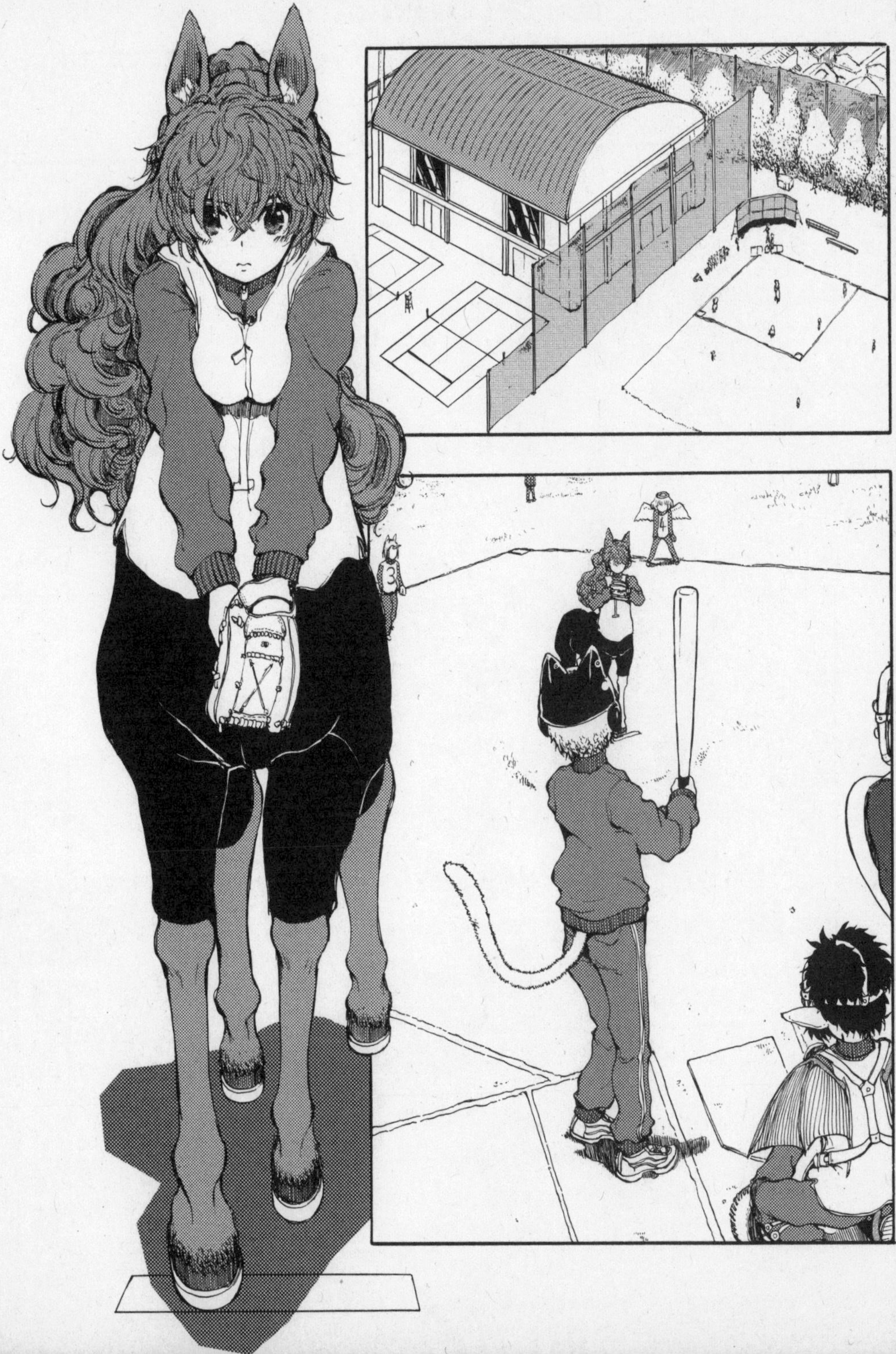

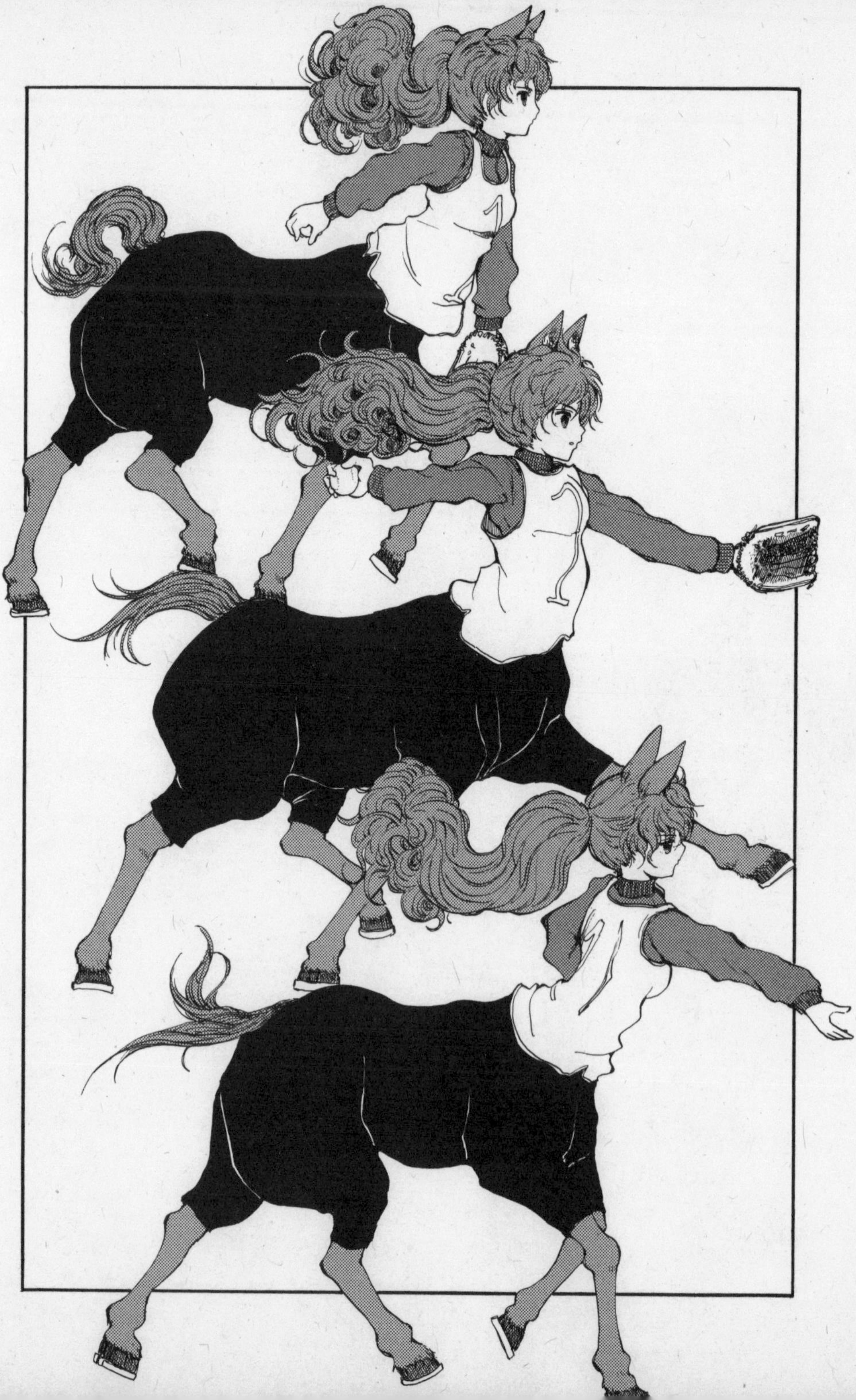

CHAPTER 9

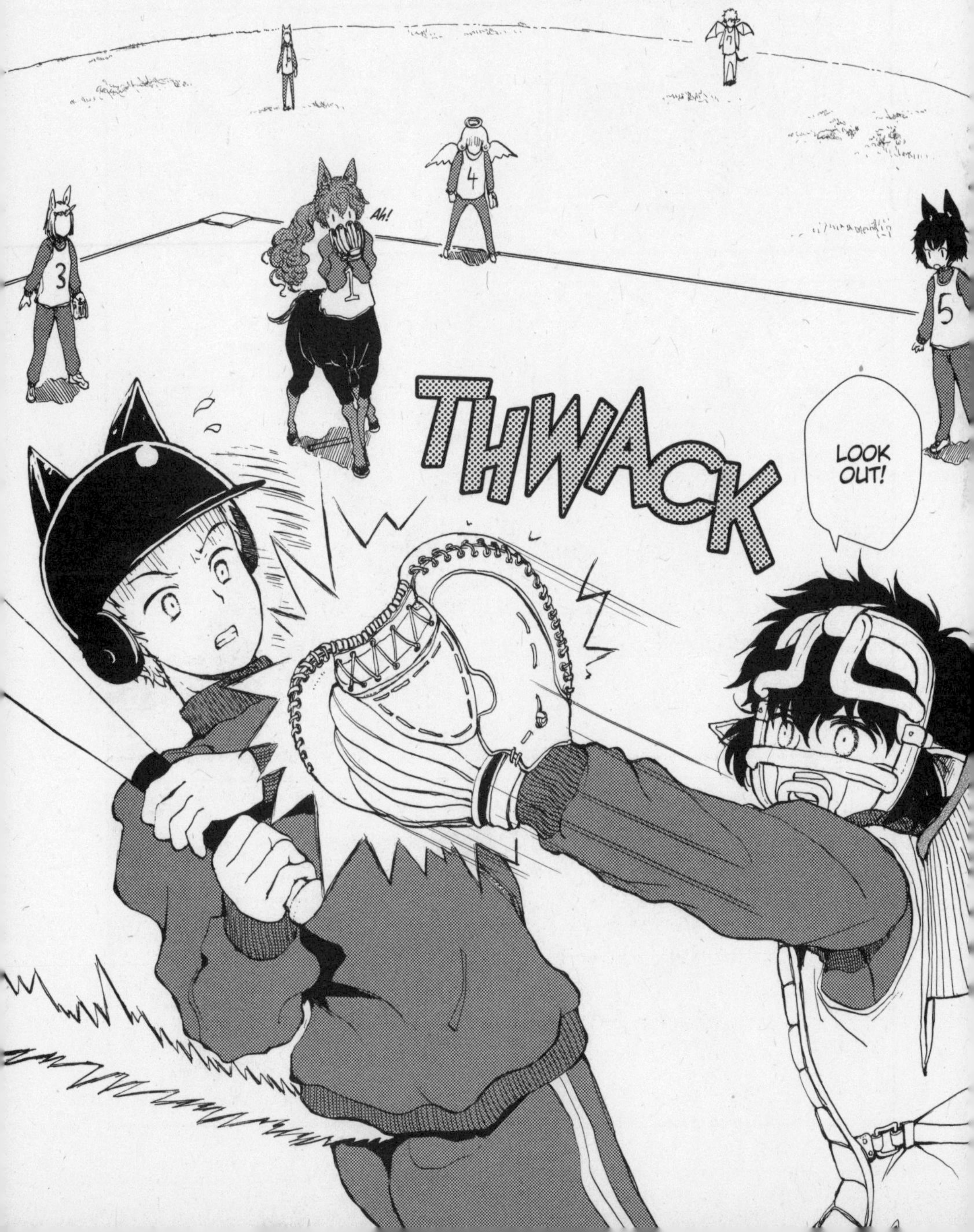
LOOK OUT!
THWACK
Ah!

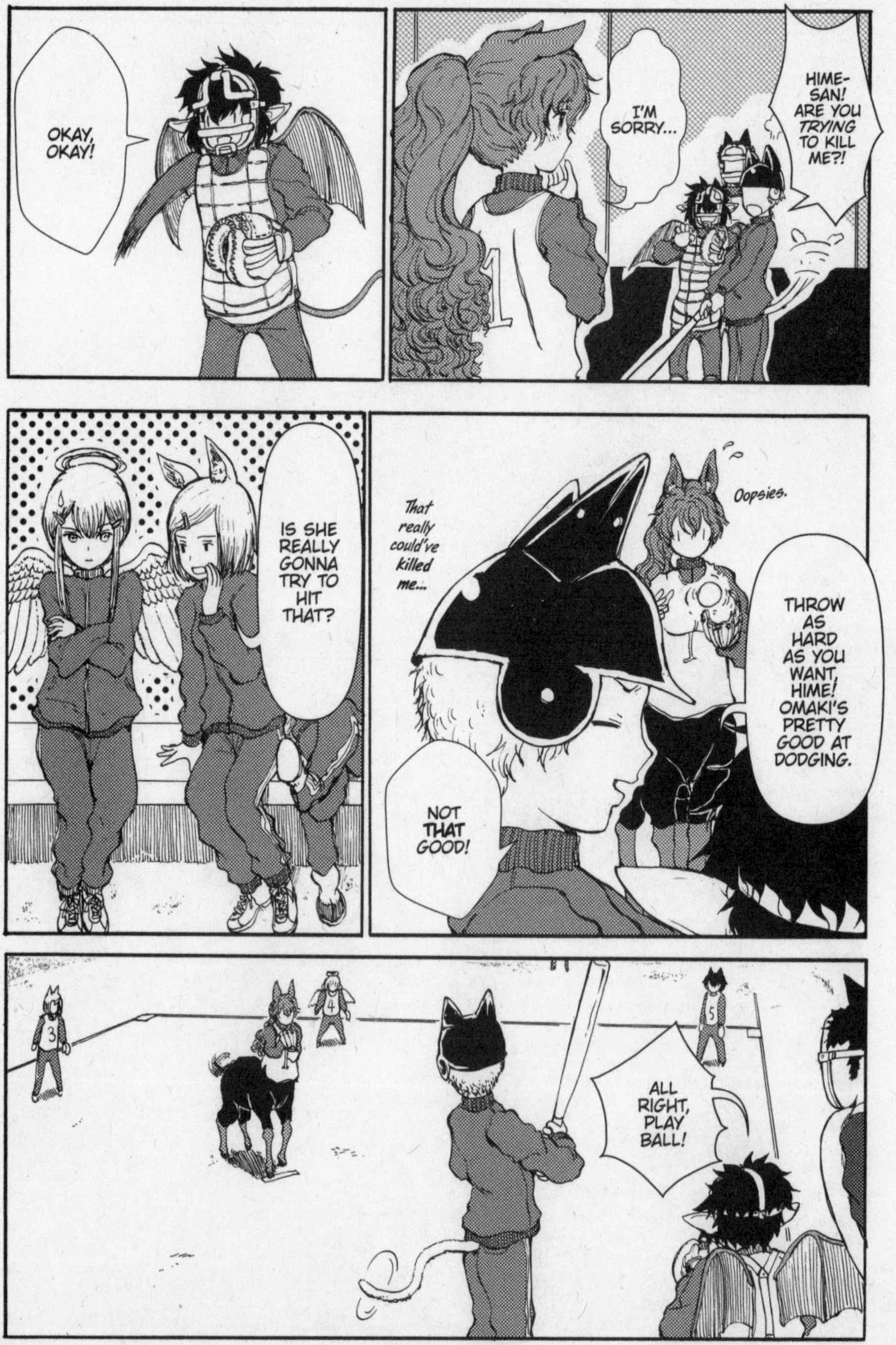
HIME-SAN! ARE YOU TRYING TO KILL ME?!
I'M SORRY...
OKAY, OKAY!
Oopsies.
THROW AS HARD AS YOU WANT, HIME! OMAKI'S PRETTY GOOD AT DODGING.
That really could've killed me...
NOT THAT GOOD!
IS SHE REALLY GONNA TRY TO HIT THAT?
ALL RIGHT, PLAY BALL!

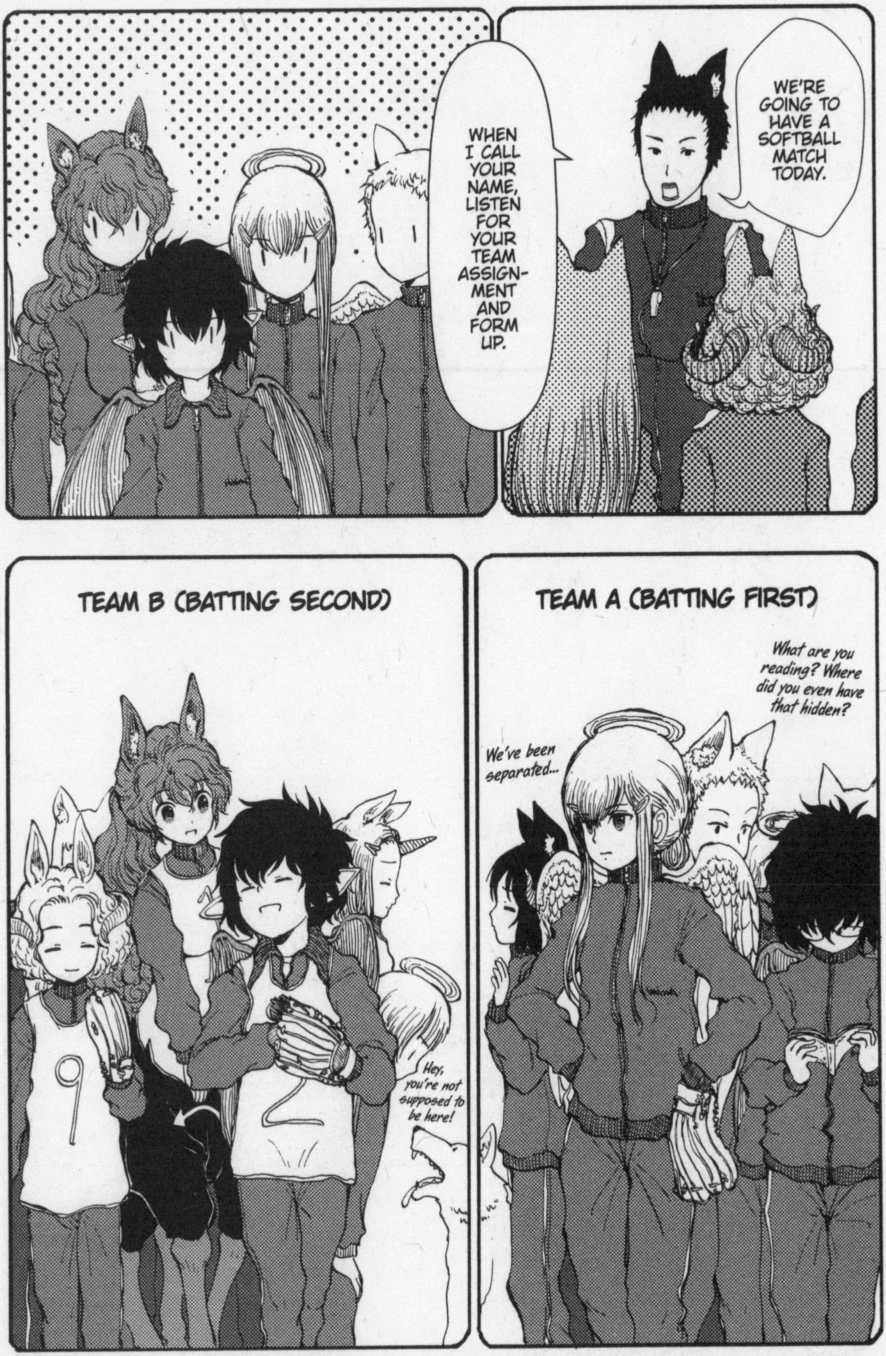
WE'RE GOING TO HAVE A SOFTBALL MATCH TODAY.
WHEN I CALL YOUR NAME, LISTEN FOR YOUR TEAM ASSIGNMENT AND FORM UP.
TEAM A (BATTING FIRST)
What are you reading? Where did you even have that hidden?
We've been separated...
TEAM B (BATTING SECOND)
Hey, you're not supposed to be here!

Class President
Ex-Softball Ace (Currently in Track/Sprinting)
Softball Club
Wind orchestra
Literary Club
Track/Shot-Putter
Kendo Club
Tea Club
Occult Research Club
THE TEAMS SEEM TO BE WELL BALANCED.
Gardening Club
Basketball Club
History Club
Lacrosse Club
Softball Club
Occult Research Club
Ex-Softball Club
Archery Club
Karate
YOU REALLY THINK THIS IS GONNA BE A DECENT MATCH?
NO MATTER WHAT BOYS SAY, THEY USUALLY HAVE **SOME** EXPERIENCE WITH BASEBALL.
Is there a position where I don't have to catch anything?
I've read some of Dokaben*. I think I know the basics.
BUT THE GIRLS WHO SAY THEY HAVE NO EXPERIENCE ARE TRULY **CLUELESS.**
WE'LL SHOOT FOR FOUR INNINGS AND STOP TEN MINUTES BEFORE THE END OF CLASS.
THE PITCHER WILL CHANGE EACH INNING.

*A play on popular 70's baseball manga Dokaben.

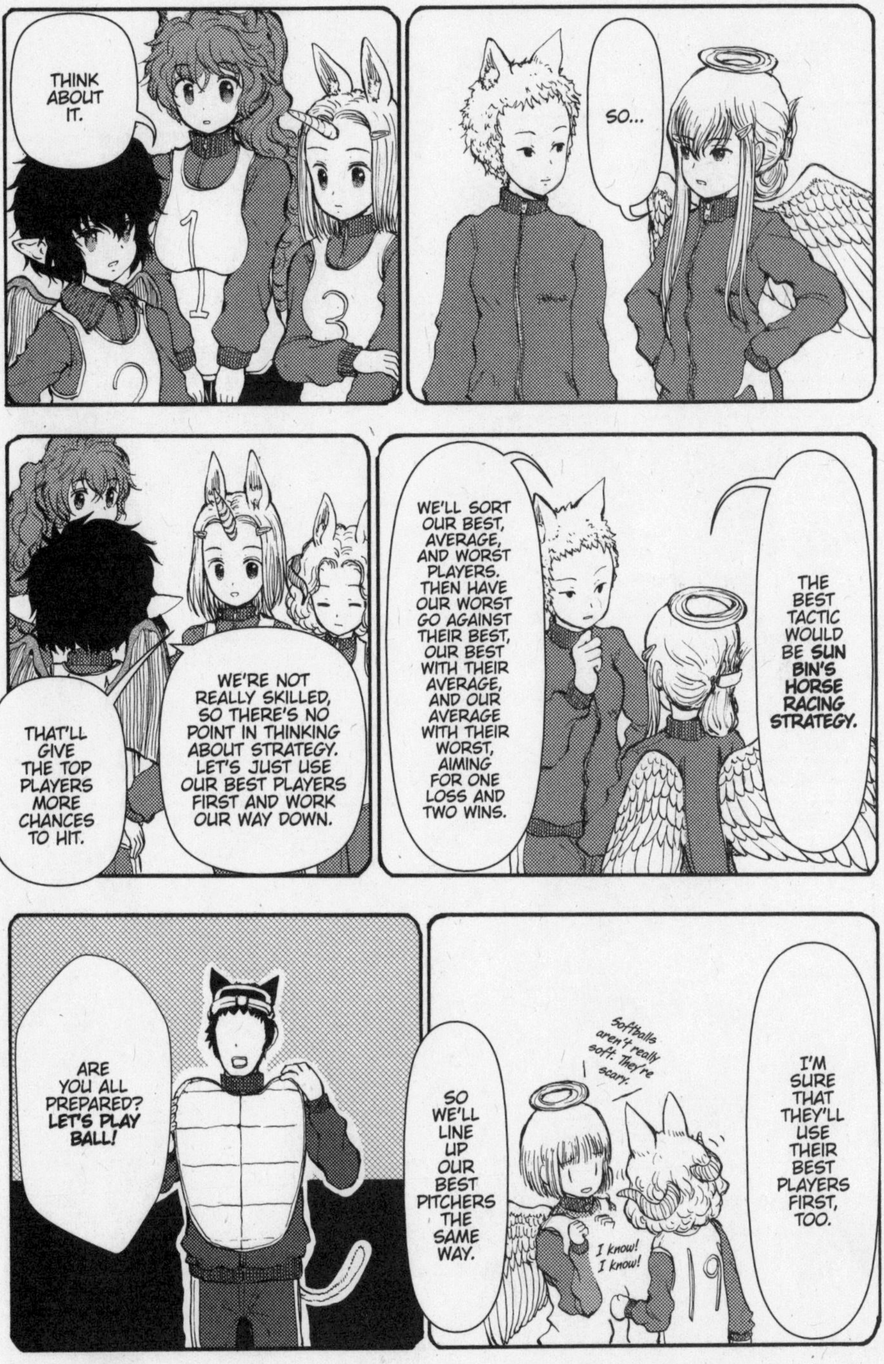
SO...
THINK ABOUT IT.
THE BEST TACTIC WOULD BE SUN BIN'S HORSE RACING STRATEGY.
WE'LL SORT OUR BEST, AVERAGE, AND WORST PLAYERS. THEN HAVE OUR WORST GO AGAINST THEIR BEST, OUR BEST WITH THEIR AVERAGE, AND OUR AVERAGE WITH THEIR WORST, AIMING FOR ONE LOSS AND TWO WINS.
WE'RE NOT REALLY SKILLED, SO THERE'S NO POINT IN THINKING ABOUT STRATEGY. LET'S JUST USE OUR BEST PLAYERS FIRST AND WORK OUR WAY DOWN.
THAT'LL GIVE THE TOP PLAYERS MORE CHANCES TO HIT.
I'M SURE THAT THEY'LL USE THEIR BEST PLAYERS FIRST, TOO.
Softballs aren't really soft. They're scary.
SO WE'LL LINE UP OUR BEST PITCHERS THE SAME WAY.
I know! I know!
ARE YOU ALL PREPARED? LET'S PLAY BALL!

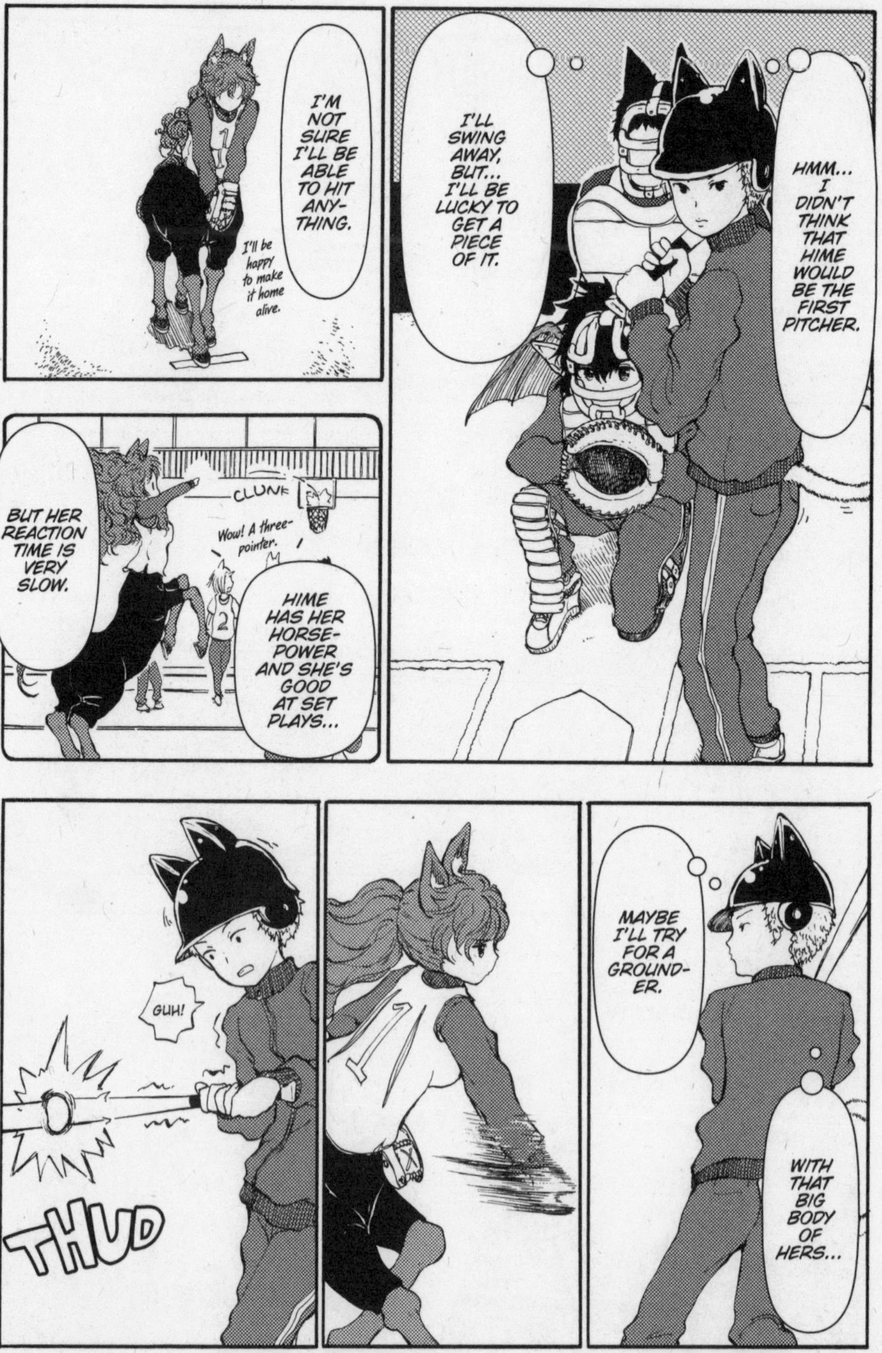
HMM... I DIDN'T THINK THAT HIME WOULD BE THE FIRST PITCHER.
I'LL SWING AWAY, BUT... I'LL BE LUCKY TO GET A PIECE OF IT.
I'M NOT SURE I'LL BE ABLE TO HIT ANYTHING.
I'll be happy to make it home alive.
CLUNK
Wow! A three-pointer.
HIME HAS HER HORSEPOWER AND SHE'S GOOD AT SET PLAYS...
BUT HER REACTION TIME IS VERY SLOW.
MAYBE I'LL TRY FOR A GROUNDER.
WITH THAT BIG BODY OF HERS...
GUH!
THUD

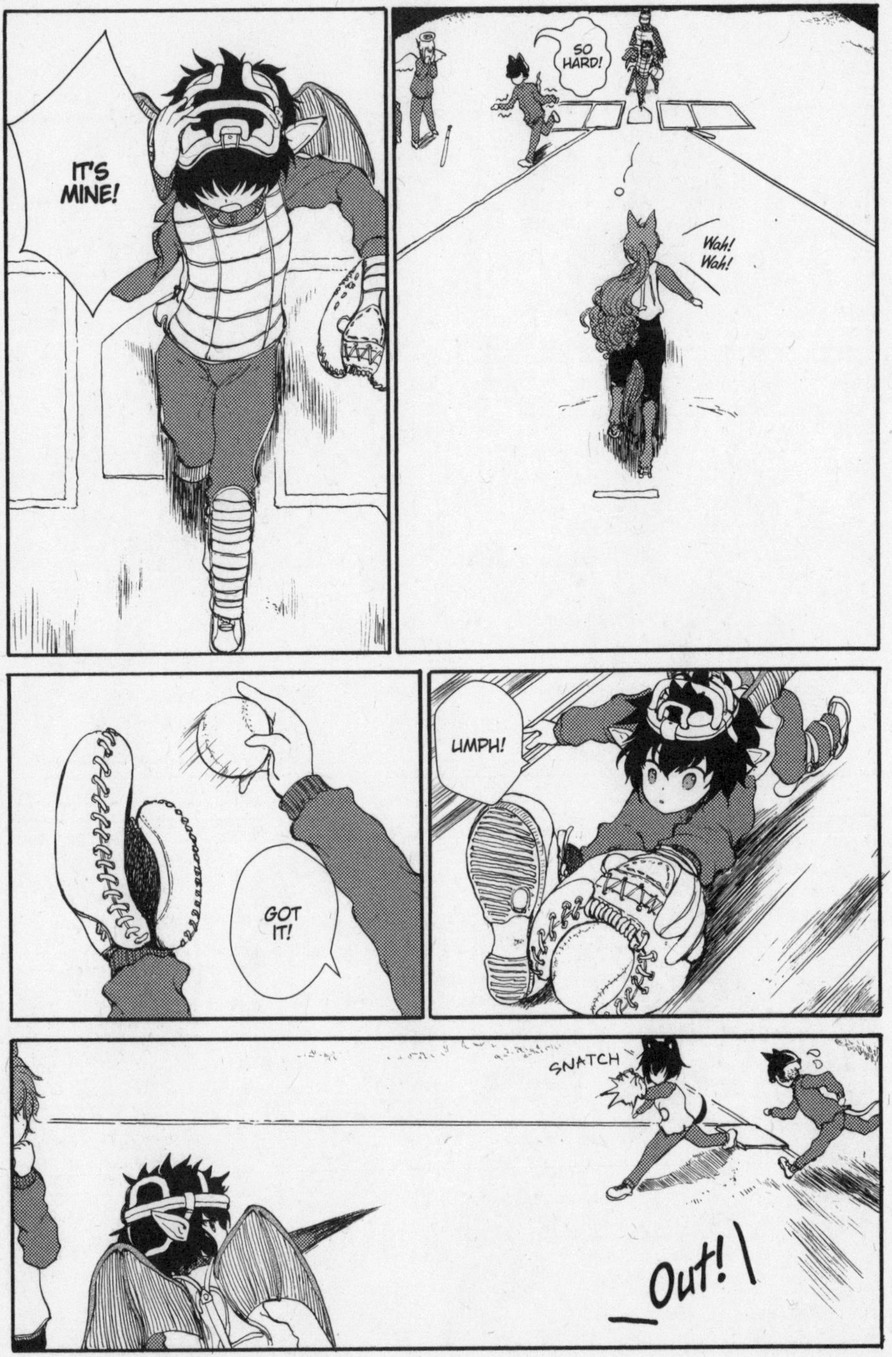
SO HARD!
Wah! Wah!
IT'S MINE!
UMPH!
GOT IT!
SNATCH
Out!

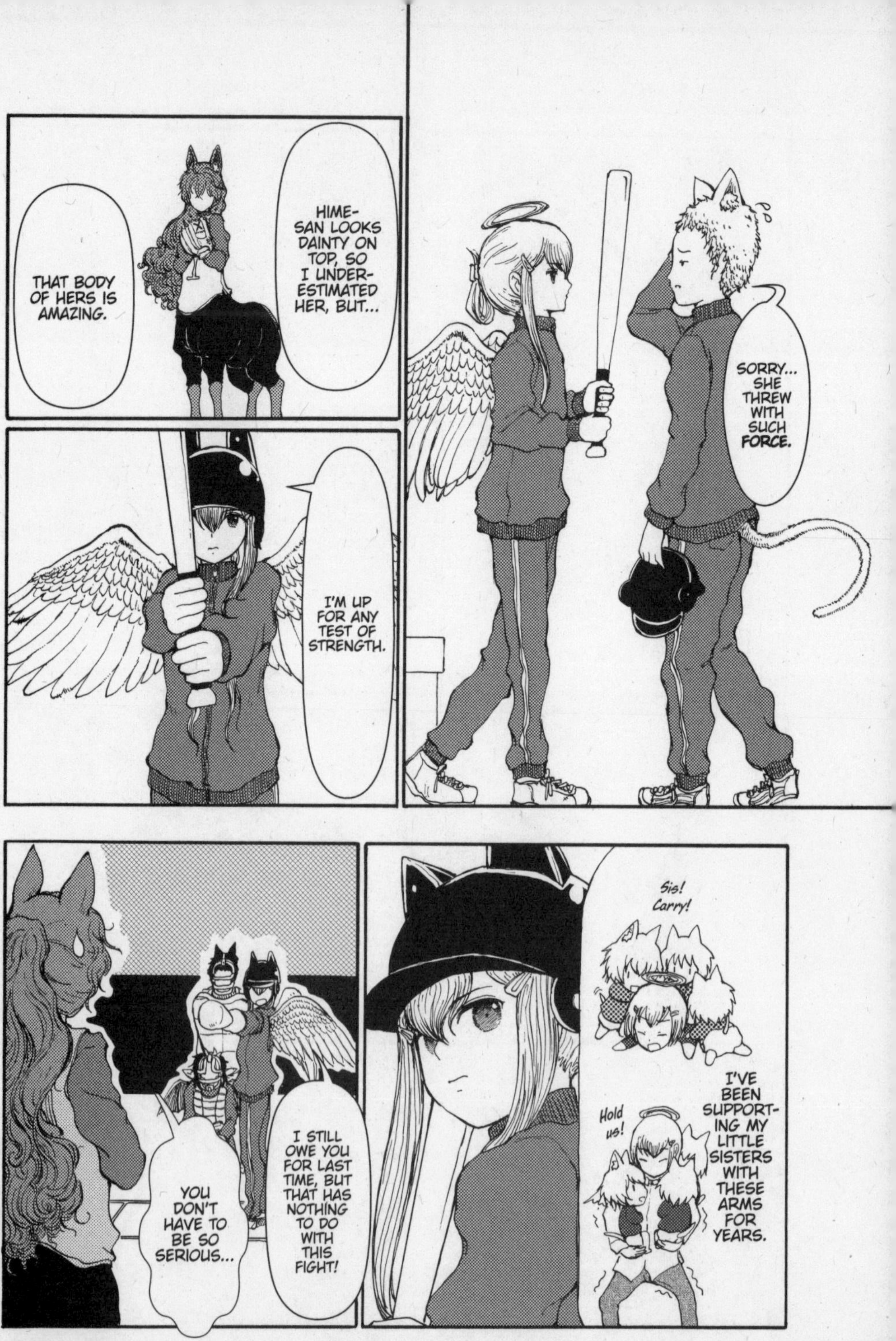
SORRY... SHE THREW WITH SUCH FORCE.
HIME-SAN LOOKS DAINTY ON TOP, SO I UNDER-ESTIMATED HER, BUT...
THAT BODY OF HERS IS AMAZING.
I'M UP FOR ANY TEST OF STRENGTH.
Sis! Carry!
I'VE BEEN SUPPORTING MY LITTLE SISTERS WITH THESE ARMS FOR YEARS.
Hold us!
I STILL OWE YOU FOR LAST TIME, BUT THAT HAS NOTHING TO DO WITH THIS FIGHT!
YOU DON'T HAVE TO BE SO SERIOUS...

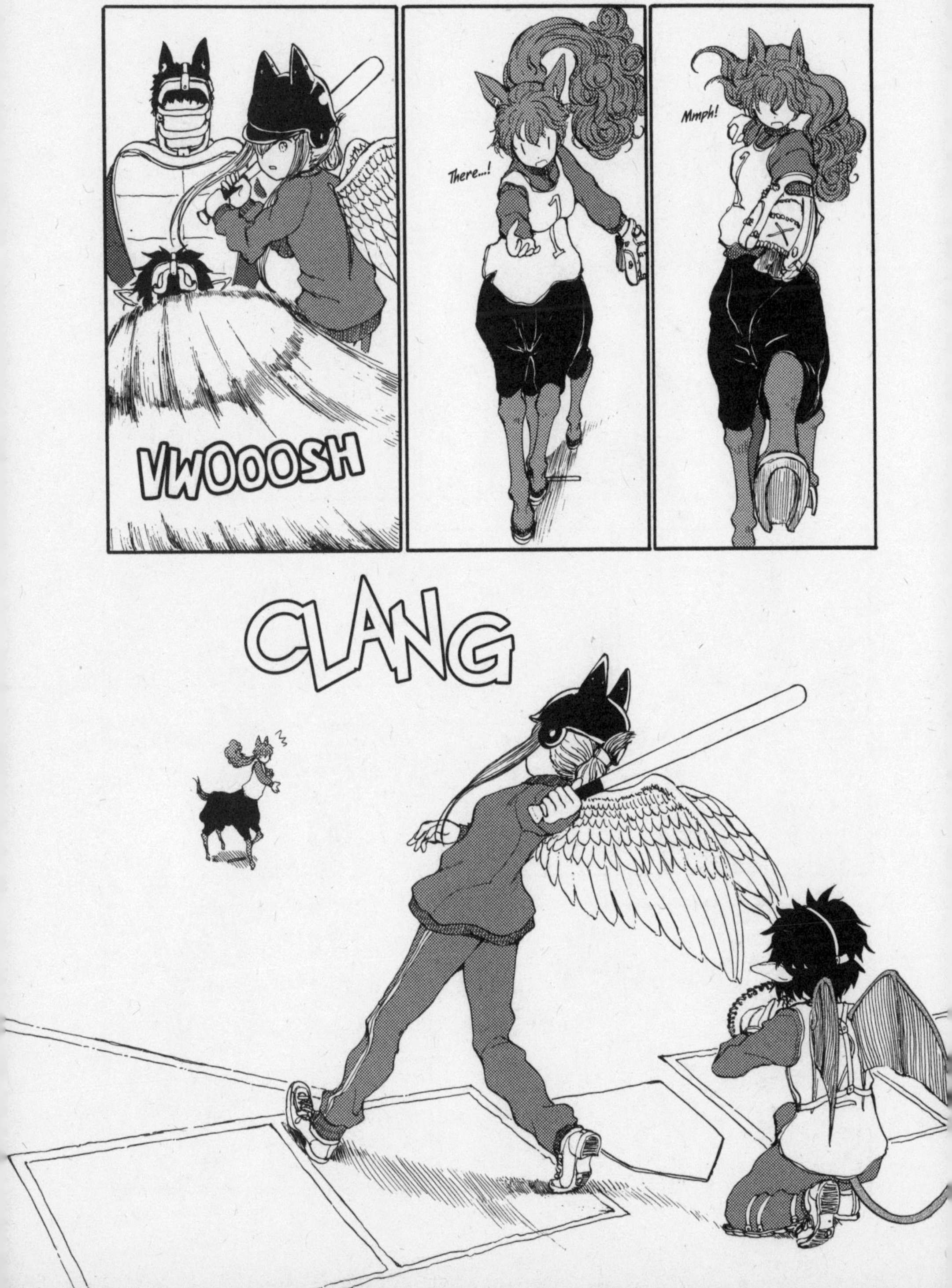
Mmph!
There...!
VWOOOSH
CLANG

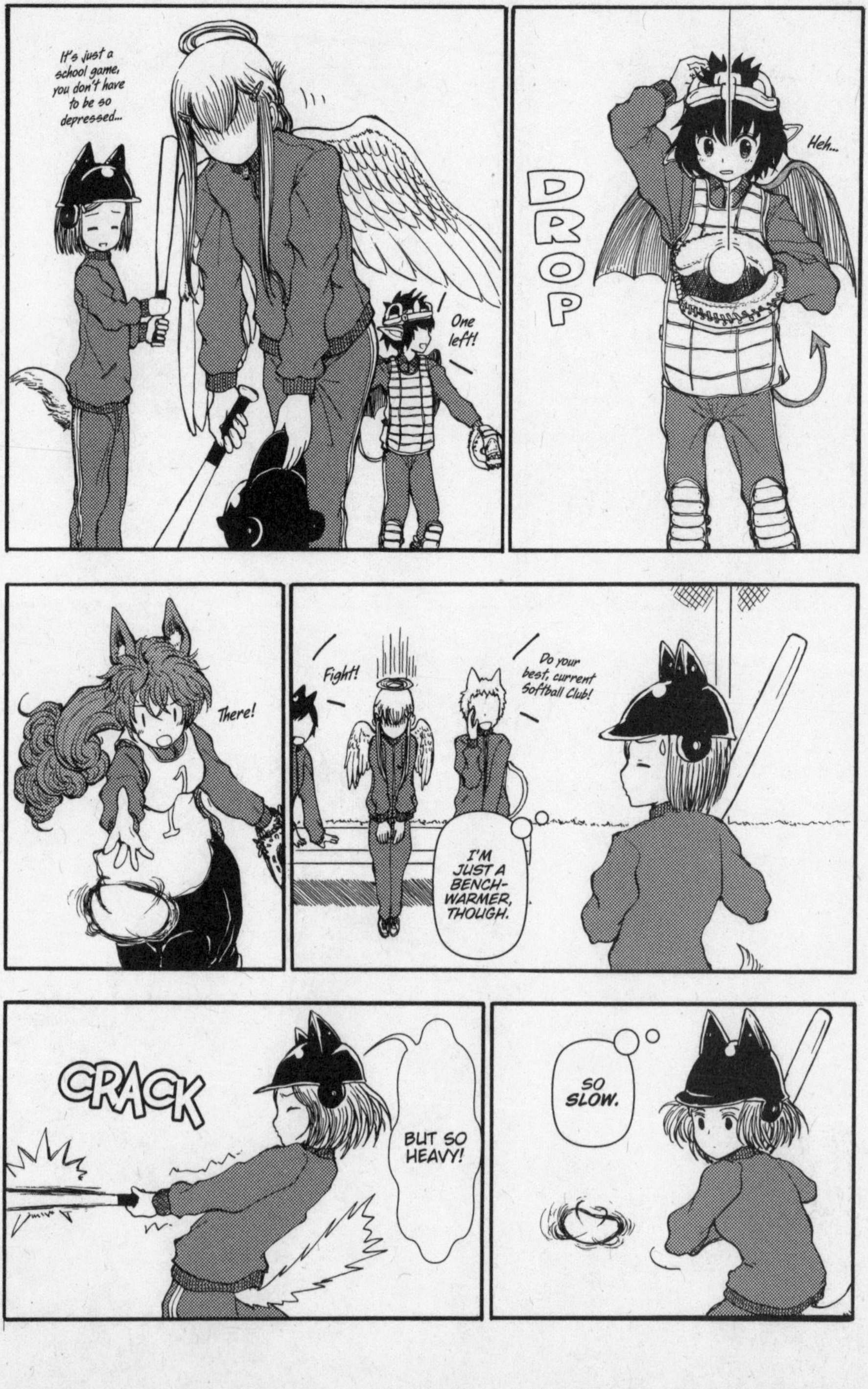
Heh...
DROP
It's just a school game, you don't have to be so depressed...
One left!
Do your best, current Softball Club!
Fight!
I'M JUST A BENCH-WARMER, THOUGH.
There!
SO SLOW.
BUT SO HEAVY!
CRACK

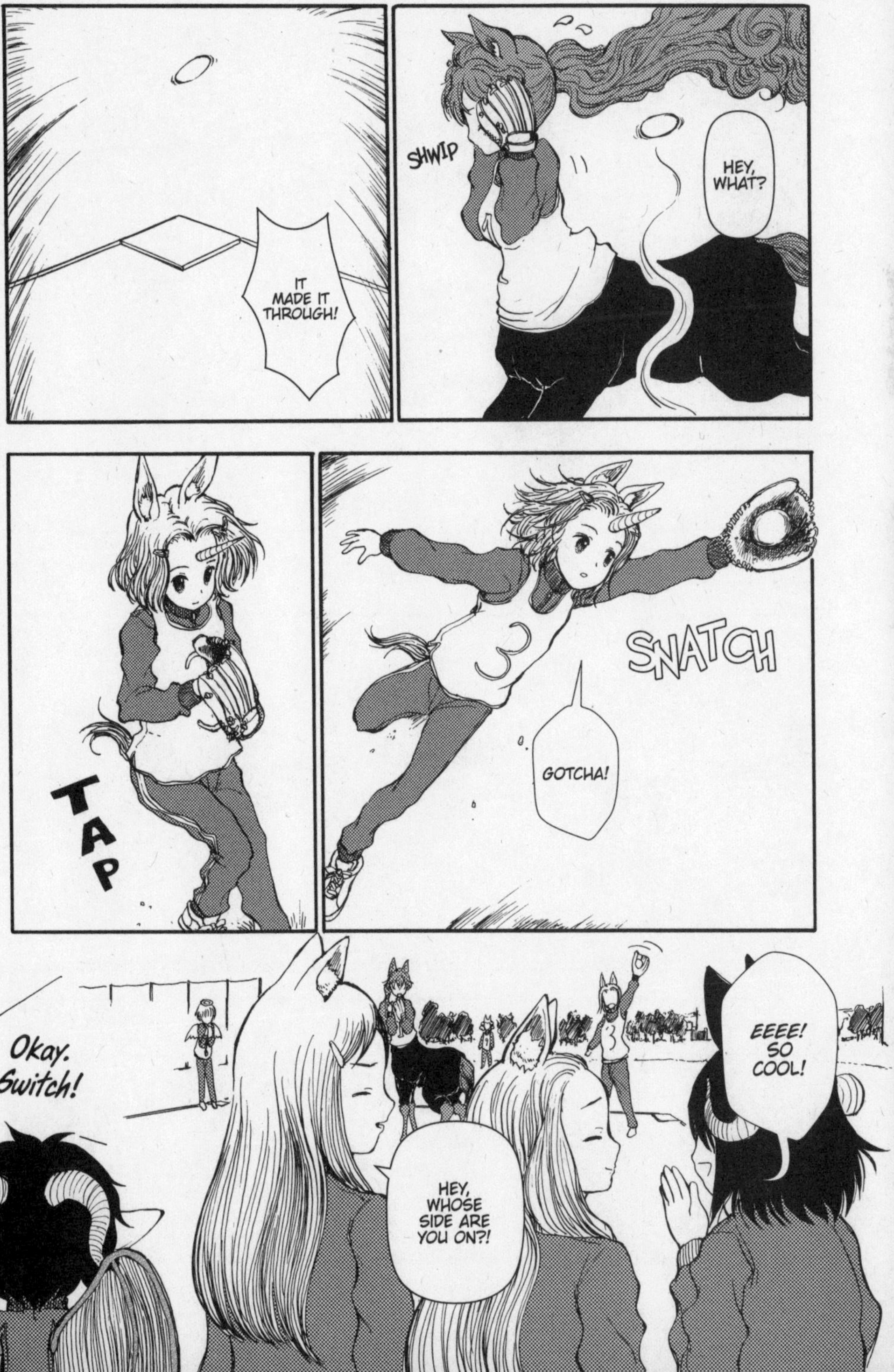
SHWIP
HEY, WHAT?
IT MADE IT THROUGH!
SNATCH
GOTCHA!
TAP
EEEE! SO COOL!
HEY, WHOSE SIDE ARE YOU ON?!
Okay. Switch!

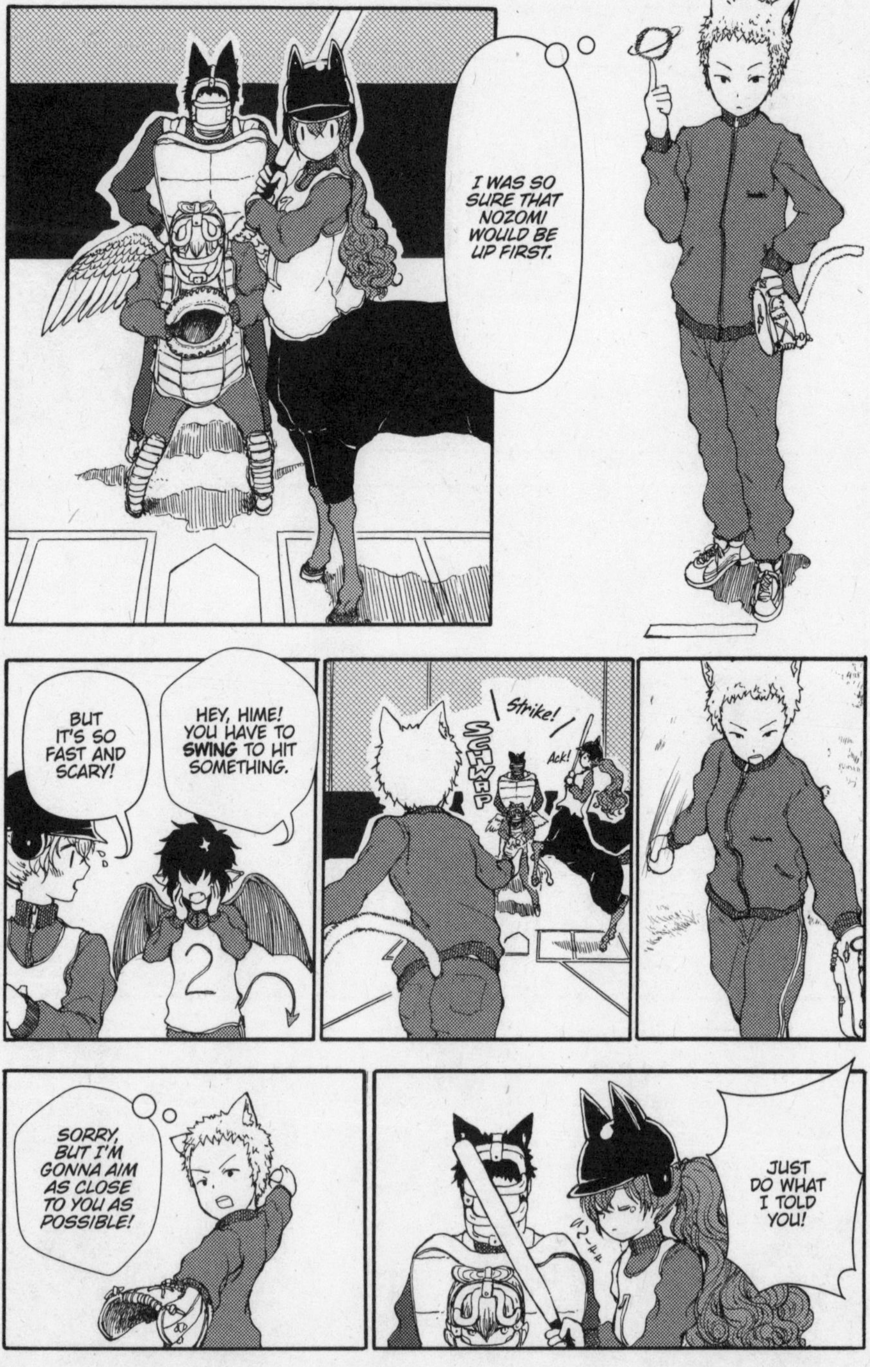
I WAS SO SURE THAT NOZOMI WOULD BE UP FIRST.
Strike!
SCHWAP
Ack!
HEY, HIME! YOU HAVE TO SWING TO HIT SOMETHING.
BUT IT'S SO FAST AND SCARY!
JUST DO WHAT I TOLD YOU!
SORRY, BUT I'M GONNA AIM AS CLOSE TO YOU AS POSSIBLE!

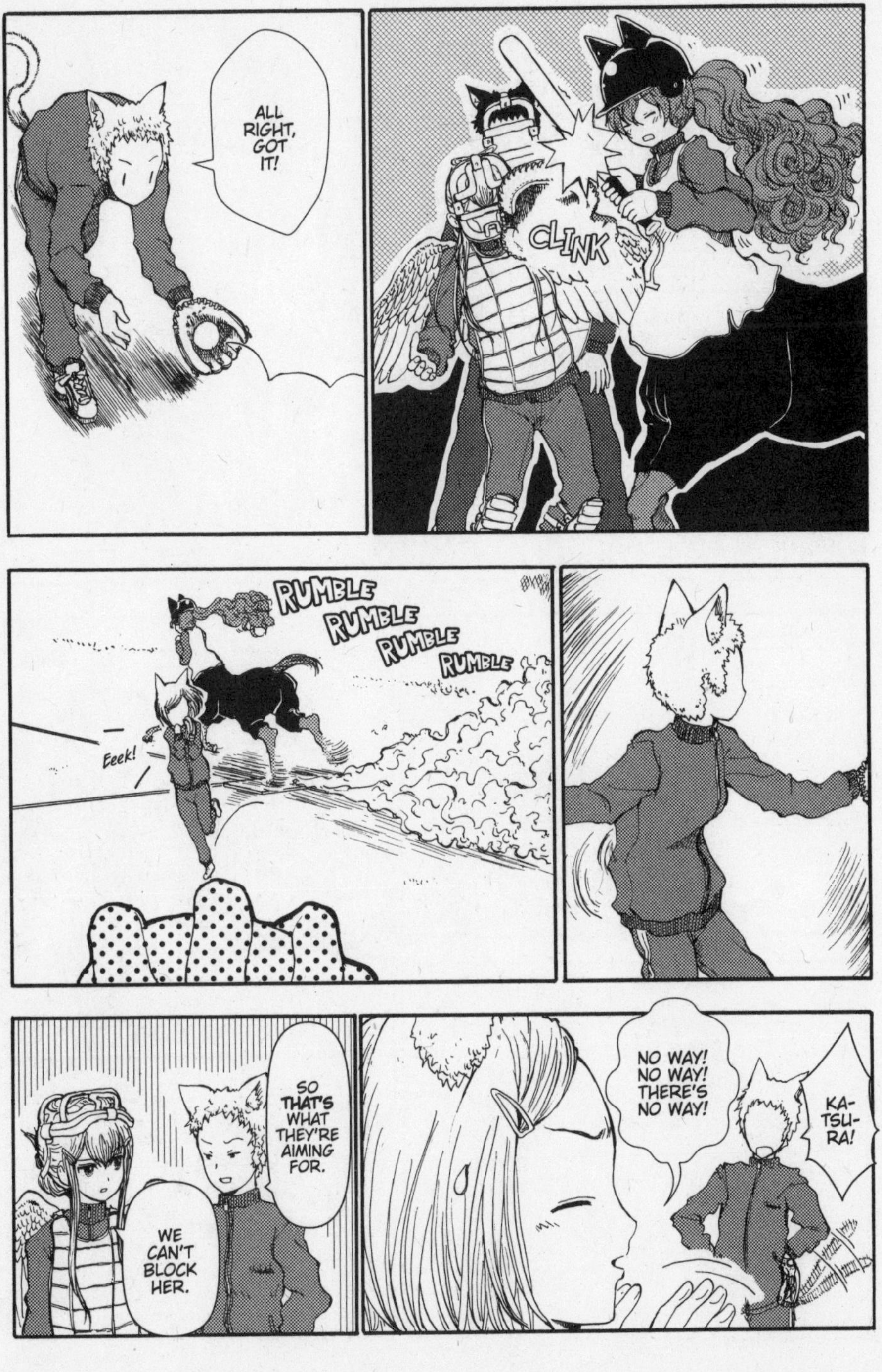
CLINK
ALL RIGHT, GOT IT!
RUMBLE RUMBLE RUMBLE RUMBLE
Eeek!
KATSU-RA!
NO WAY! NO WAY! THERE'S NO WAY!
SO THAT'S WHAT THEY'RE AIMING FOR.
WE CAN'T BLOCK HER.

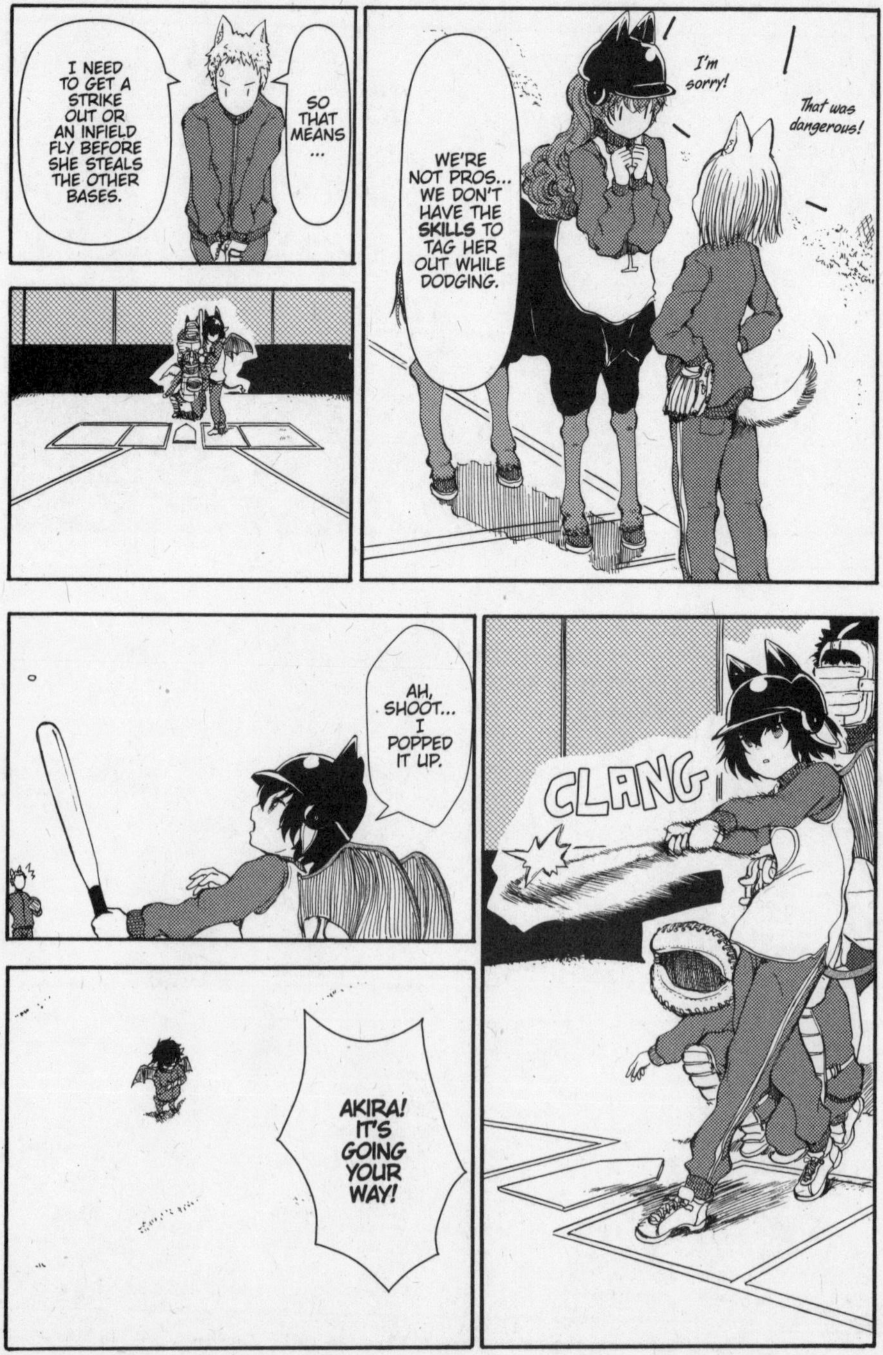

That was dangerous!
I'm sorry!
WE'RE NOT PROS... WE DON'T HAVE THE **SKILLS** TO TAG HER OUT WHILE DODGING.
SO THAT MEANS ...
I NEED TO GET A STRIKE OUT OR AN INFIELD FLY BEFORE SHE STEALS THE OTHER BASES.
CLANG
AH, SHOOT... I POPPED IT UP.
AKIRA! IT'S GOING YOUR WAY!

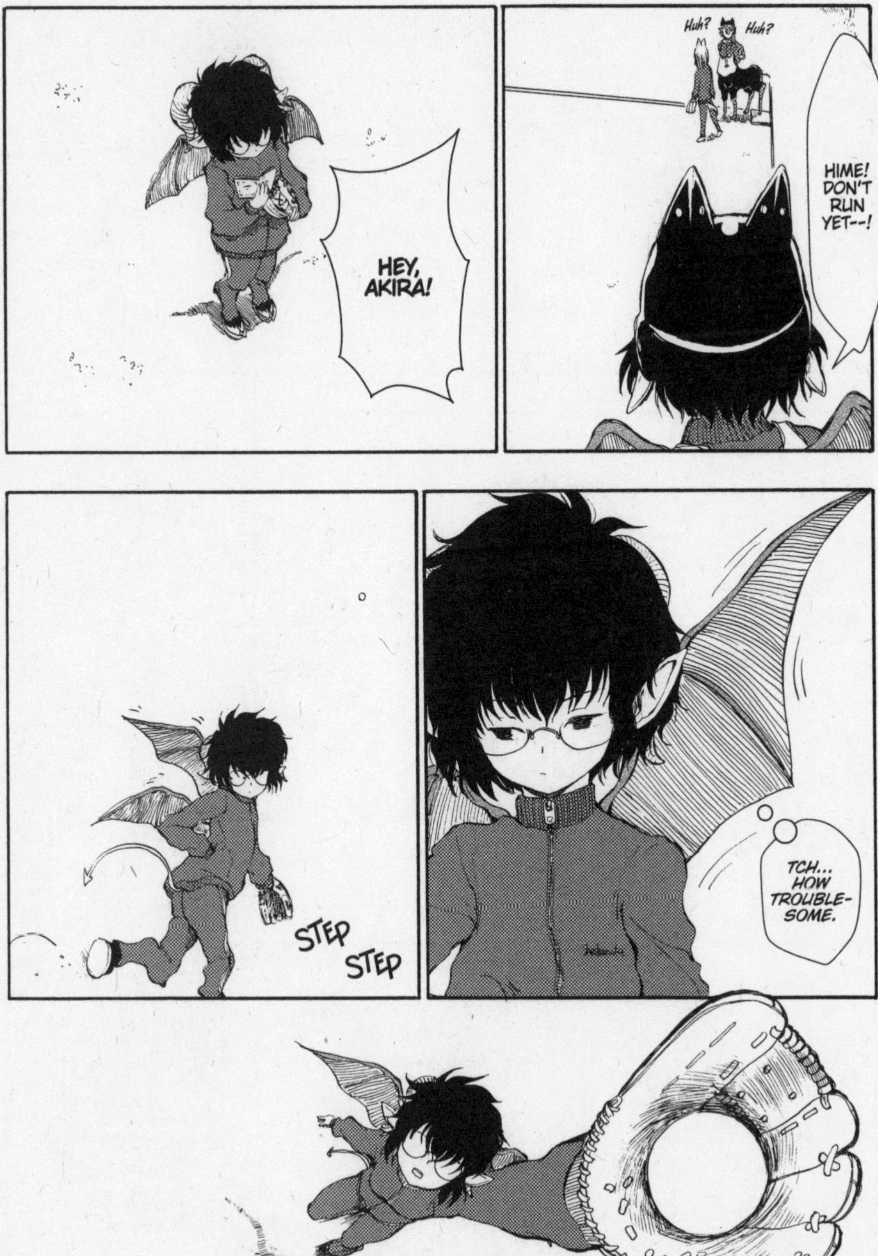
Huh?
Huh?
HIME! DON'T RUN YET--!
HEY, AKIRA!
TCH... HOW TROUBLE-SOME.
STEP STEP
SNATCH

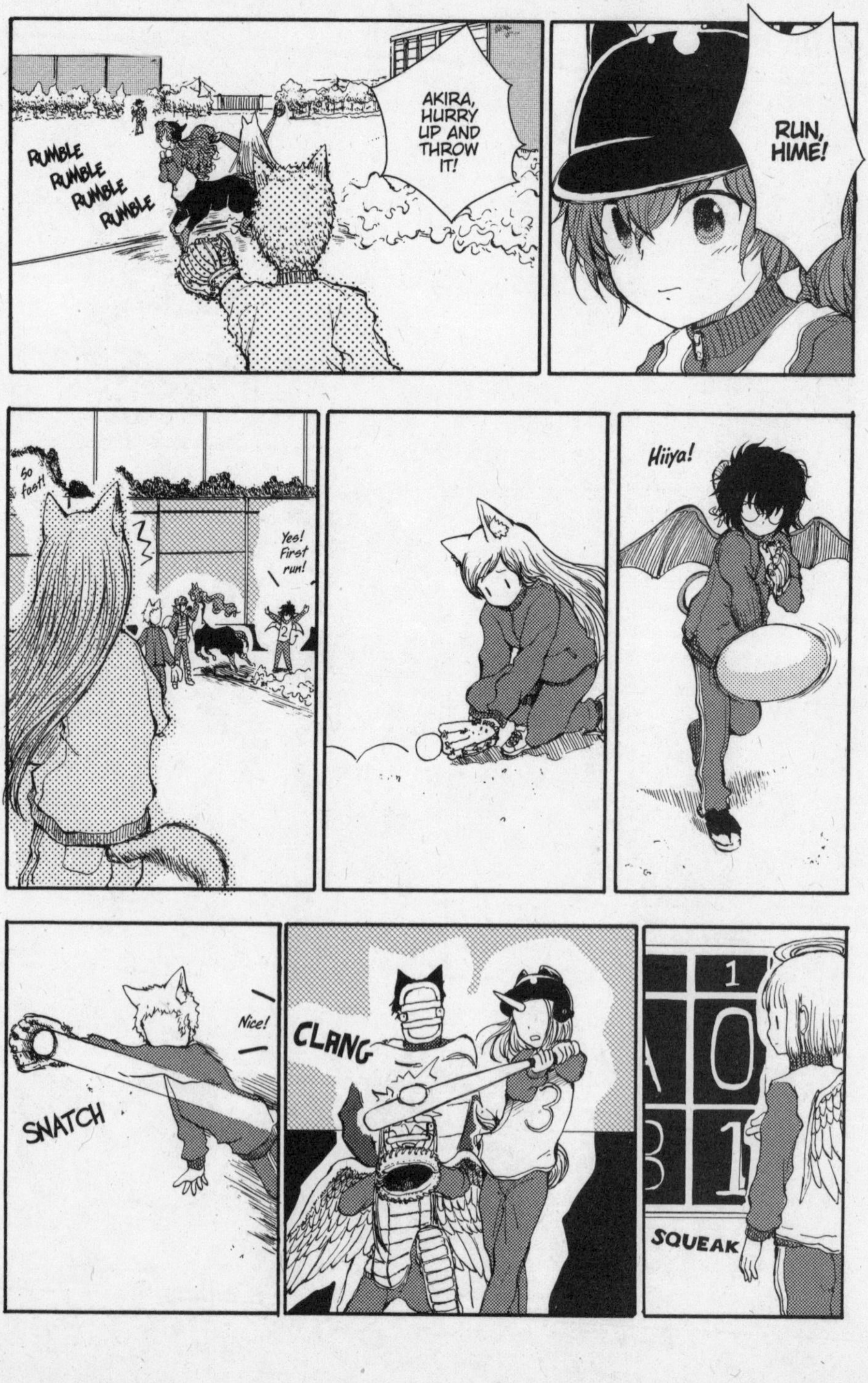
RUN, HIME!
AKIRA, HURRY UP AND THROW IT!
RUMBLE RUMBLE RUMBLE RUMBLE
Hiiya!
So fast!
Yes! First run!
SQUEAK
CLANG
Nice!
SNATCH

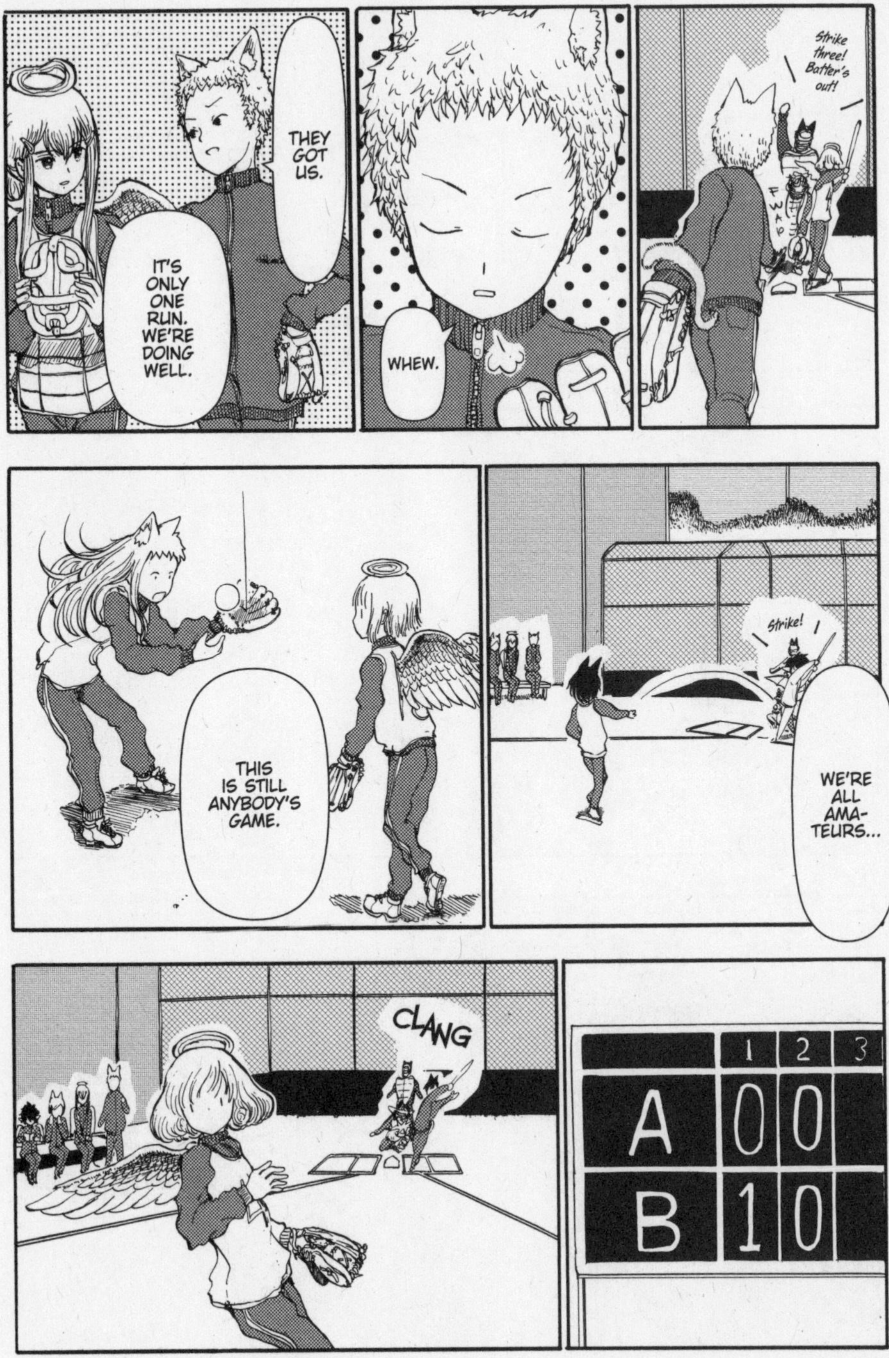
Strike three! Batter's out!
FWAP
WHEW.
THEY GOT US.
IT'S ONLY ONE RUN. WE'RE DOING WELL.
Strike!
WE'RE ALL AMATEURS...
THIS IS STILL ANYBODY'S GAME.
1 2 3
A 0 0
B 1 0
CLANG

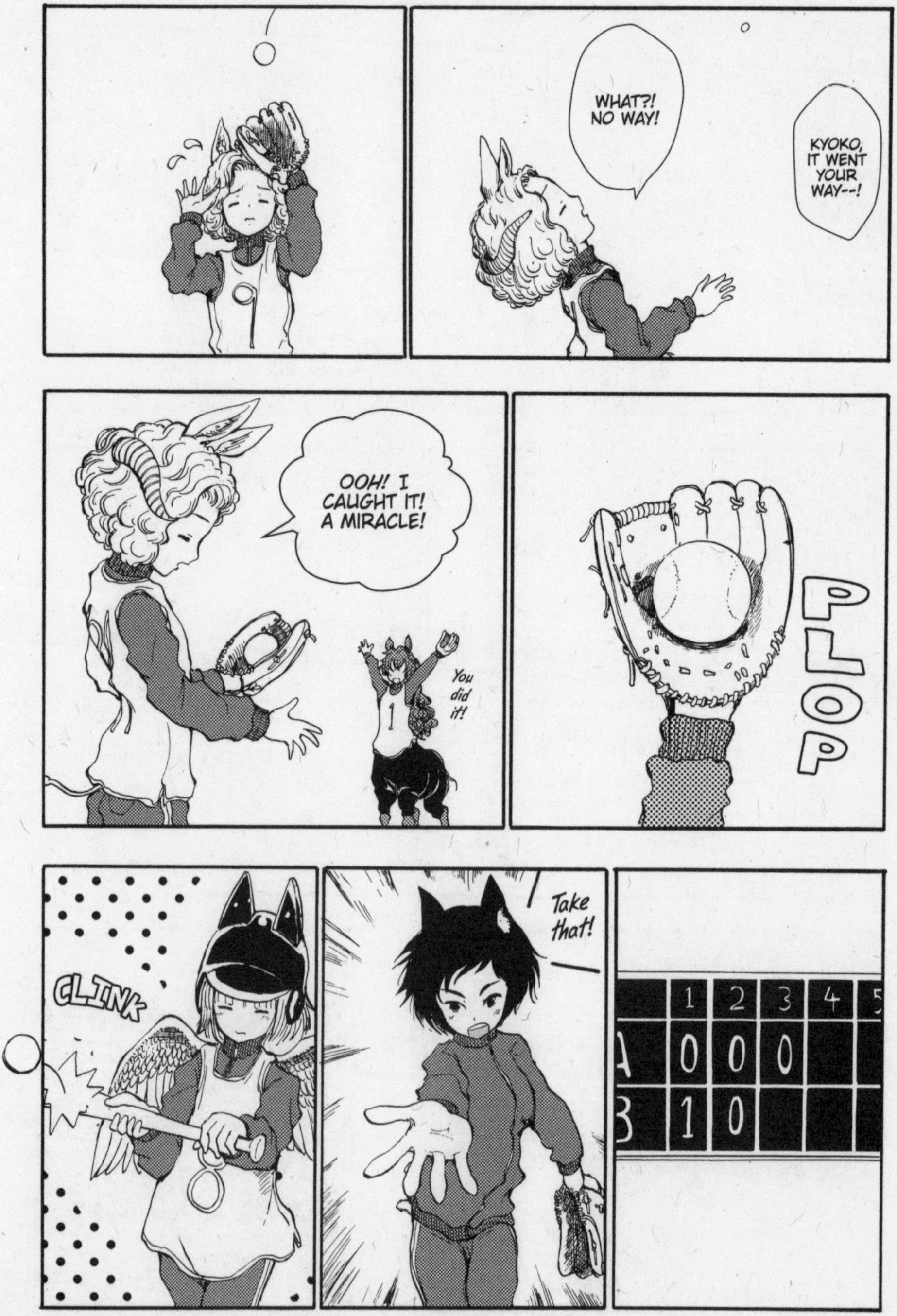
KYOKO, IT WENT YOUR WAY--!
WHAT?! NO WAY!
PLOP
OOH! I CAUGHT IT! A MIRACLE!
You did it!
1 2 3 4 5
A 0 0 0
B 1 0
Take that!
CLINK

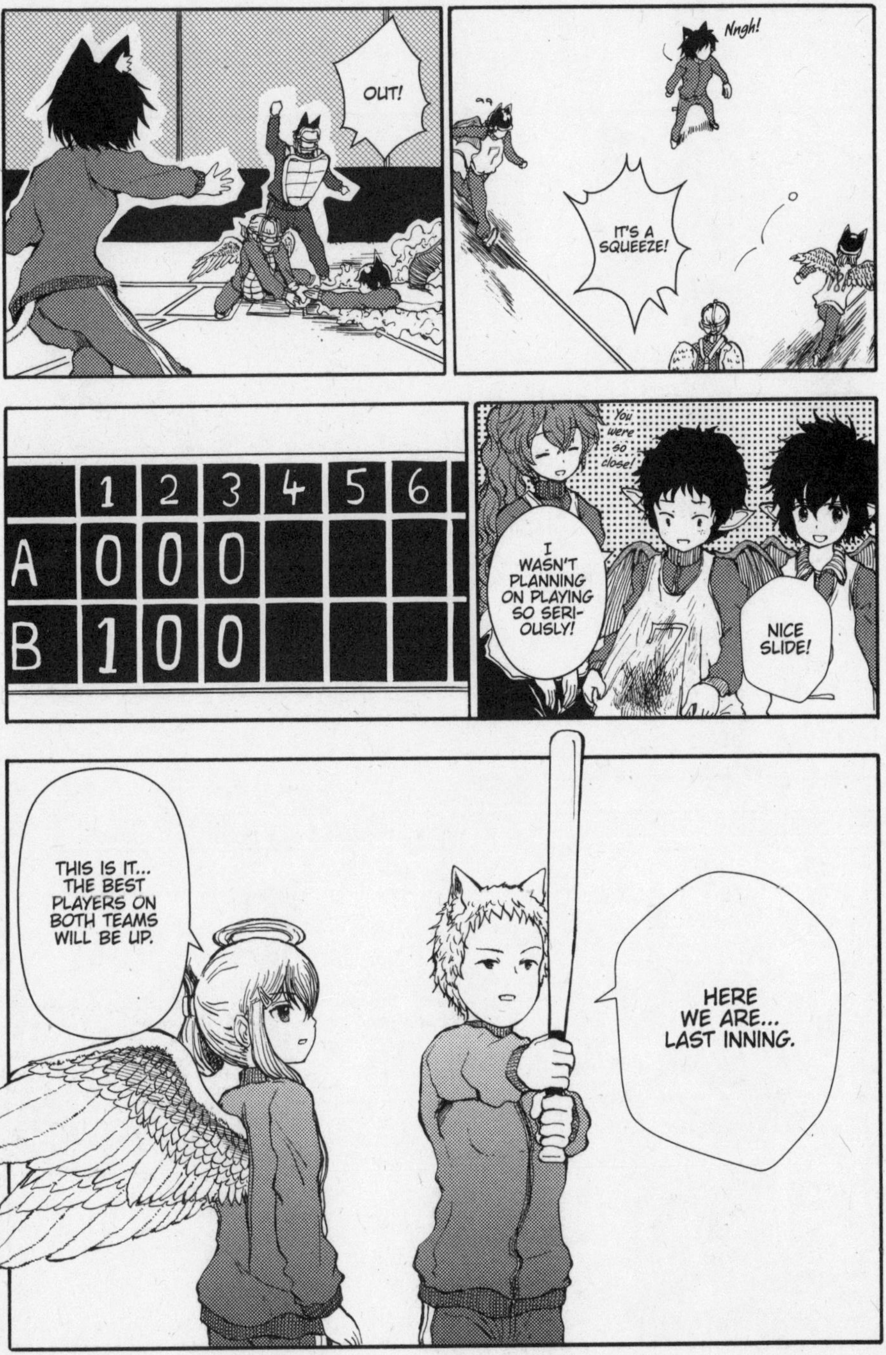
Nngh!
IT'S A SQUEEZE!
OUT!
You were so close!
NICE SLIDE!
I WASN'T PLANNING ON PLAYING SO SERI-OUSLY!
1 2 3 4 5 6
A 0 0 0
B 1 0 0
HERE WE ARE... LAST INNING.
THIS IS IT... THE BEST PLAYERS ON BOTH TEAMS WILL BE UP.

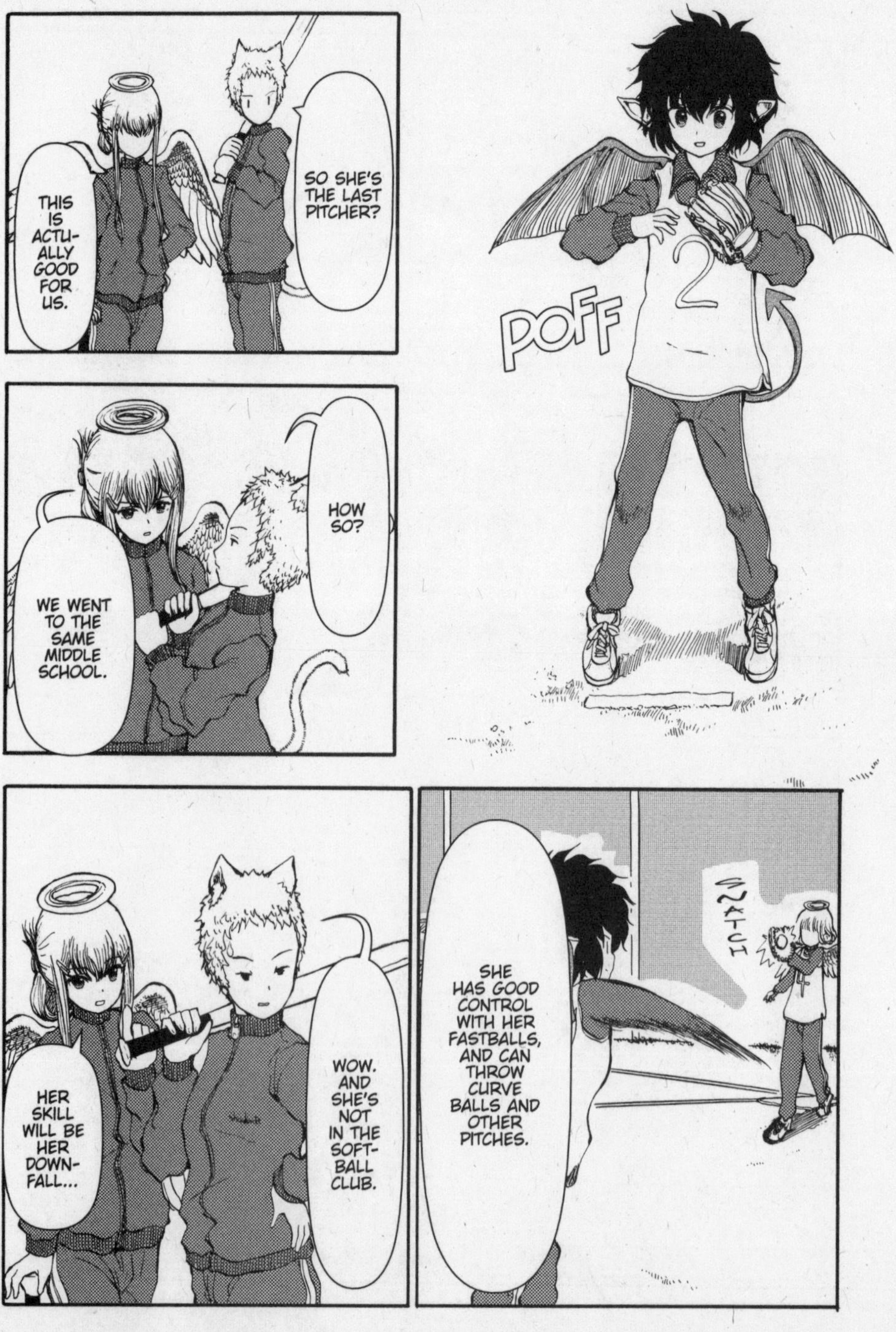
POFF
SO SHE'S THE LAST PITCHER?
THIS IS ACTUALLY GOOD FOR US.
HOW SO?
WE WENT TO THE SAME MIDDLE SCHOOL.
SNATCH
SHE HAS GOOD CONTROL WITH HER FASTBALLS, AND CAN THROW CURVE BALLS AND OTHER PITCHES.
WOW. AND SHE'S NOT IN THE SOFT-BALL CLUB.
HER SKILL WILL BE HER DOWN-FALL...

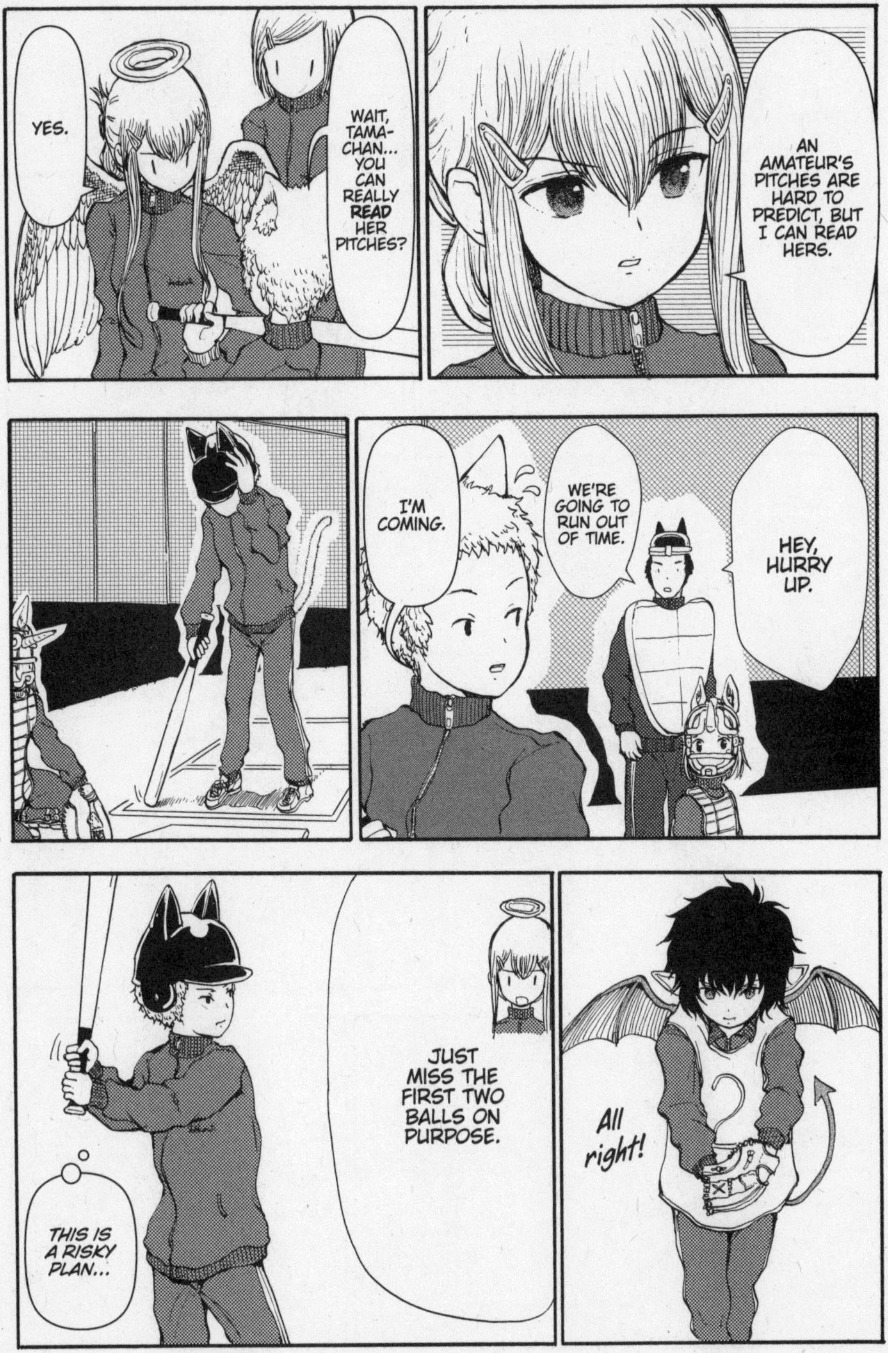
AN AMATEUR'S PITCHES ARE HARD TO PREDICT, BUT I CAN READ HERS.
WAIT, TAMA-CHAN... YOU CAN REALLY READ HER PITCHES?
YES.
HEY, HURRY UP.
WE'RE GOING TO RUN OUT OF TIME.
I'M COMING.
All right!
JUST MISS THE FIRST TWO BALLS ON PURPOSE.
THIS IS A RISKY PLAN...

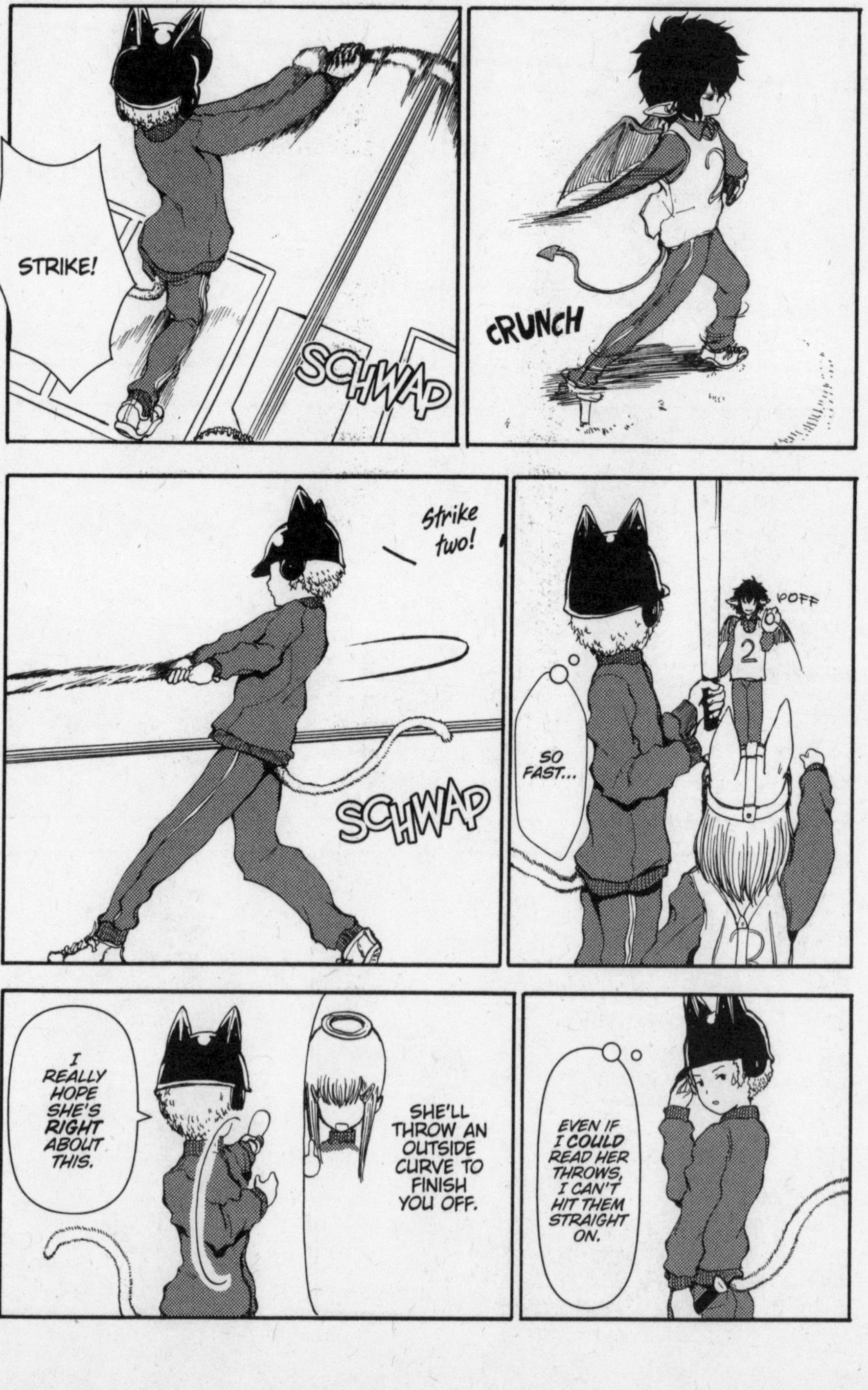
CRUNCH
STRIKE!
SCHWAP
POFF
SO FAST...
Strike two!
SCHWAP
EVEN IF I COULD READ HER THROWS, I CAN'T HIT THEM STRAIGHT ON.
SHE'LL THROW AN OUTSIDE CURVE TO FINISH YOU OFF.
I REALLY HOPE SHE'S RIGHT ABOUT THIS.

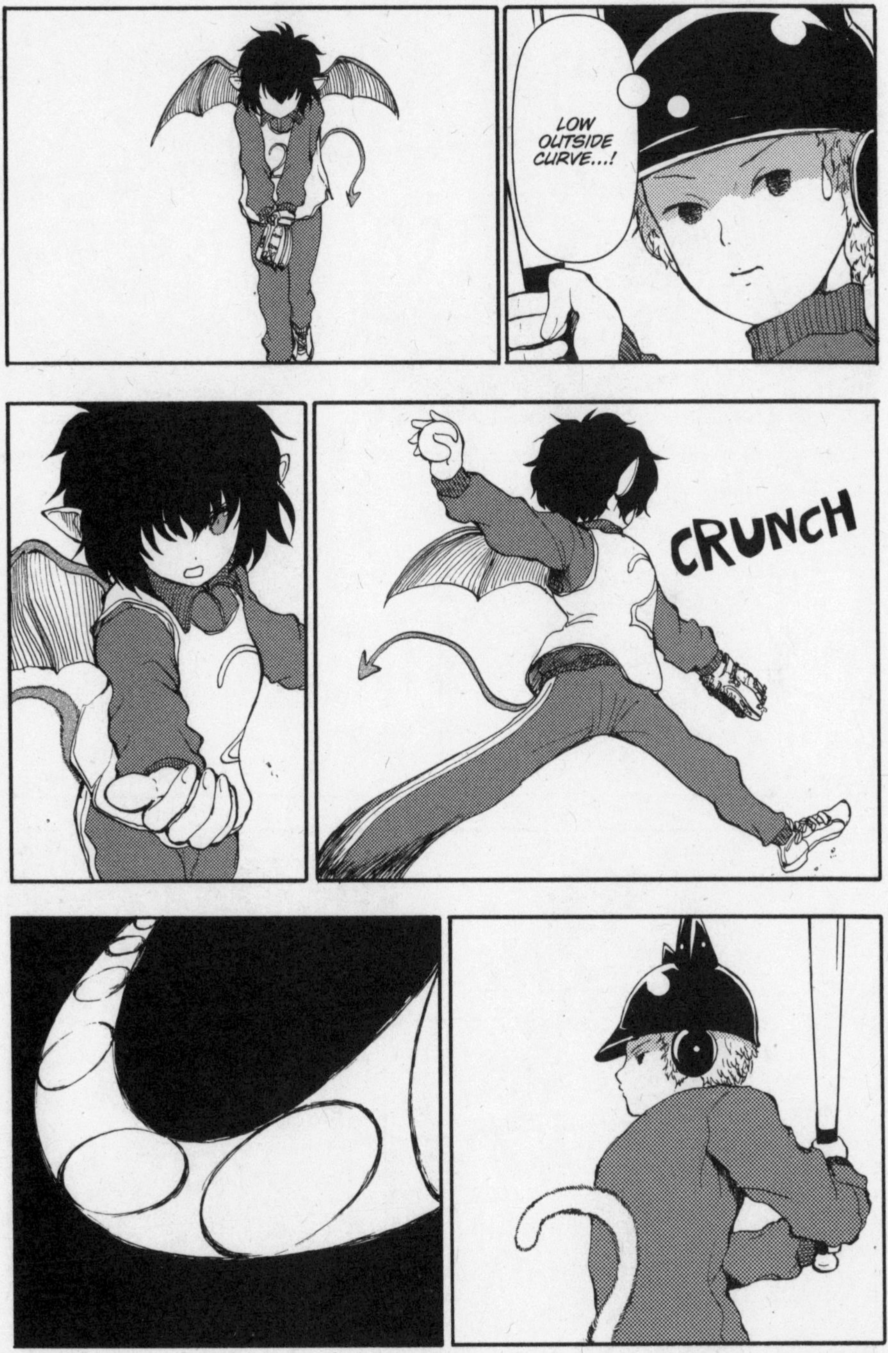
LOW OUTSIDE CURVE...!
CRUNCH

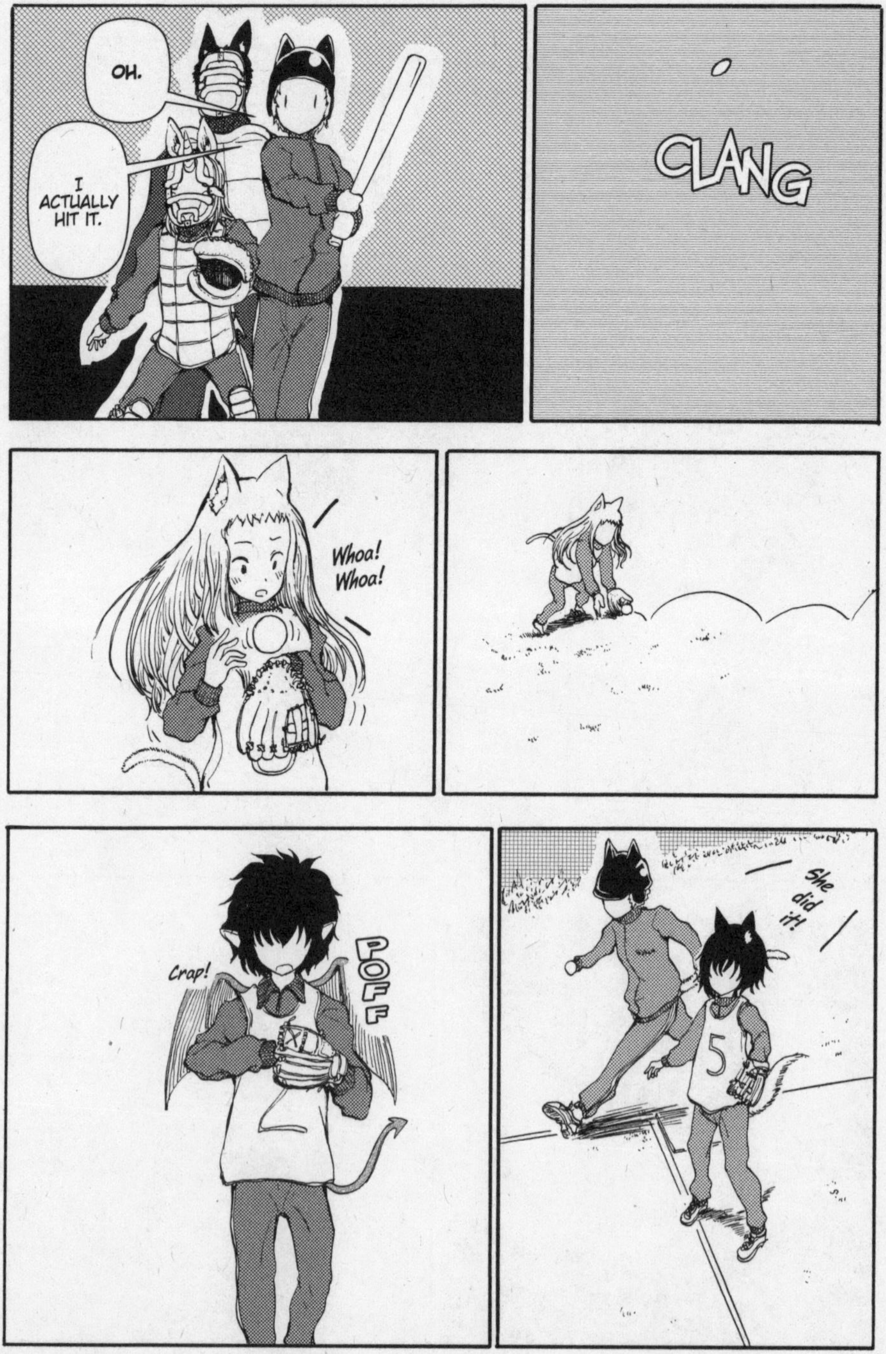
CLANG
OH.
I ACTUALLY HIT IT.
Whoa! Whoa!
She did it!
POFF
Crap!

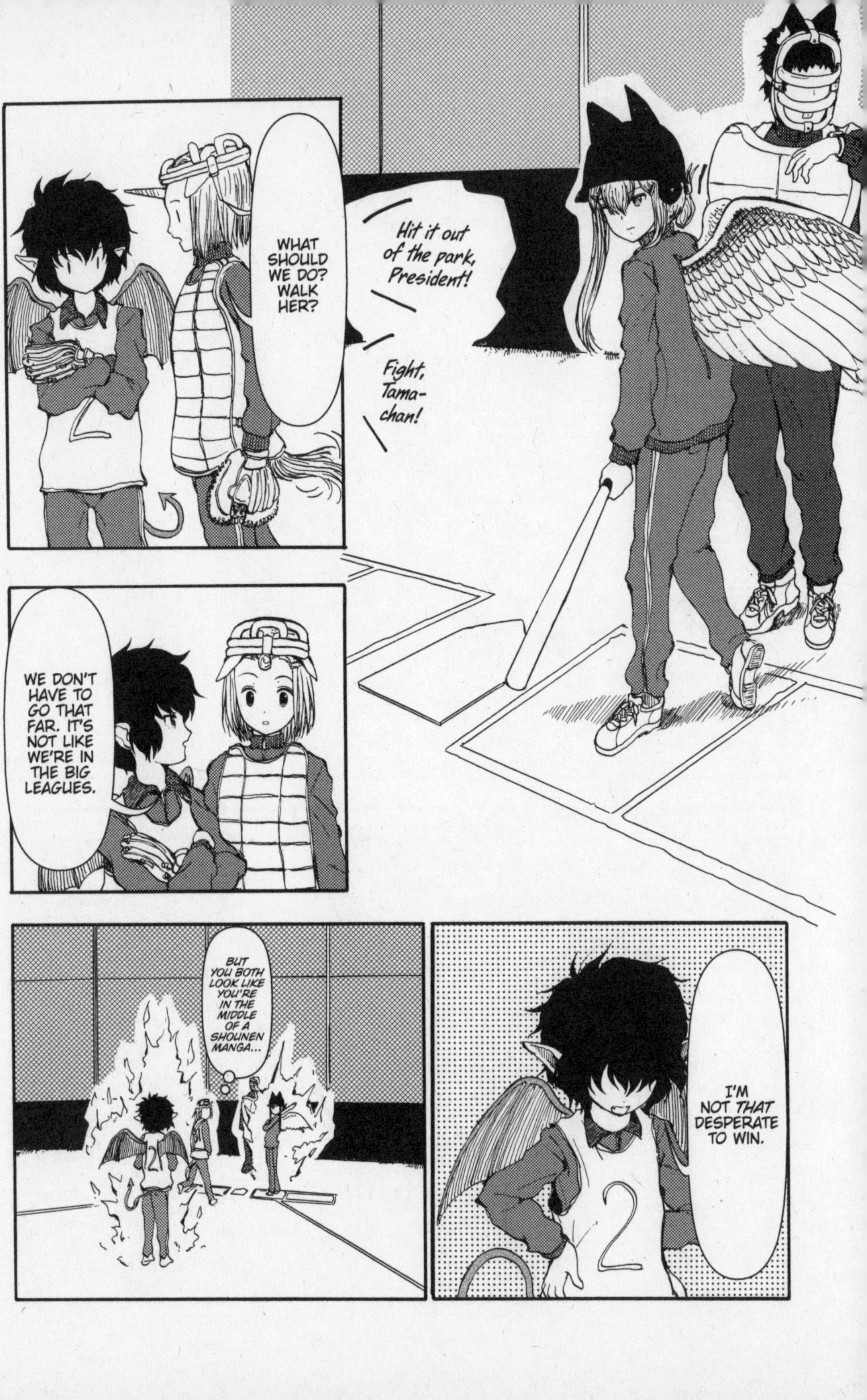
Hit it out of the park, President!
Fight, Tama-chan!
WHAT SHOULD WE DO? WALK HER?
WE DON'T HAVE TO GO THAT FAR. IT'S NOT LIKE WE'RE IN THE BIG LEAGUES.
I'M NOT *THAT* DESPERATE TO WIN.
BUT YOU BOTH LOOK LIKE YOU'RE IN THE MIDDLE OF A SHOUNEN MANGA...

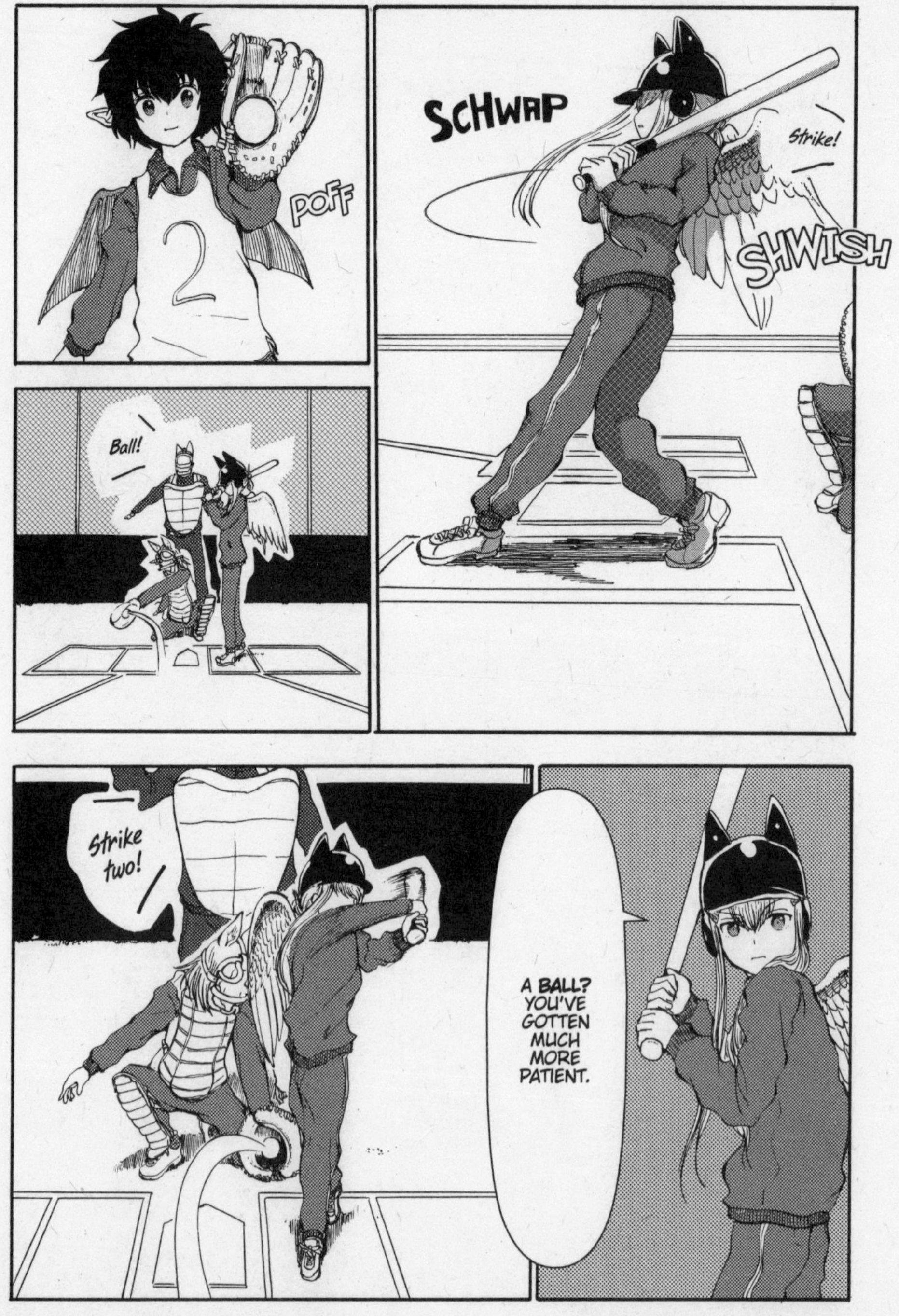
SCHWAP
Strike!
SHWISH
POFF
Ball!
A BALL? YOU'VE GOTTEN MUCH MORE PATIENT.
Strike two!

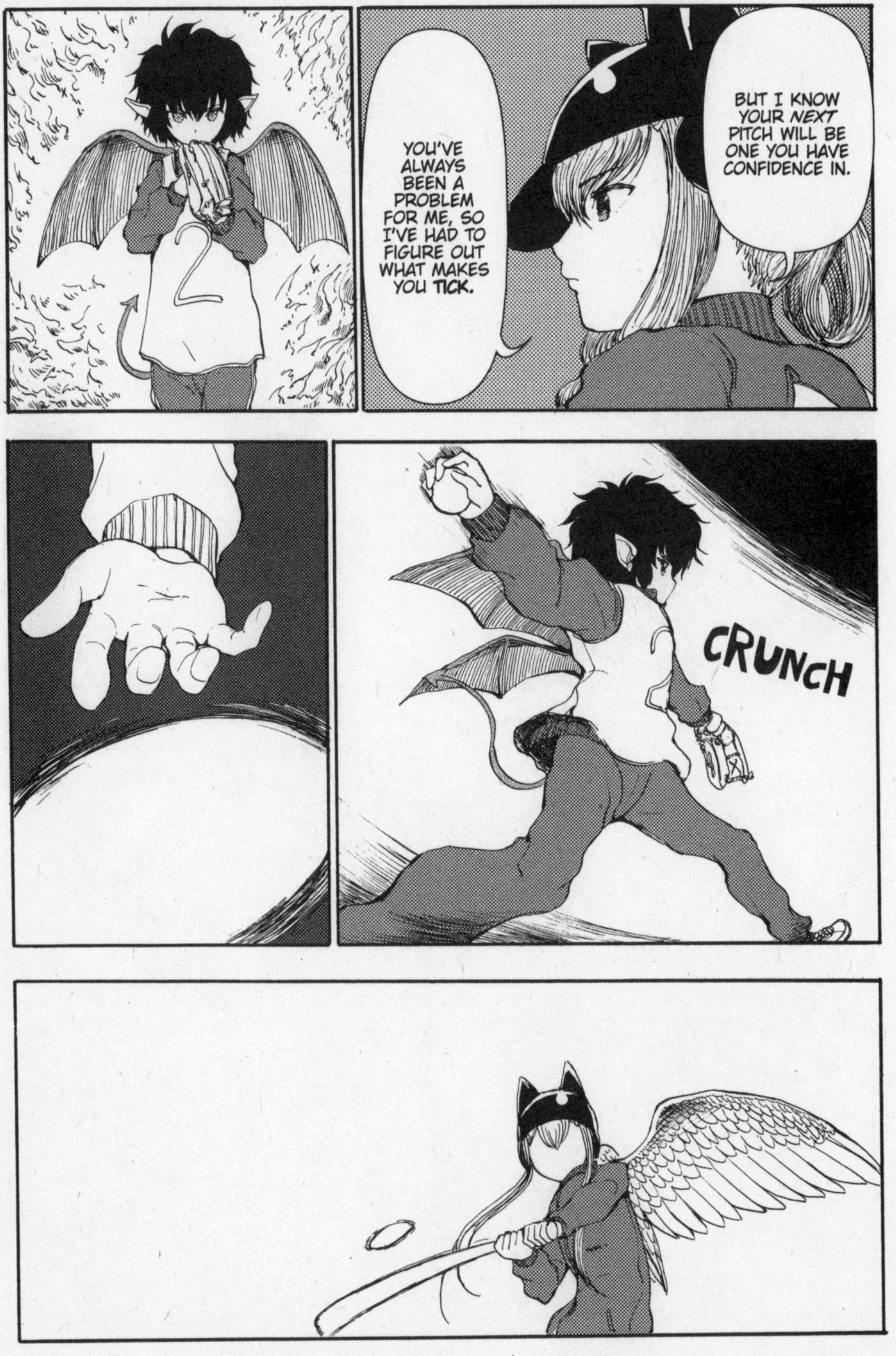

YOU'VE ALWAYS BEEN A PROBLEM FOR ME, SO I'VE HAD TO FIGURE OUT WHAT MAKES YOU TICK.
BUT I KNOW YOUR NEXT PITCH WILL BE ONE YOU HAVE CONFIDENCE IN.
CRUNCH

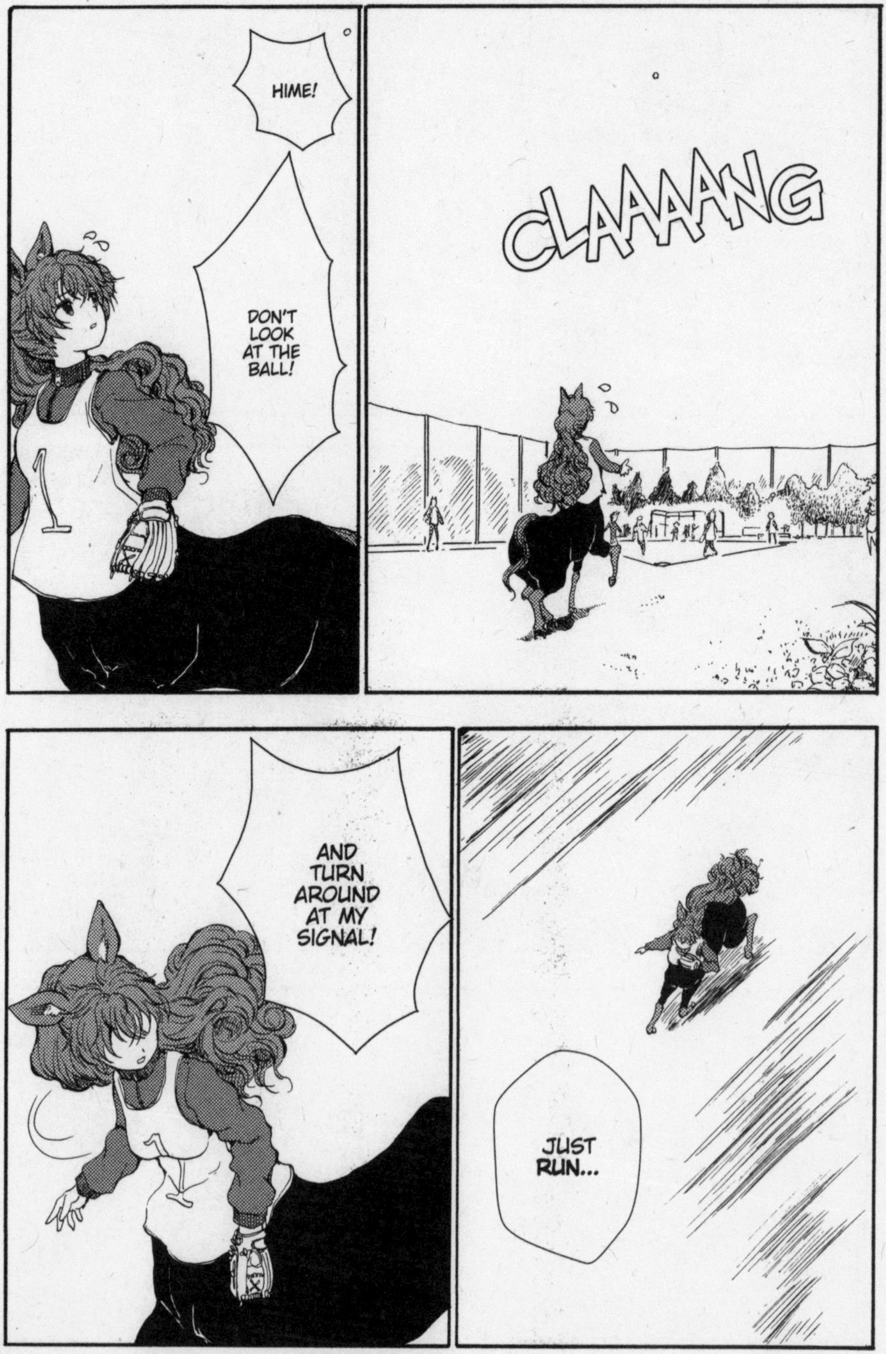
CLAAAANG
HIME!
DON'T LOOK AT THE BALL!
JUST RUN...
AND TURN AROUND AT MY SIGNAL!

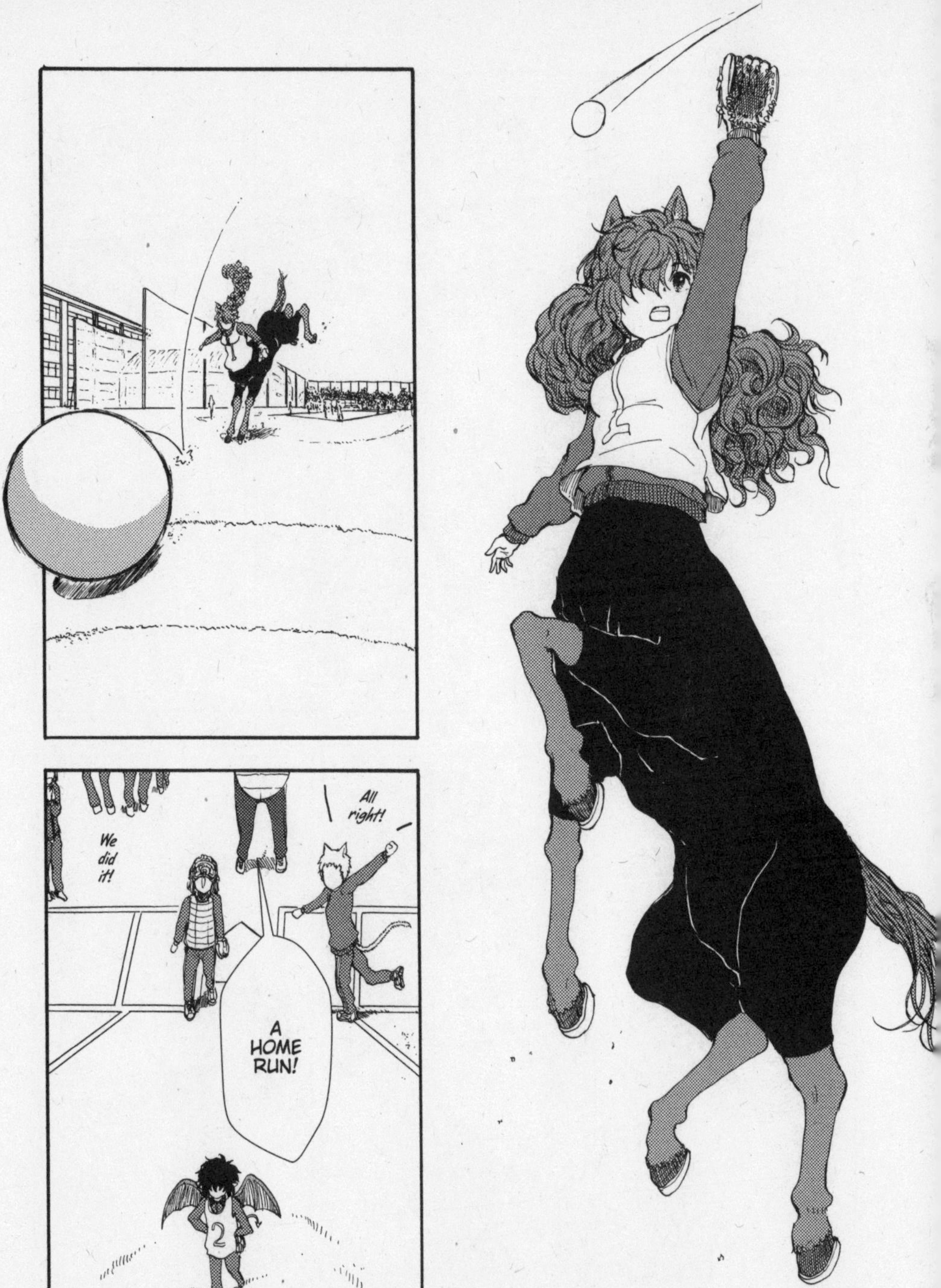
All right!
We did it!
A HOME RUN!

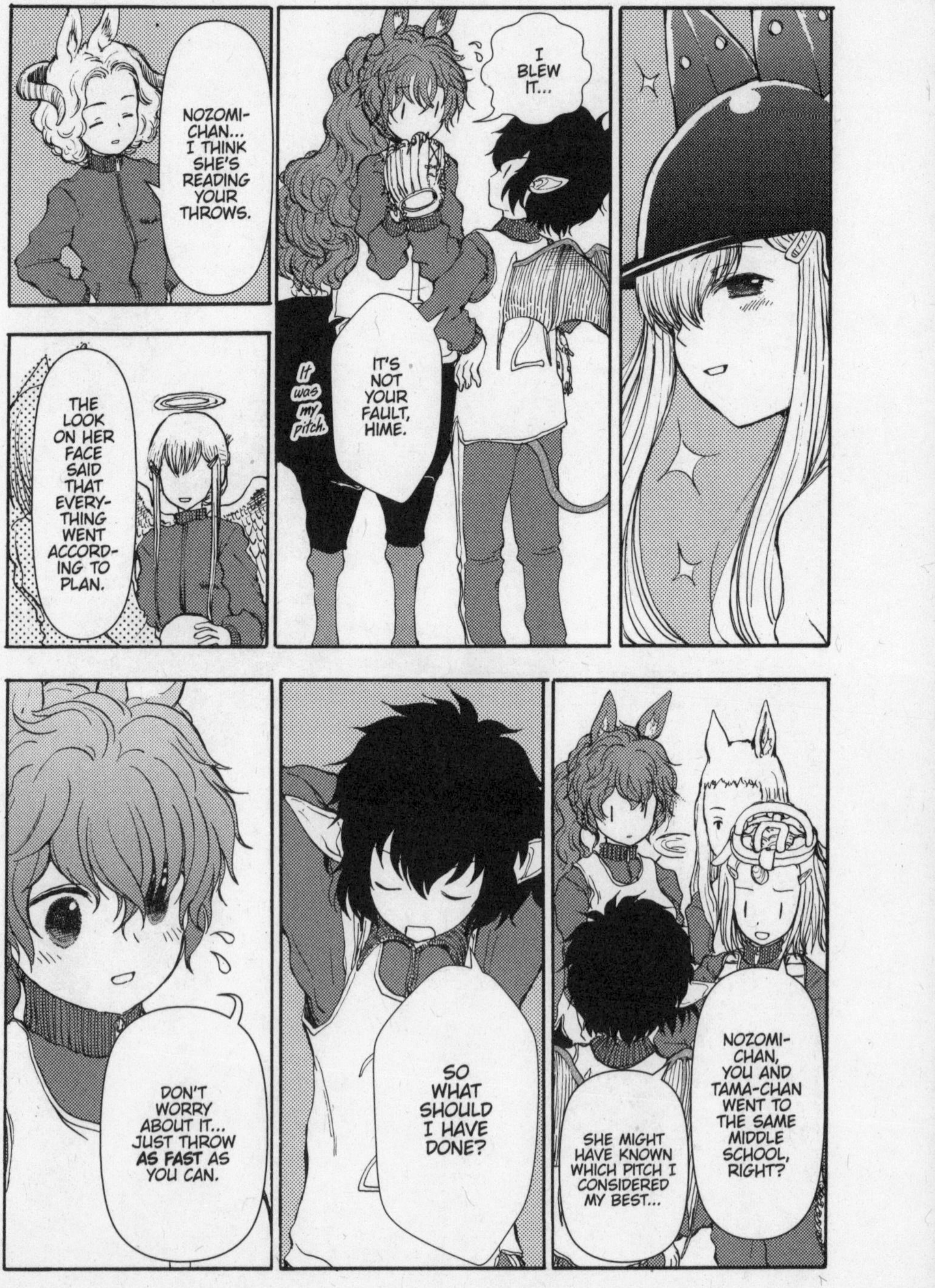
I BLEW IT...
IT'S NOT YOUR FAULT, HIME.
It was my pitch.
NOZOMI-CHAN... I THINK SHE'S READING YOUR THROWS.
THE LOOK ON HER FACE SAID THAT EVERYTHING WENT ACCORDING TO PLAN.
NOZOMI-CHAN, YOU AND TAMA-CHAN WENT TO THE SAME MIDDLE SCHOOL, RIGHT?
SHE MIGHT HAVE KNOWN WHICH PITCH I CONSIDERED MY BEST...
SO WHAT SHOULD I HAVE DONE?
DON'T WORRY ABOUT IT... JUST THROW AS FAST AS YOU CAN.

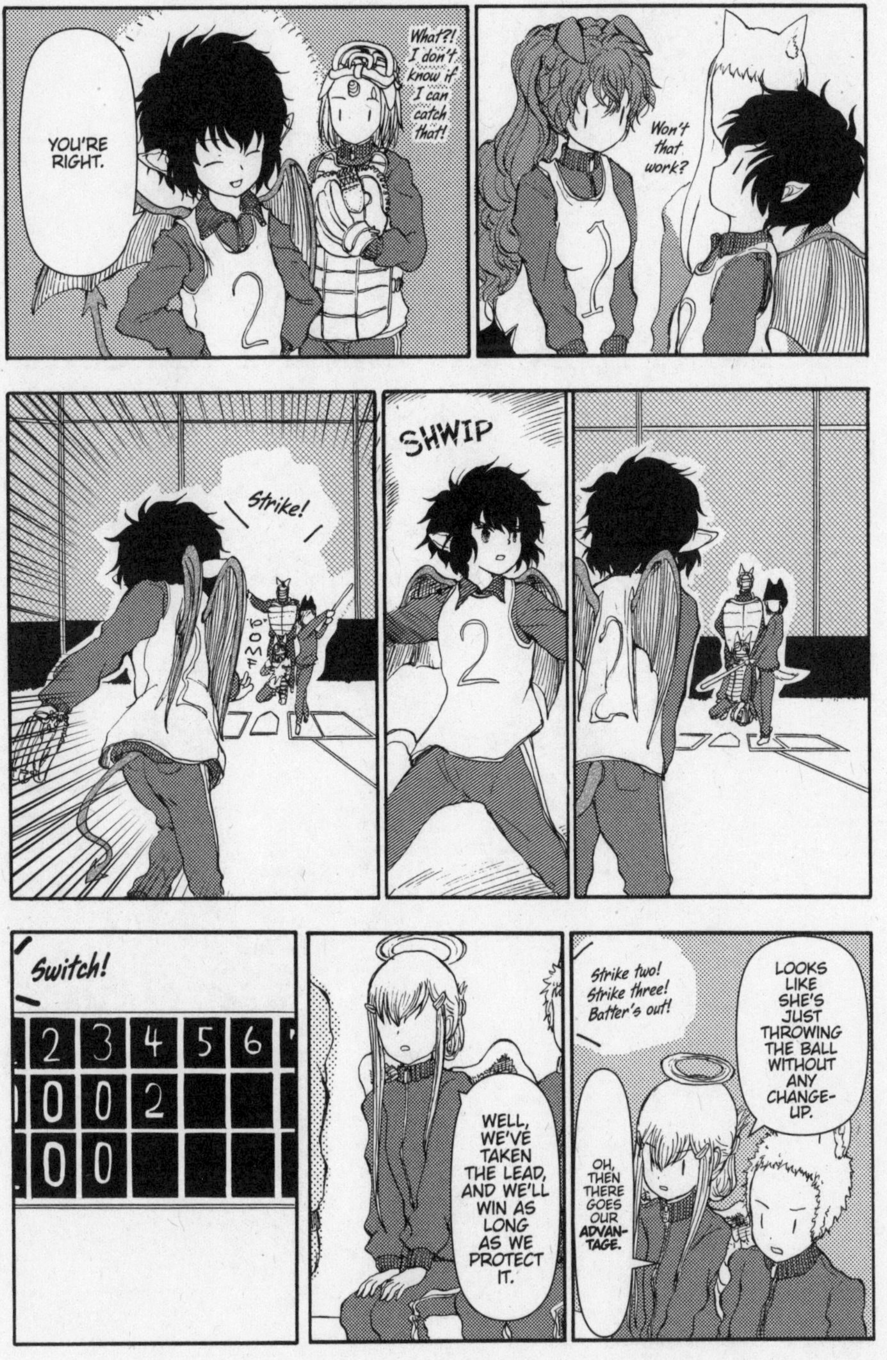
Won't that work?
What?! I don't know if I can catch that!
YOU'RE RIGHT.
SHWIP
Strike!
POMF
LOOKS LIKE SHE'S JUST THROWING THE BALL WITHOUT ANY CHANGE-UP.
Strike two! Strike three! Batter's out!
OH, THEN THERE GOES OUR ADVANTAGE.
WELL, WE'VE TAKEN THE LEAD, AND WE'LL WIN AS LONG AS WE PROTECT IT.
Switch!

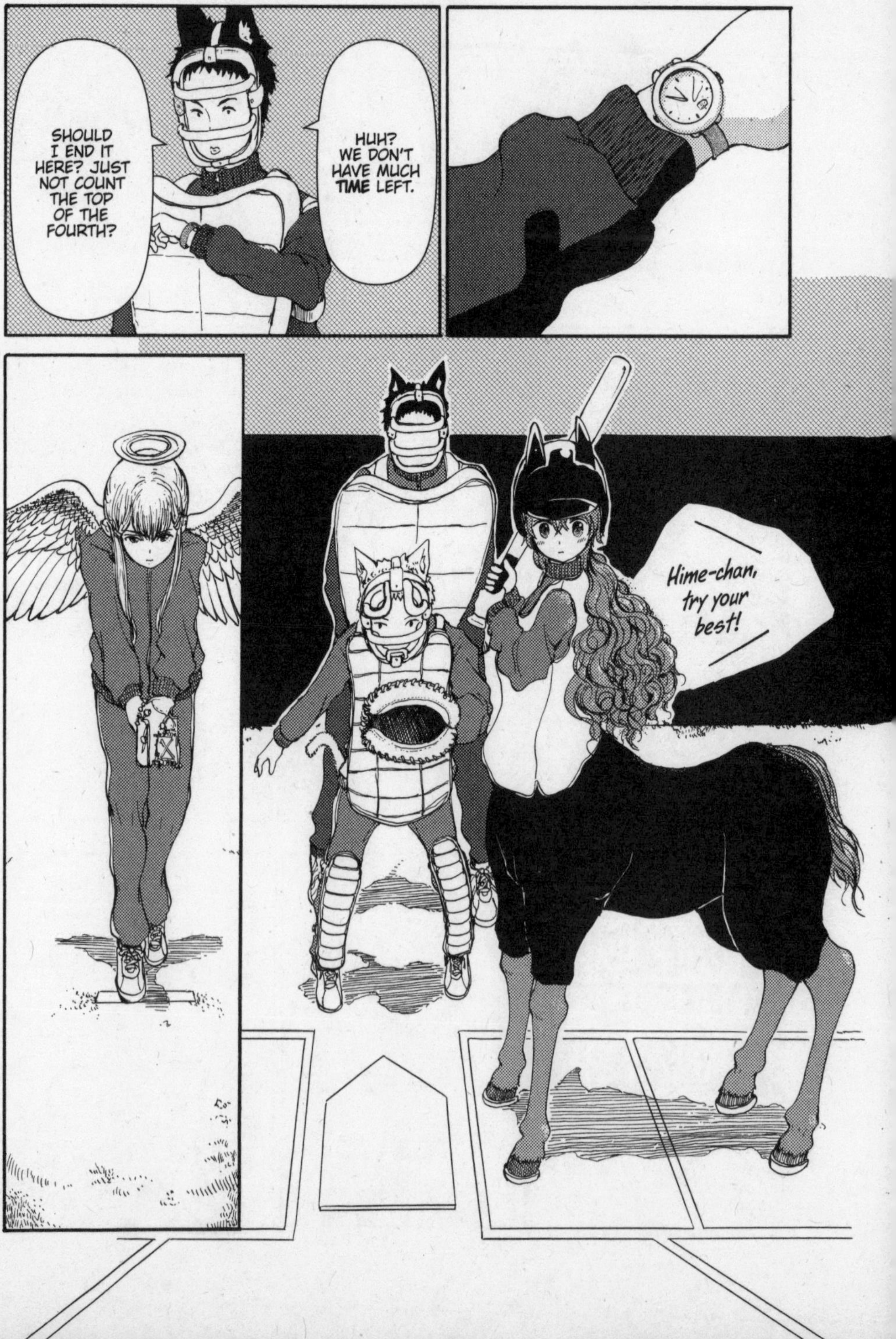
HUH? WE DON'T HAVE MUCH TIME LEFT.
SHOULD I END IT HERE? JUST NOT COUNT THE TOP OF THE FOURTH?
Hime-chan, try your best!

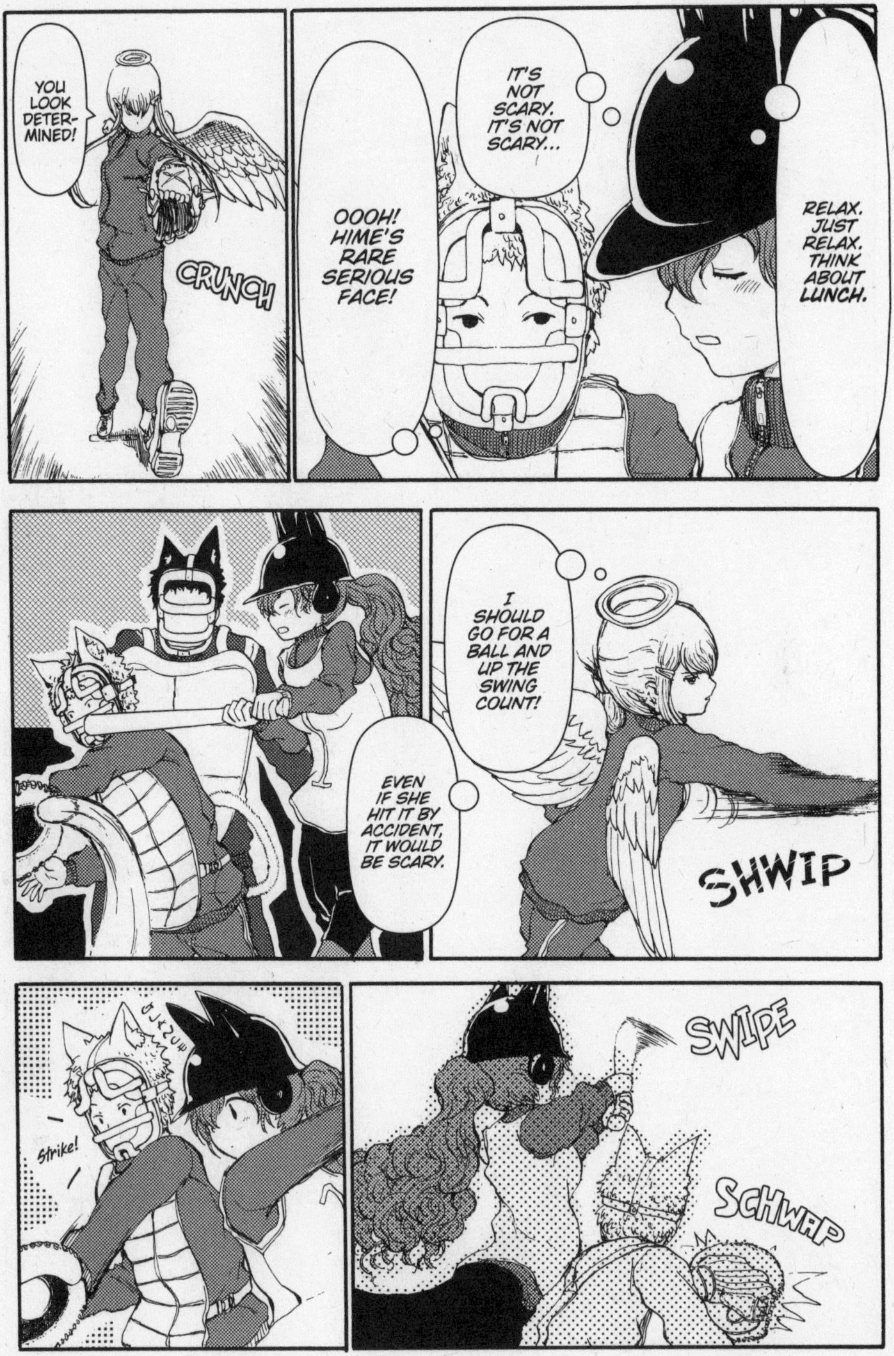

RELAX. JUST RELAX. THINK ABOUT LUNCH.
IT'S NOT SCARY. IT'S NOT SCARY...
OOOH! HIME'S RARE SERIOUS FACE!
YOU LOOK DETERMINED!
CRUNCH
I SHOULD GO FOR A BALL AND UP THE SWING COUNT!
SHWIP
EVEN IF SHE HIT IT BY ACCIDENT, IT WOULD BE SCARY.
SWIPE
SCHWAP
Strike!

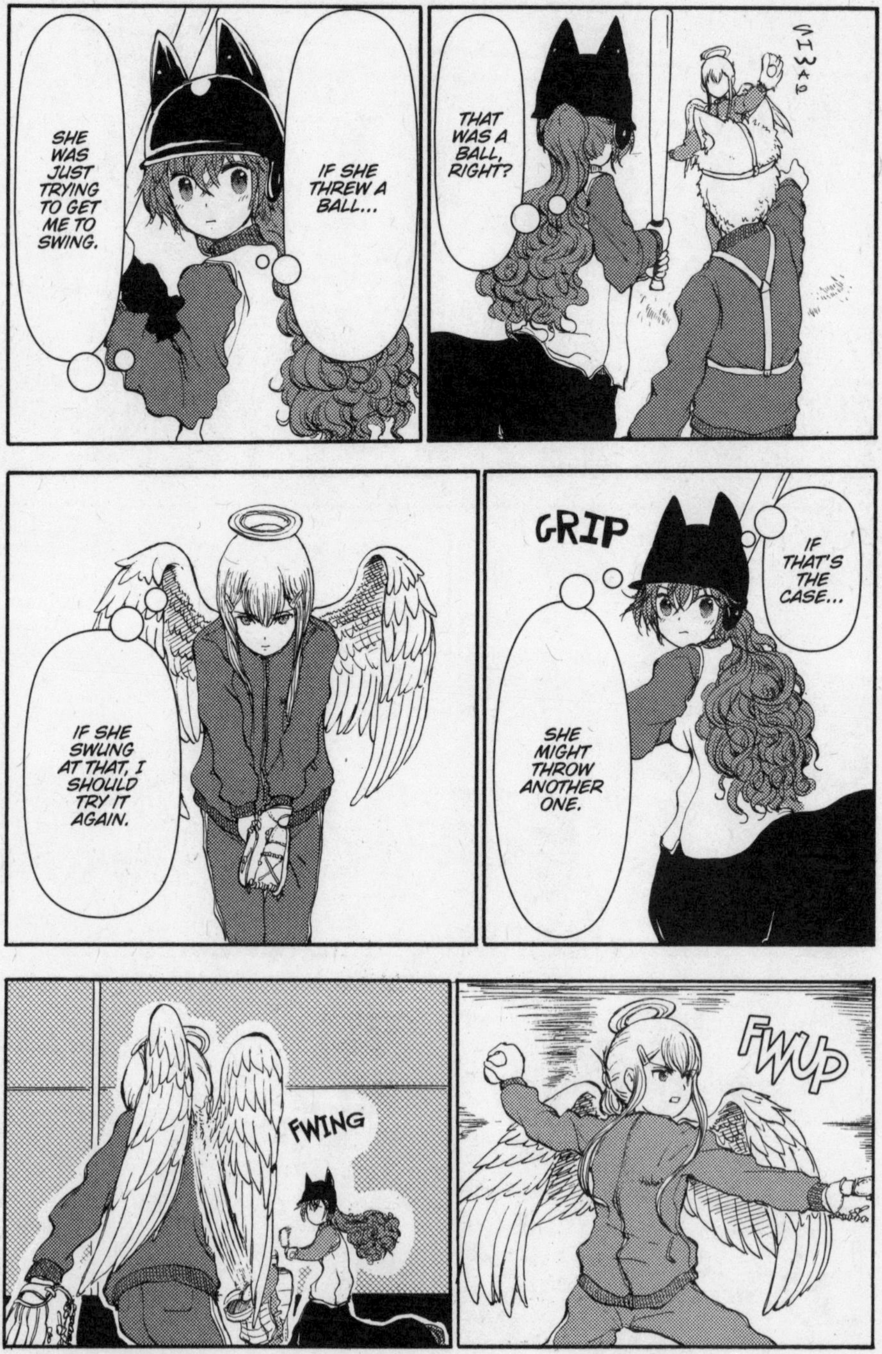
SHWAP
THAT WAS A BALL, RIGHT?
IF SHE THREW A BALL...
SHE WAS JUST TRYING TO GET ME TO SWING.
IF THAT'S THE CASE...
GRIP
SHE MIGHT THROW ANOTHER ONE.
IF SHE SWUNG AT THAT, I SHOULD TRY IT AGAIN.
FWUP
FWING

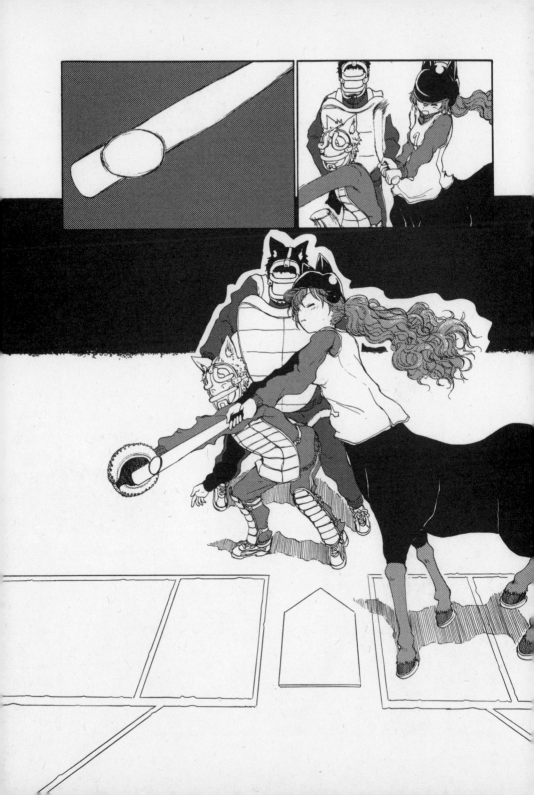

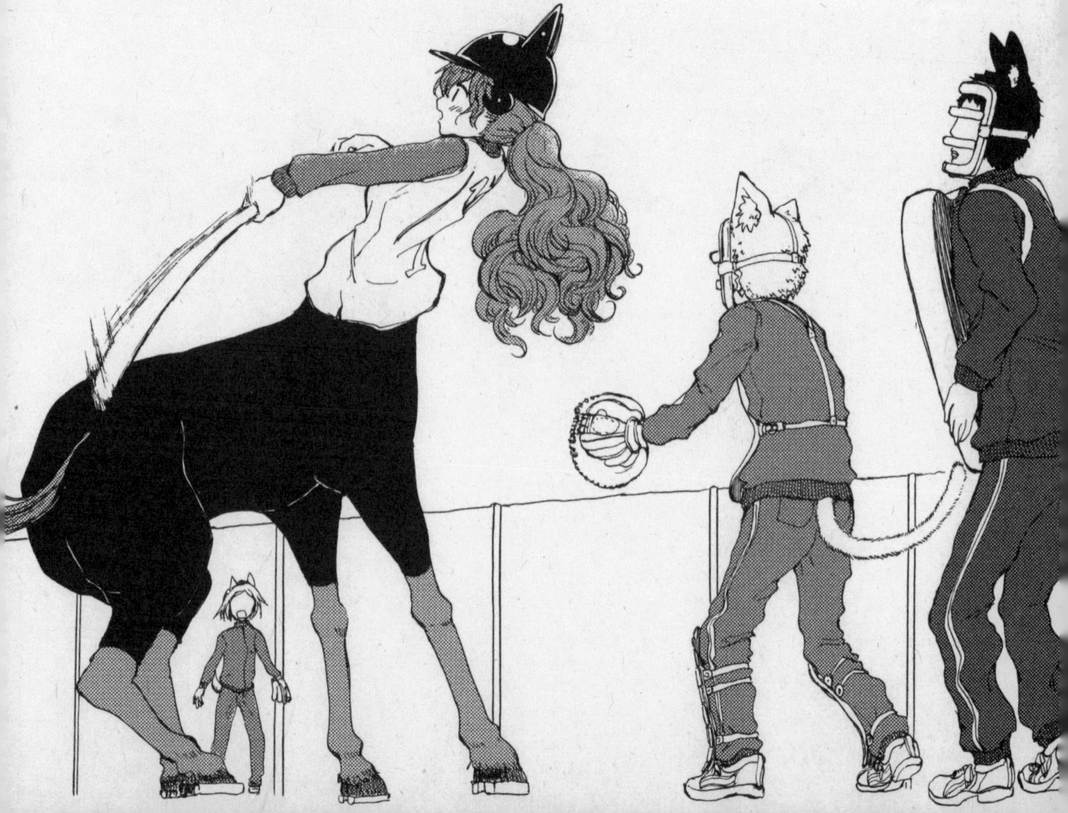

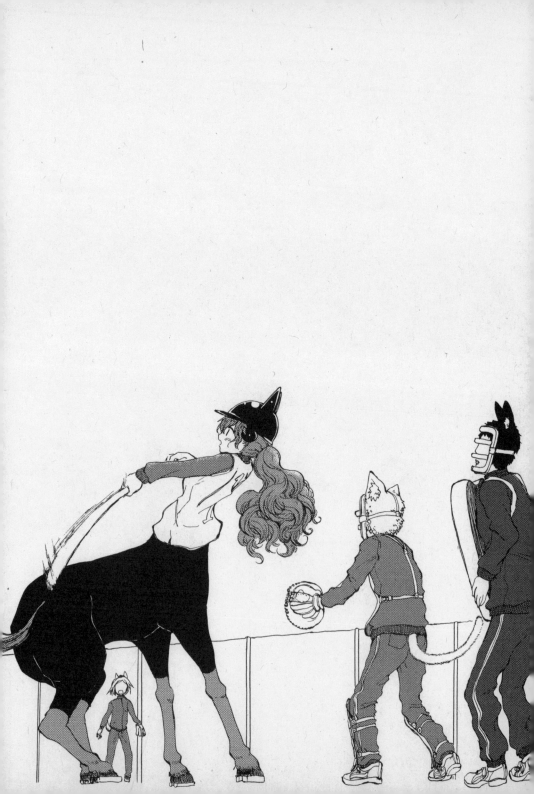

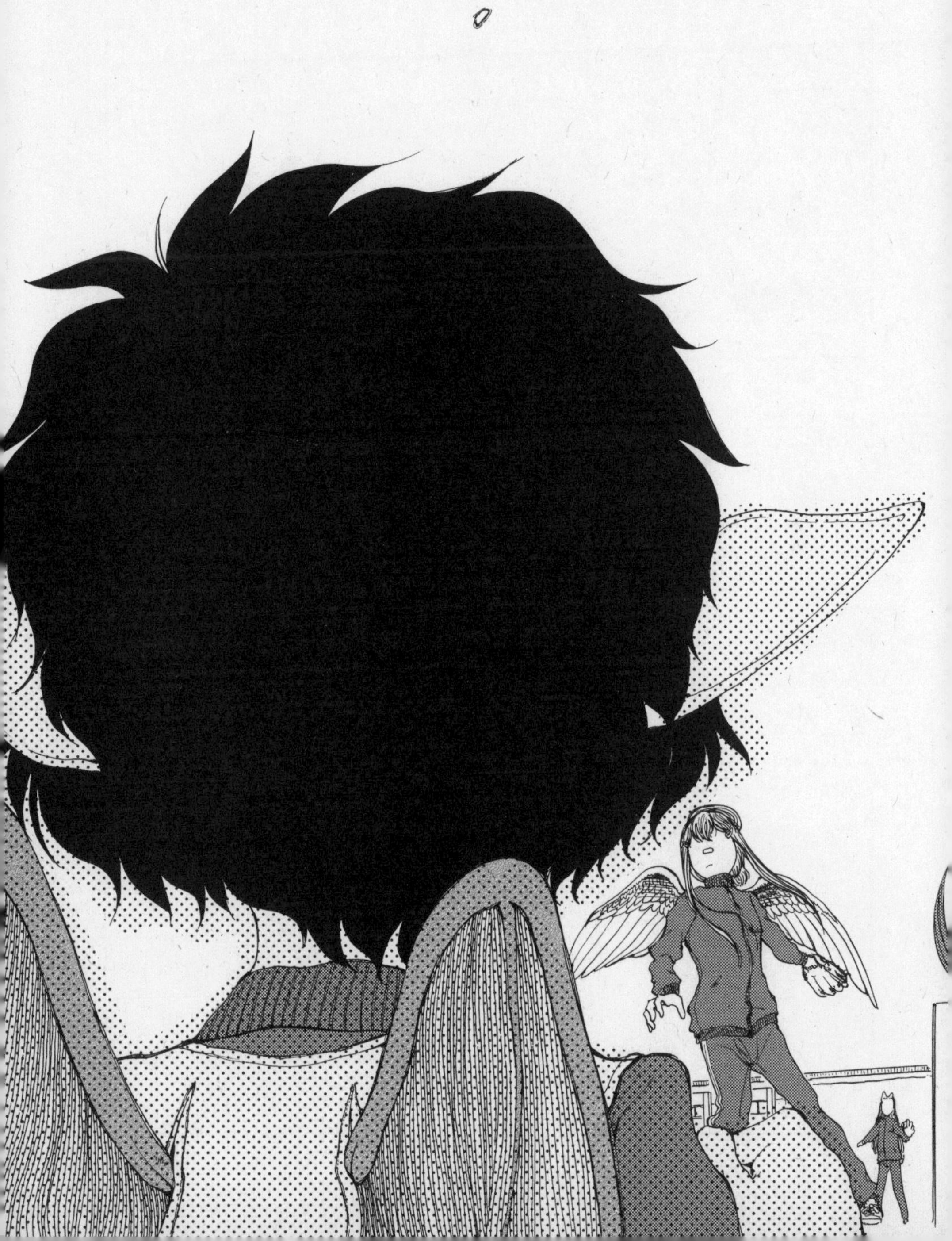

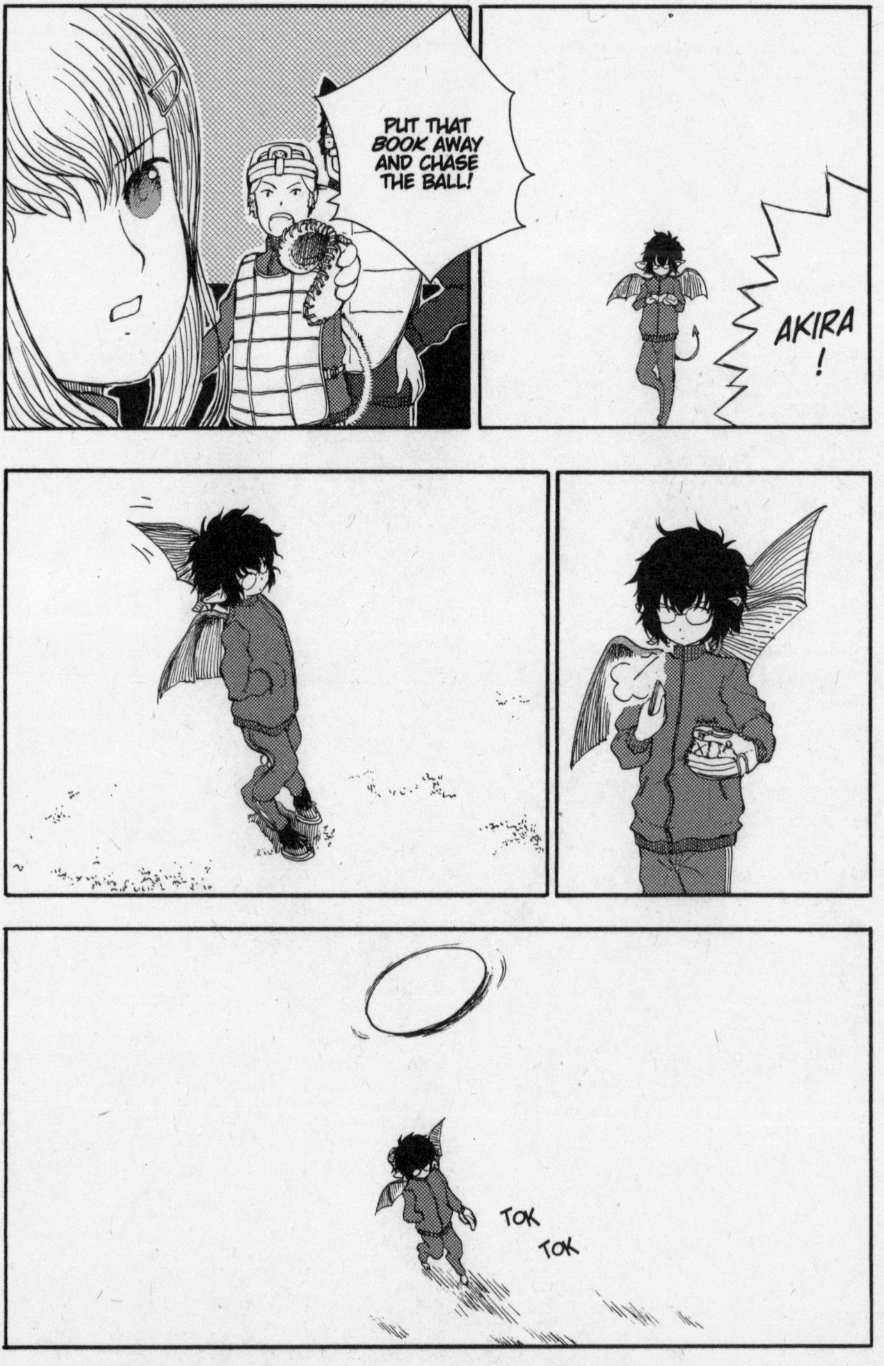
AKIRA !
PUT THAT BOOK AWAY AND CHASE THE BALL!
TOK TOK

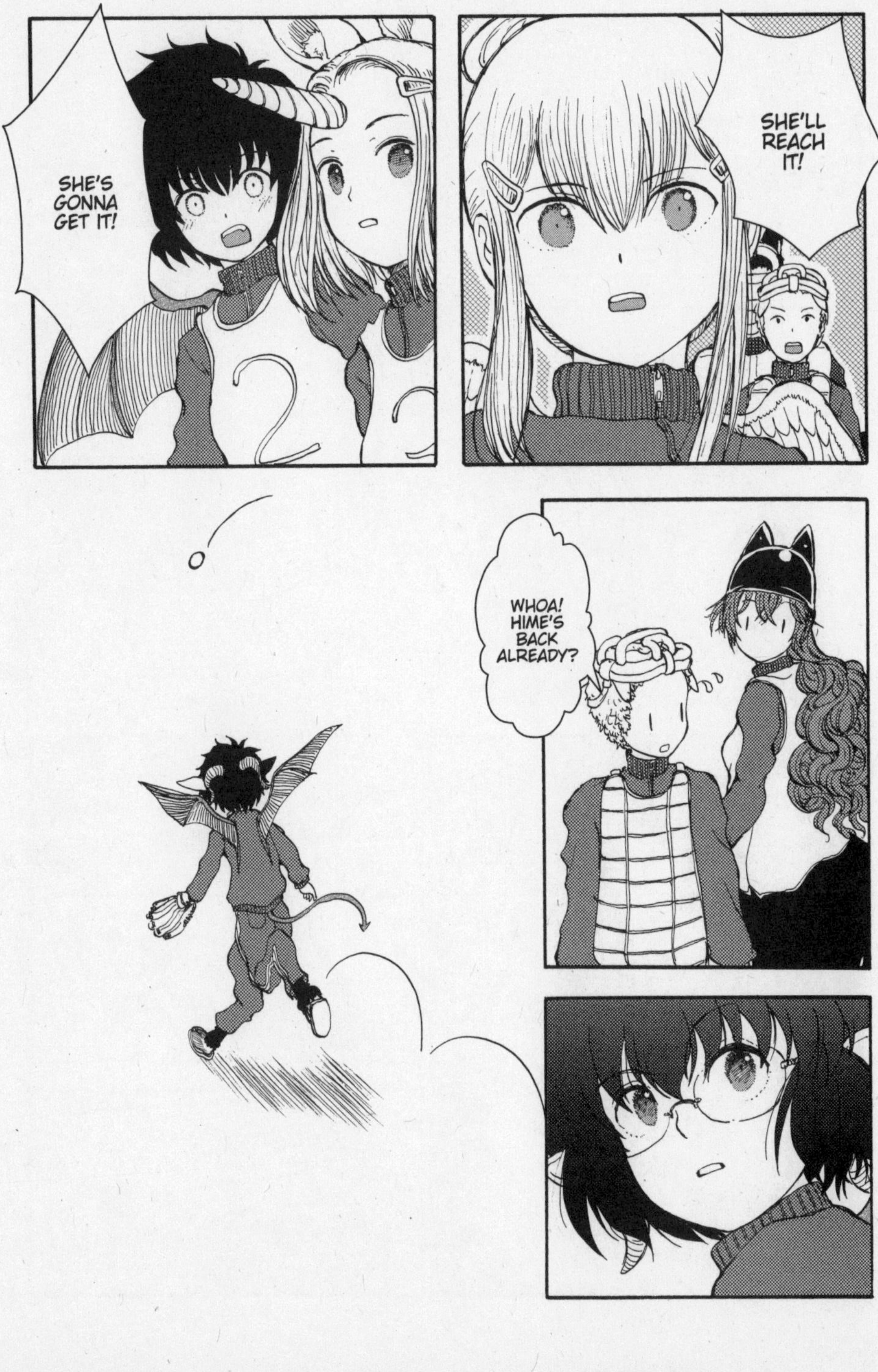
SHE'LL REACH IT!
SHE'S GONNA GET IT!
WHOA! HIME'S BACK ALREADY?

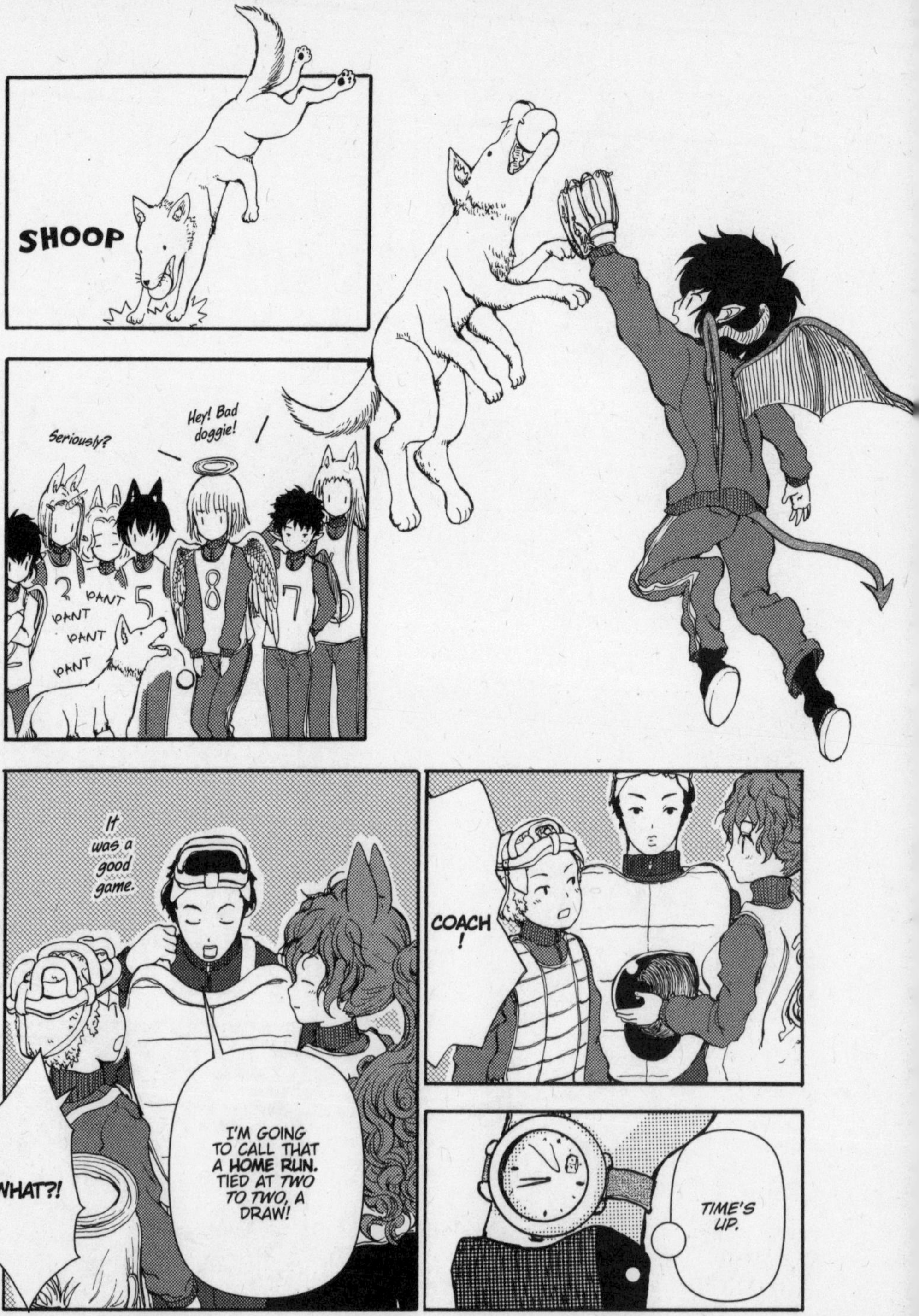
SHOOP
Hey! Bad doggie!
Seriously?
PANT
PANT
PANT
PANT
COACH!
TIME'S UP.
It was a good game.
I'M GOING TO CALL THAT A HOME RUN. TIED AT TWO TO TWO, A DRAW!
WHAT?!

A Centaur's Life

SUPERNATURAL BEINGS: GODS

SINCE THE DAWN OF HUMANITY, PEOPLE HAVE TRIED TO EXPLAIN THE UNKNOWN AS A PRODUCT OF SUPERNATURAL BEINGS, AND OVER TIME THEY'VE STRENGTHENED THOSE BEINGS WITH THE POWER OF THEIR BELIEFS. THESE BEINGS ARE KNOWN AS GODS. THESE GODS TAKE ON DIFFERENT FORMS AND ROLES DEPENDING ON THE CULTURE AND RELIGION OF THEIR WORSHIPPERS. THESE ARE SOME OF THE MOST POPULAR INCARNATIONS OF THE SUPERNATURAL ENTITIES WE KNOW AS GODS:

① A FORMLESS LIGHT OR FIRE. FREQUENTLY FOUND IN MONOTHEISTIC RELIGIONS.

② A CREATURE THAT IS PART ANIMAL AND PART HUMAN BUT DOES NOT LOOK LIKE ANY MODERN HUMAN RACE.

③ A BEING WHO TAKES ON A SHAPE THAT COMBINES THE LOOK OF MULTIPLE MODERN RACES. COMMON IN POLYTHEISTIC RELIGIONS.

④ TAKES THE FORM OF THE RAREST EXTANT SPECIES AND IS OFTEN DEPICTED WITH CLOUDS OR LIGHT BELOW HIS TORSO.

⑤ LOOKS EXACTLY LIKE ANY MODERN HUMAN RACE. COMPARATIVELY INDIVIDUALISTIC AND DEPICTED DIFFERENTLY DEPENDING ON THE NATURE AND CULTURE OF WORSHIPPERS.

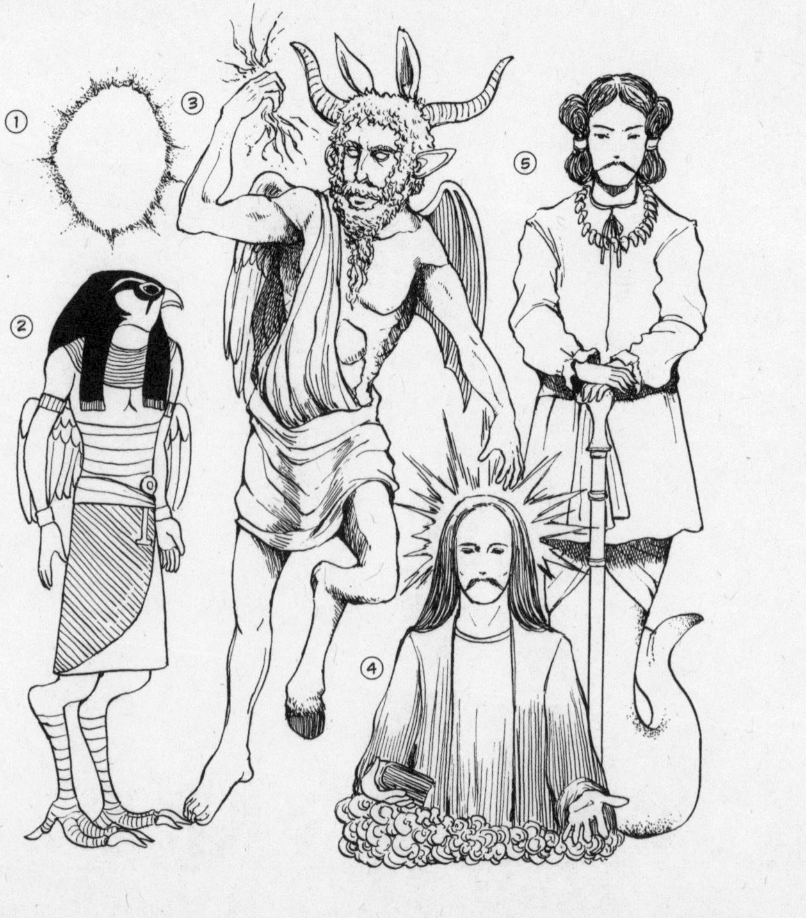
①
②
③
④
⑤

CHAPTER 10

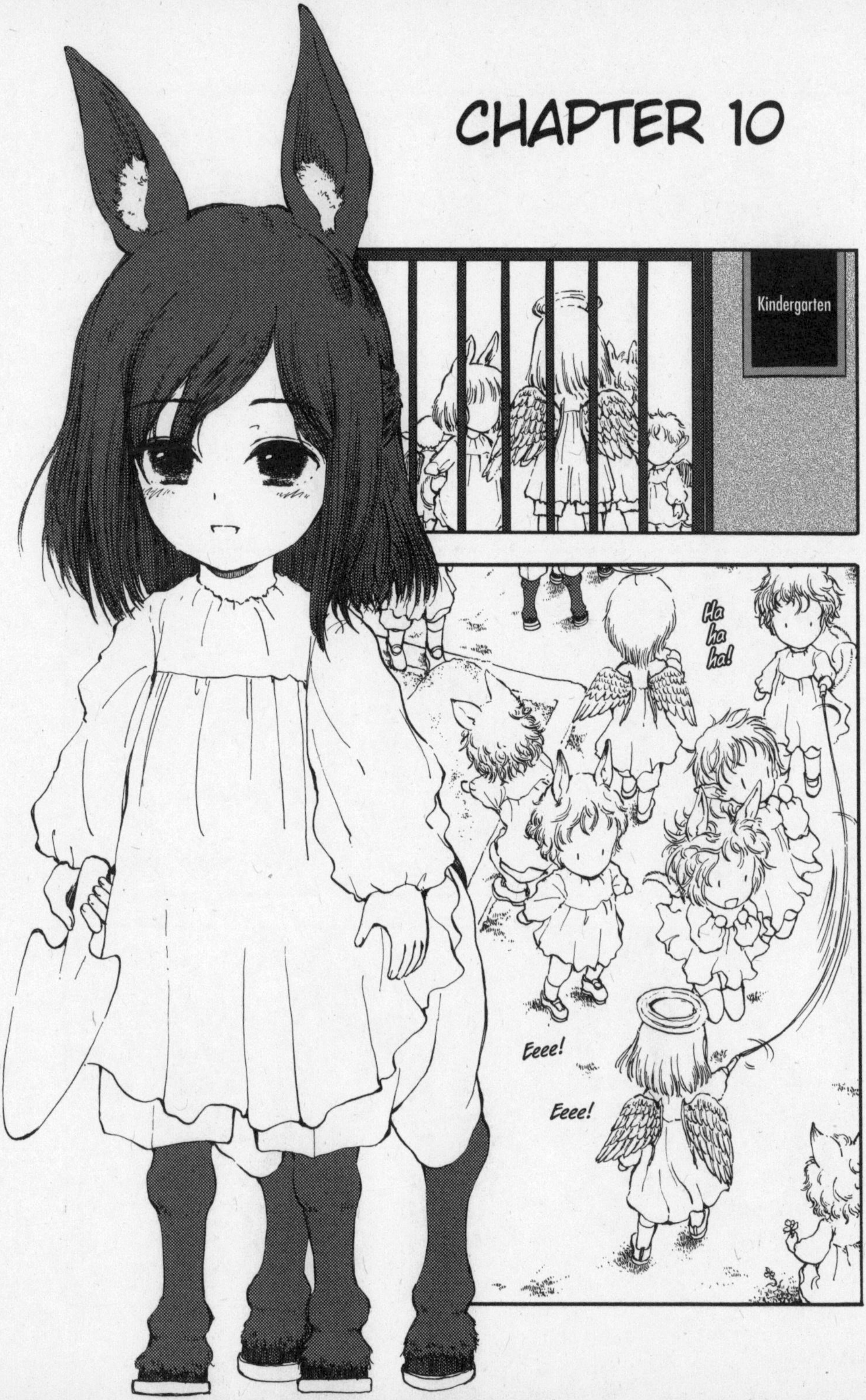
Kindergarten
Ha ha ha!
Eeee!
Eeee!

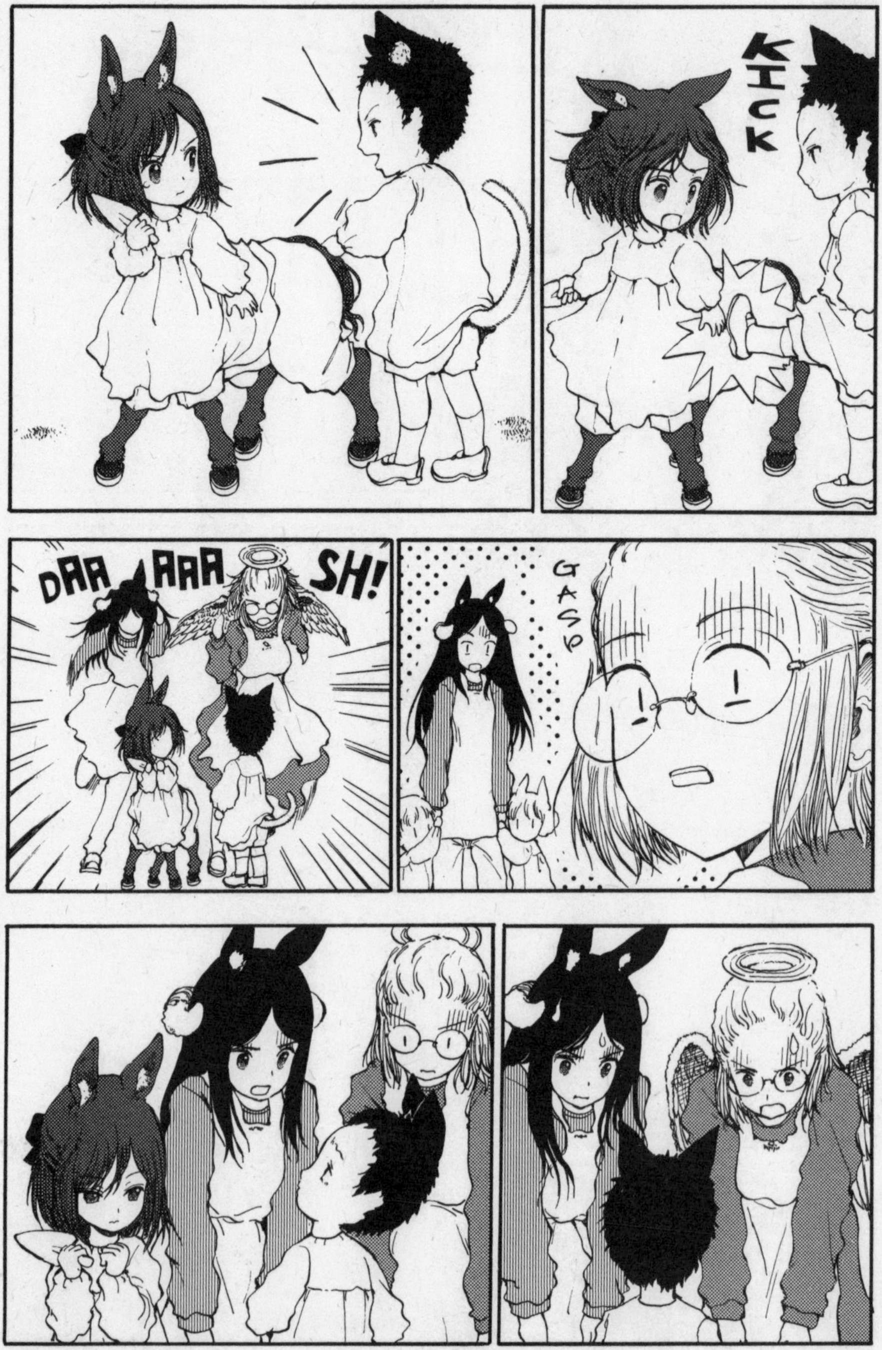
KICK
GASP
DAA AAA SH!

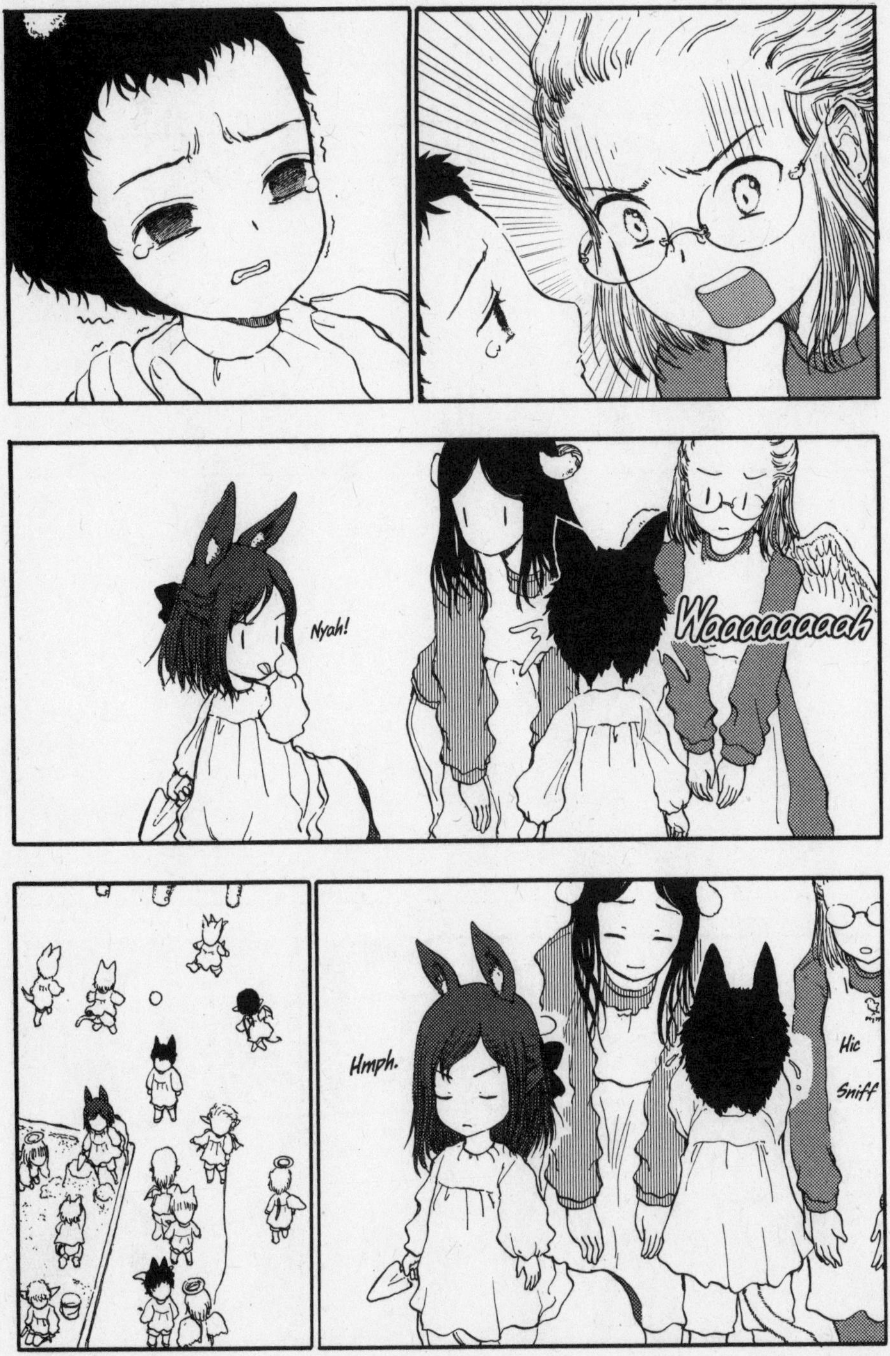

Waaaaaaaah
Nyah!
Hic
Sniff
Hmph.

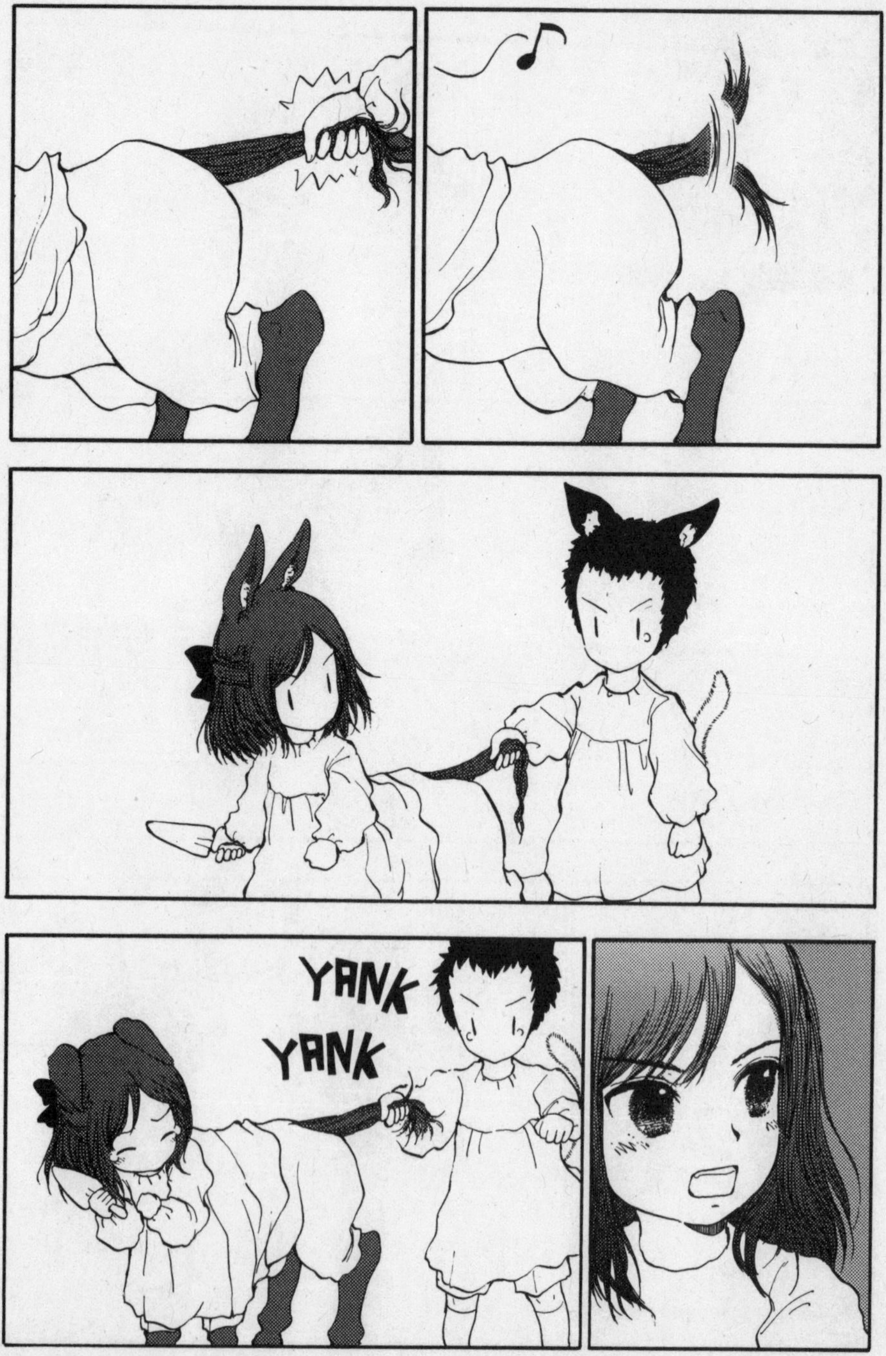
YANK
YANK

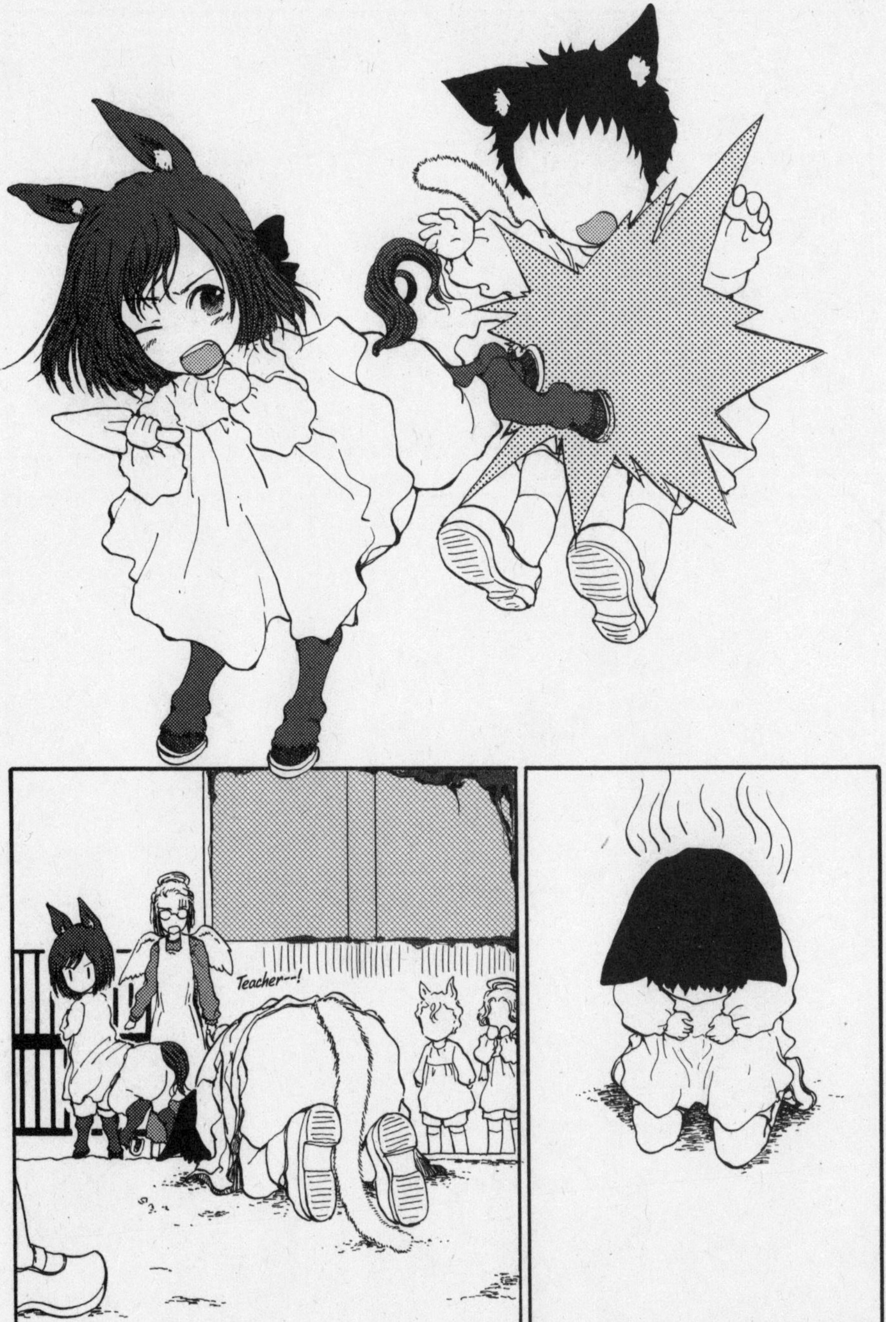
Teacher--!

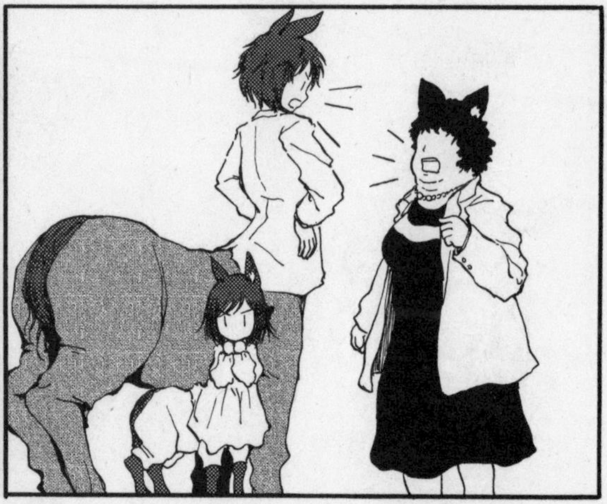

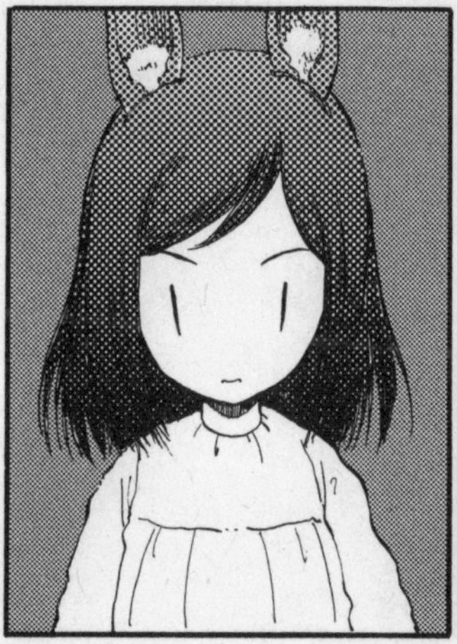

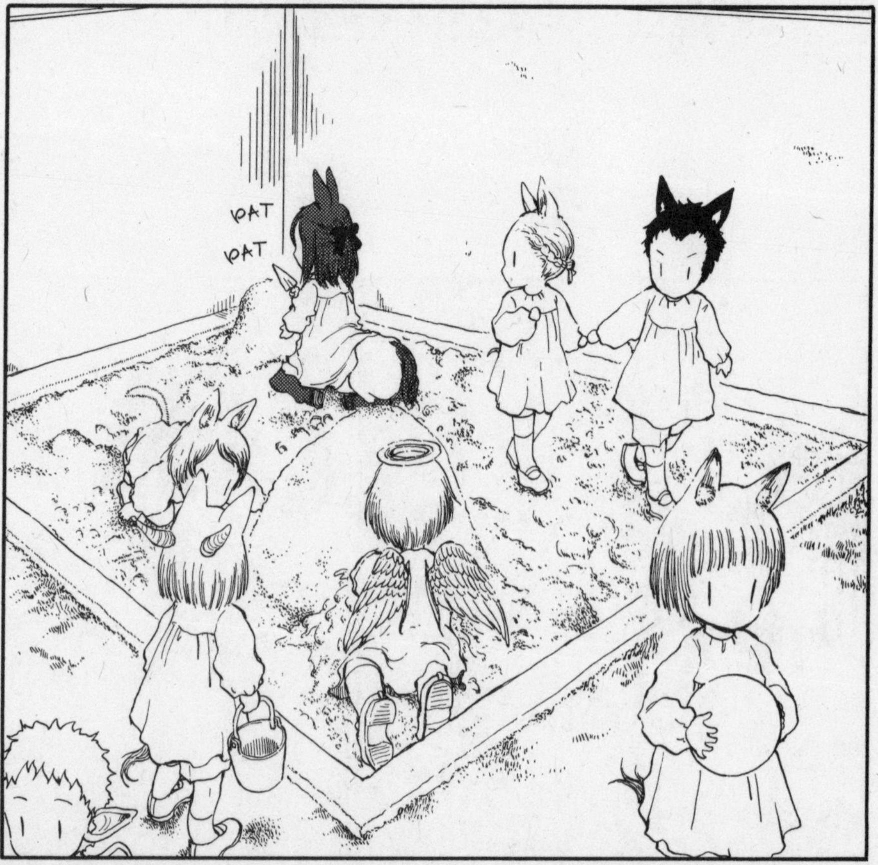
PAT
PAT

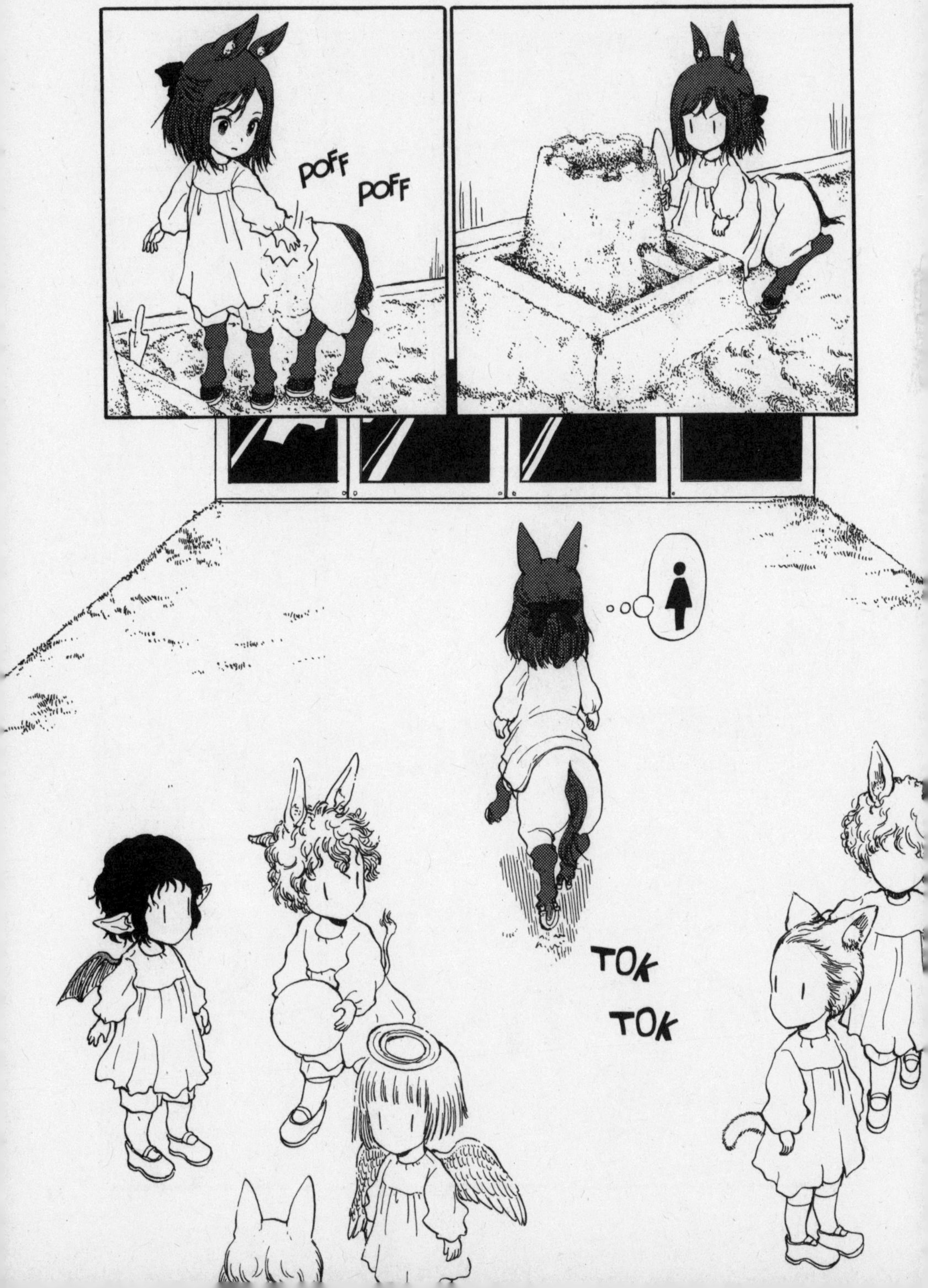
POFF
POFF
TOK
TOK

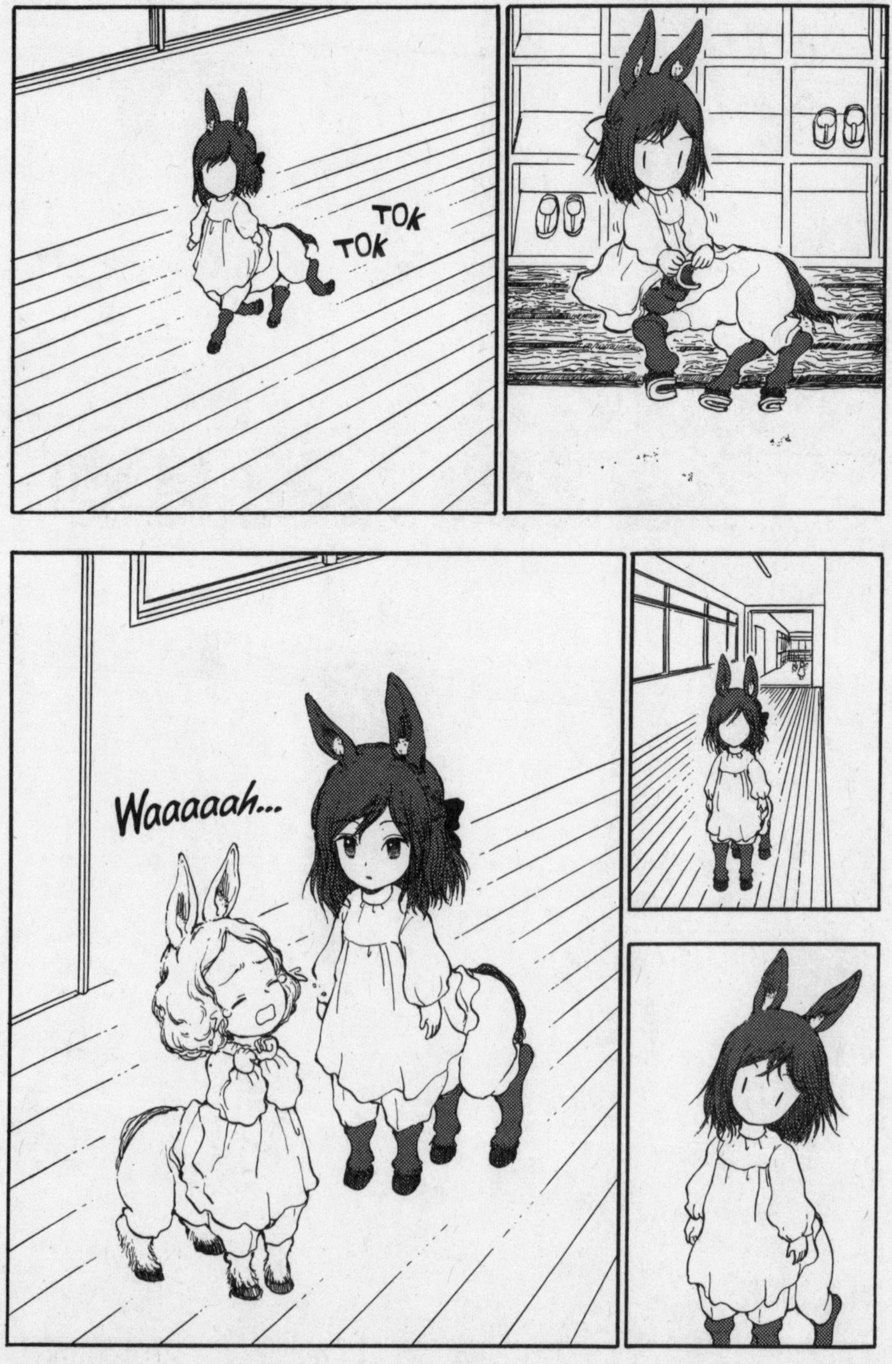
TOK
TOK
Waaaaah...

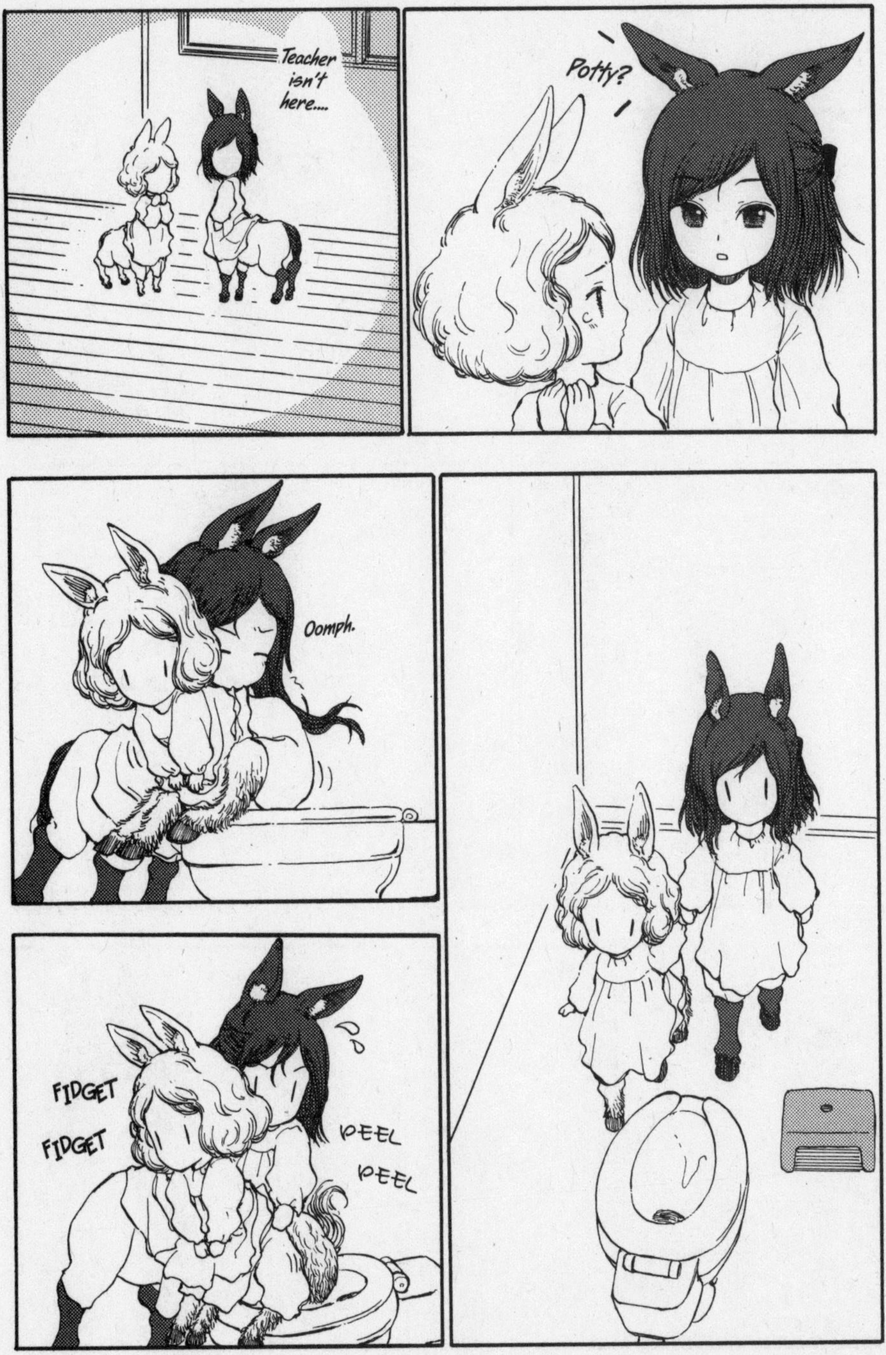
Potty?
Teacher isn't here....
Oomph.
FIDGET
FIDGET
PEEL
PEEL

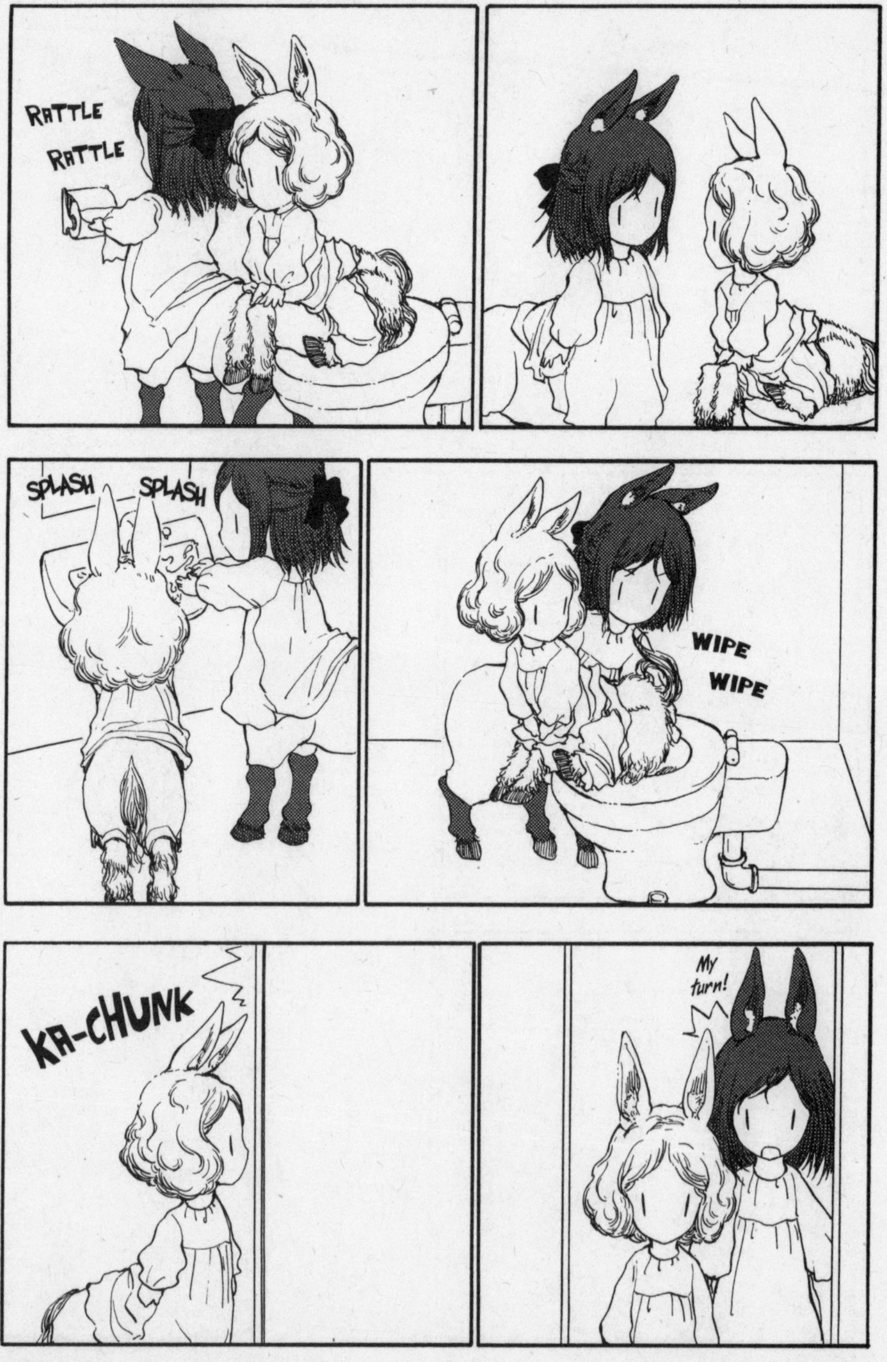
RATTLE
RATTLE
WIPE
WIPE
SPLASH
SPLASH
My turn!
KA-CHUNK

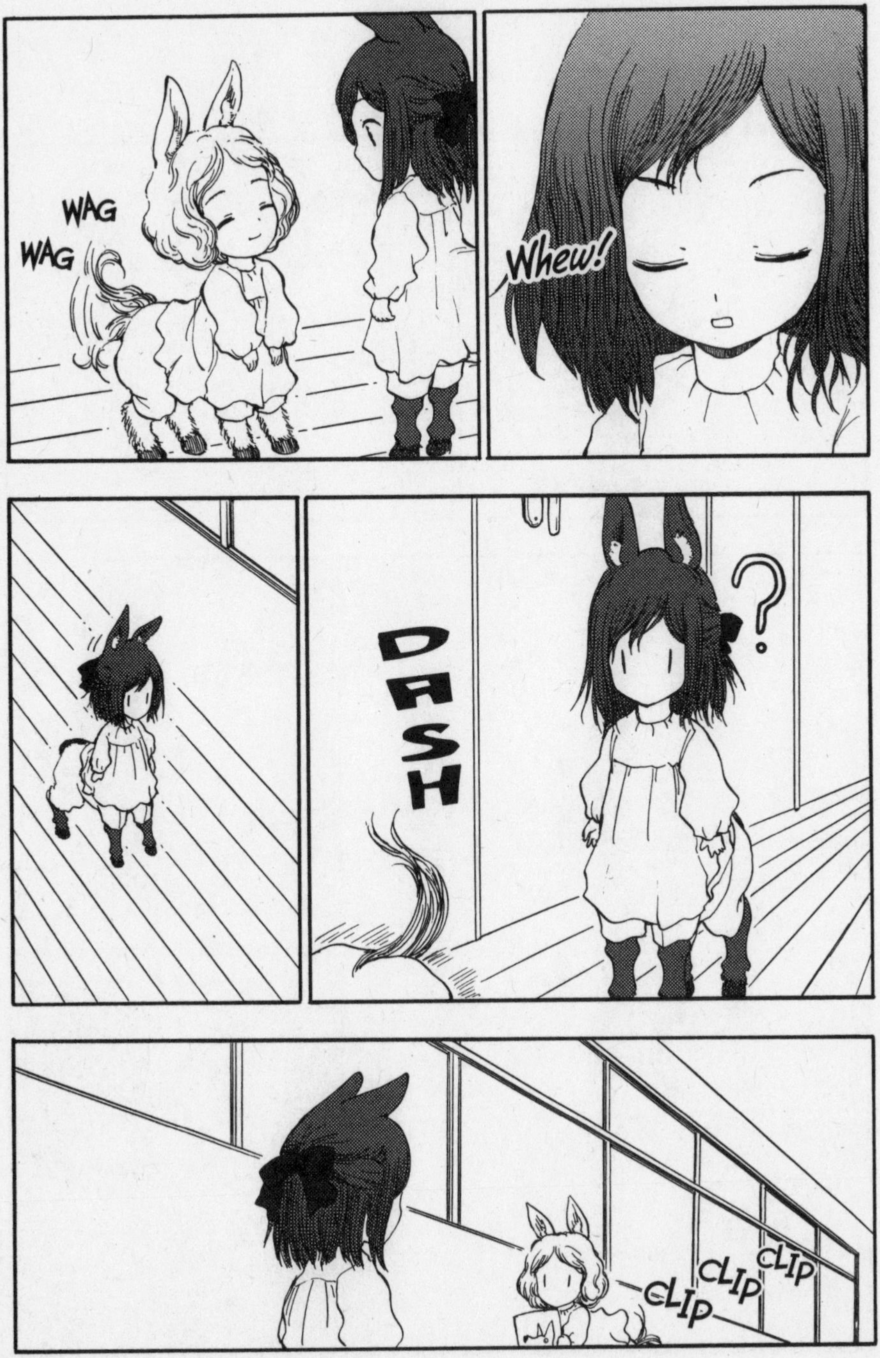
Whew!
WAG
WAG
?
DASH
CLIP
CLIP
CLIP

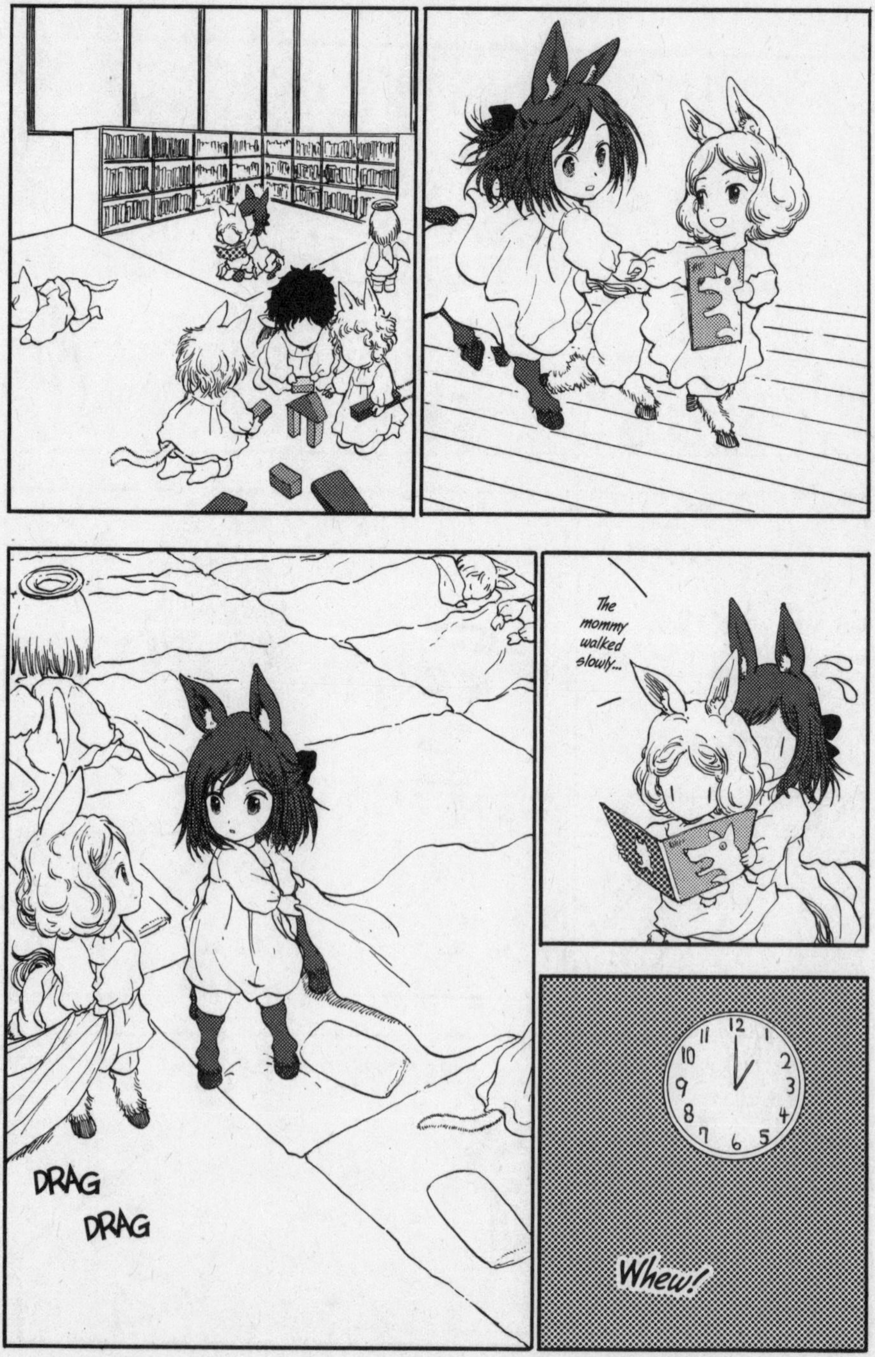
The mommy walked slowly...
Whew!
DRAG
DRAG

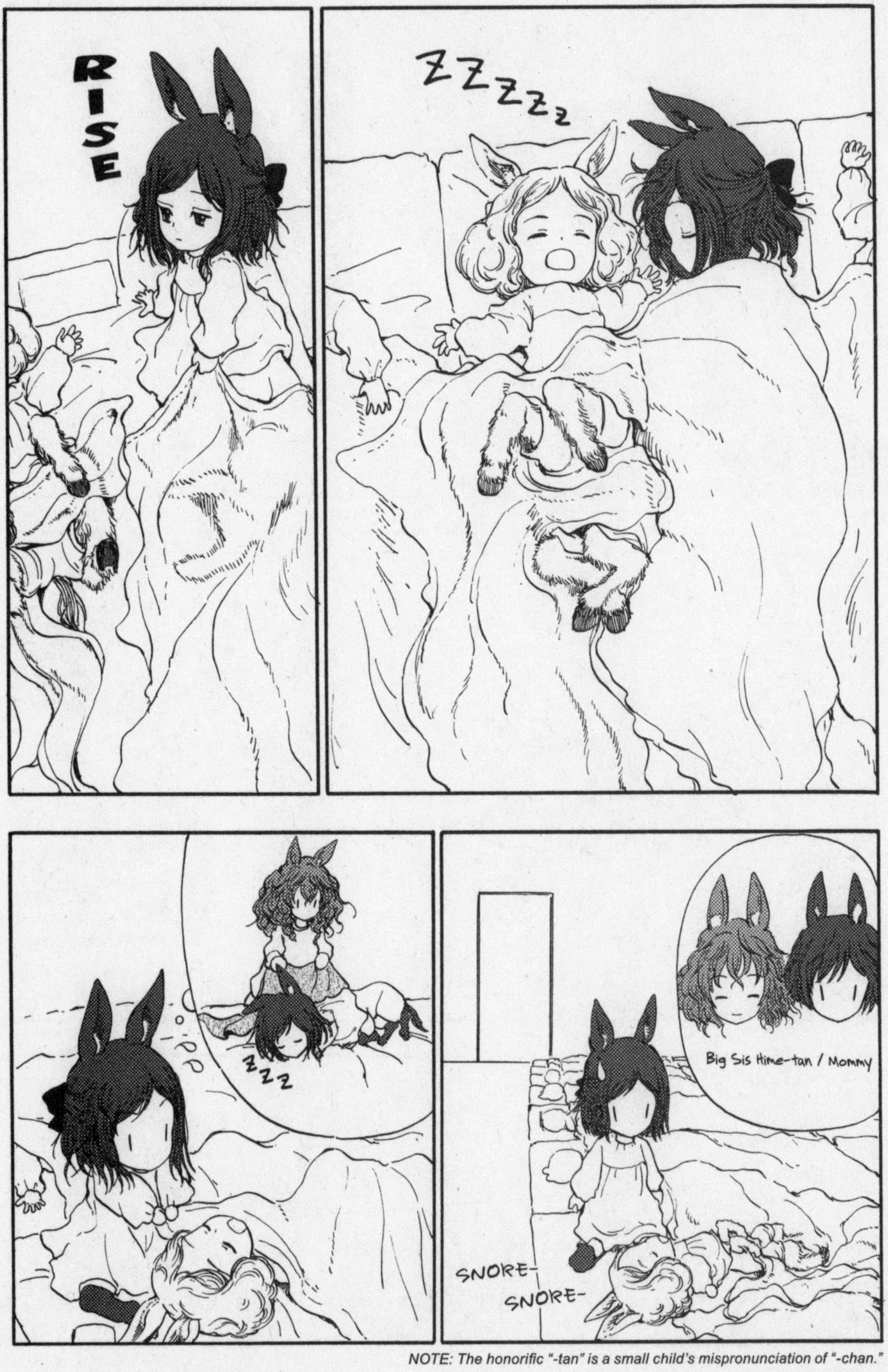
ZZZzzz
RISE
Big Sis Hime-tan / Mommy
SNORE-
SNORE-
ZZZ

NOTE: The honorific "-tan" is a small child's mispronunciation of "-chan."

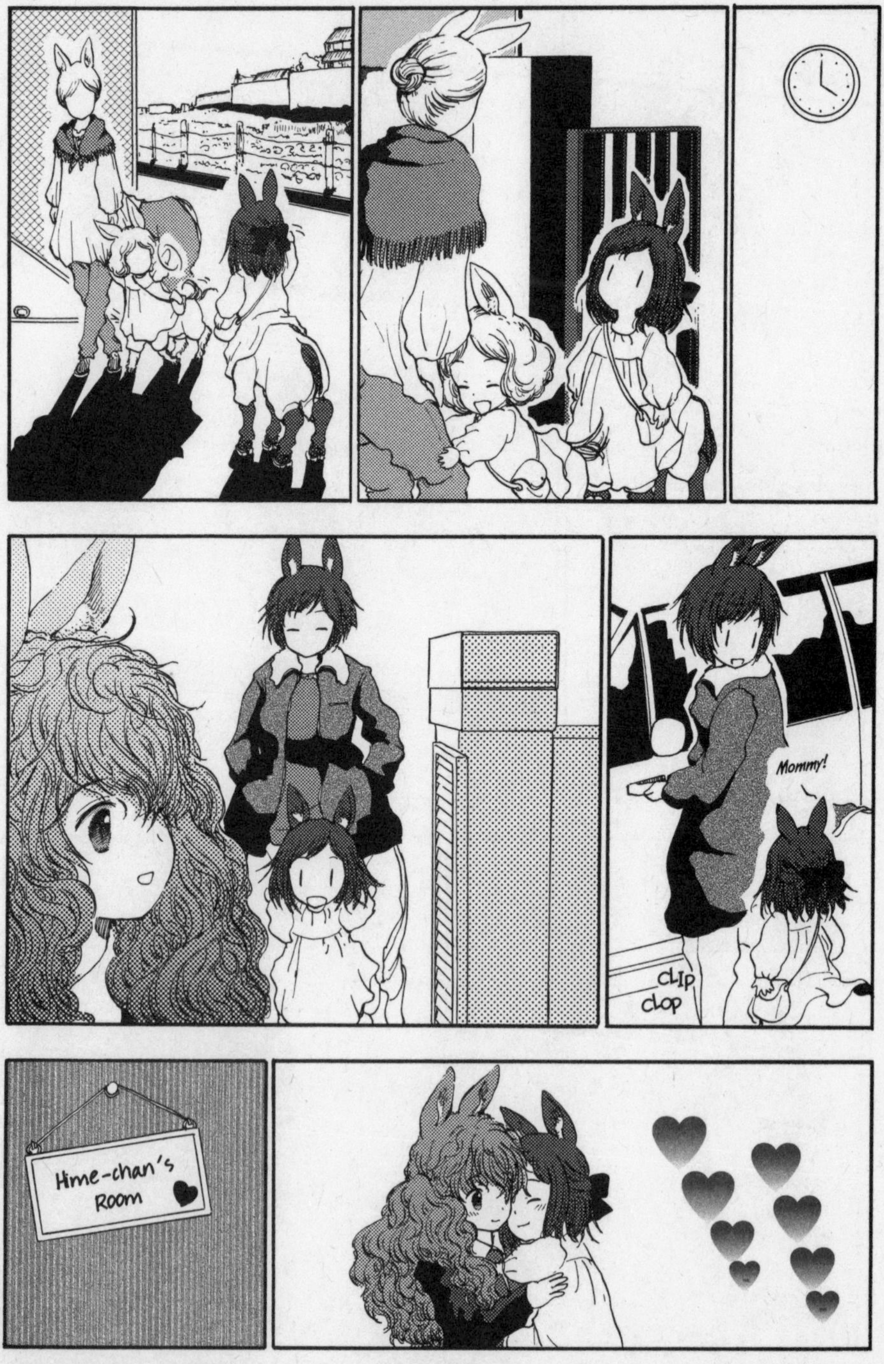
Mommy!
CLIP
clop
Hime-chan's Room

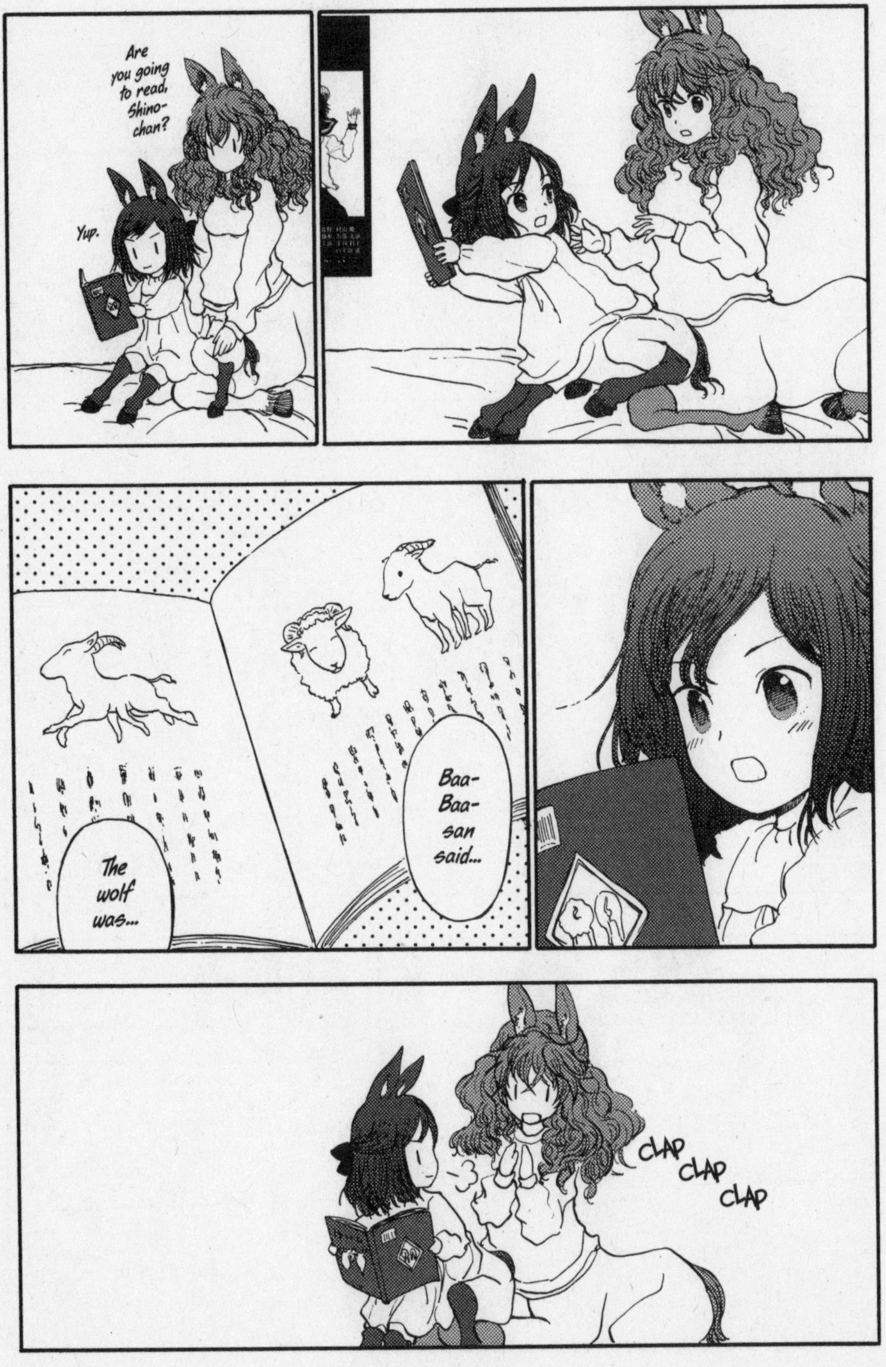
Are you going to read, Shino-chan?
Yup.
Baa-Baa-san said...
The wolf was...
CLAP
CLAP
CLAP

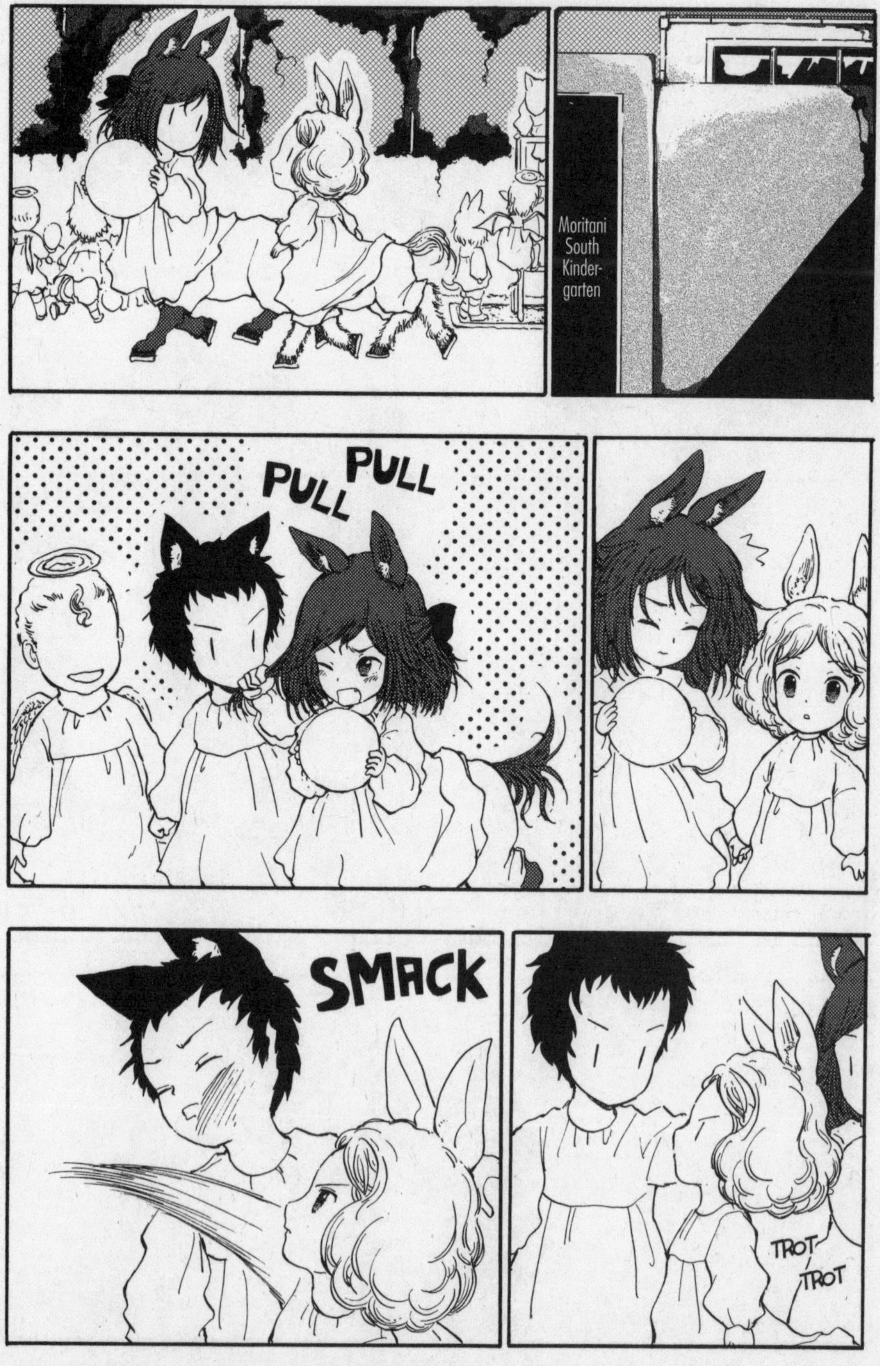
Moritani South Kinder-garten
PULL PULL
TROT TROT
SMACK

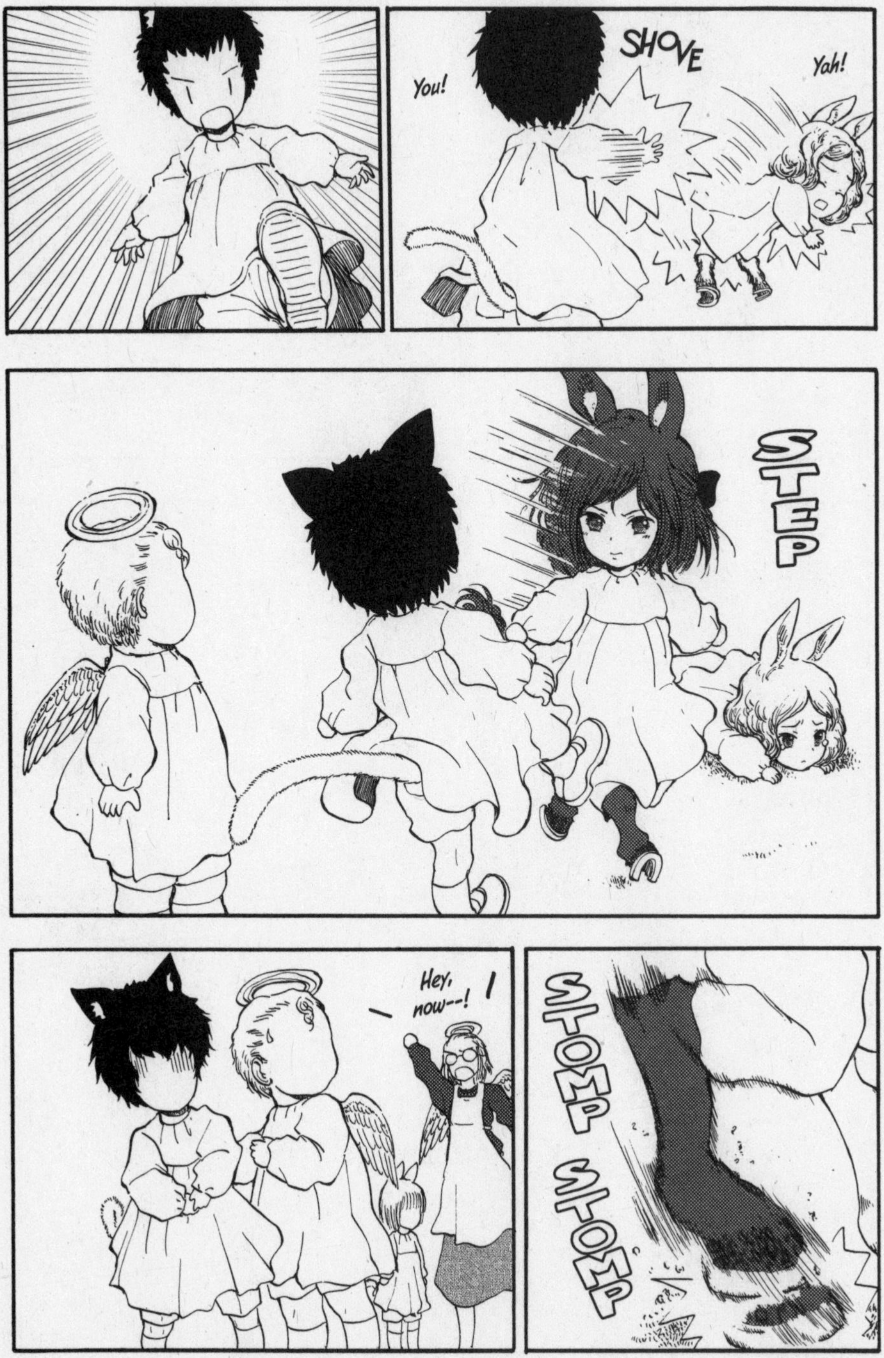
Yah!
SHOVE
You!
STEP
STOMP STOMP
Hey, now--!

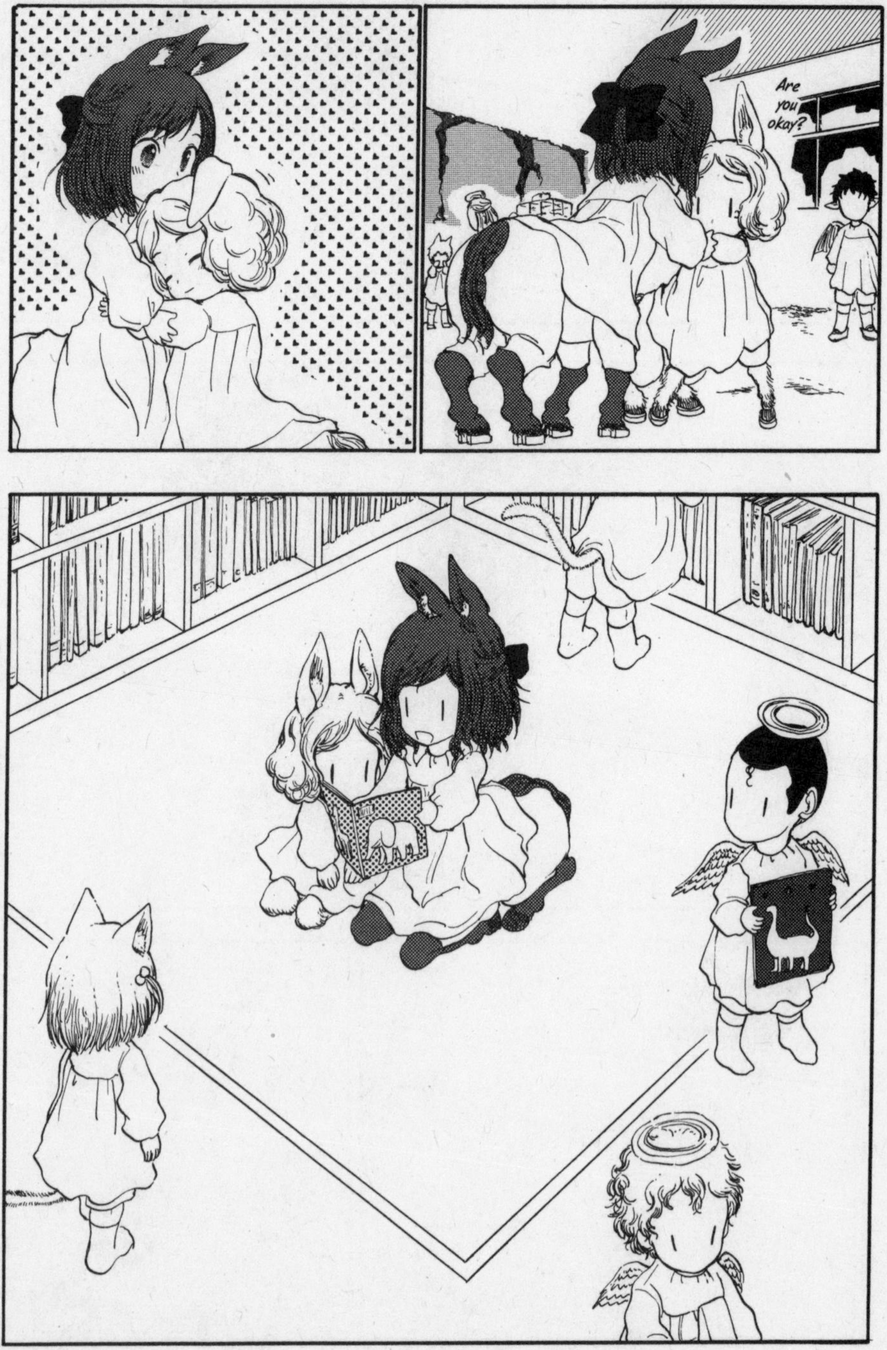
Are you okay?

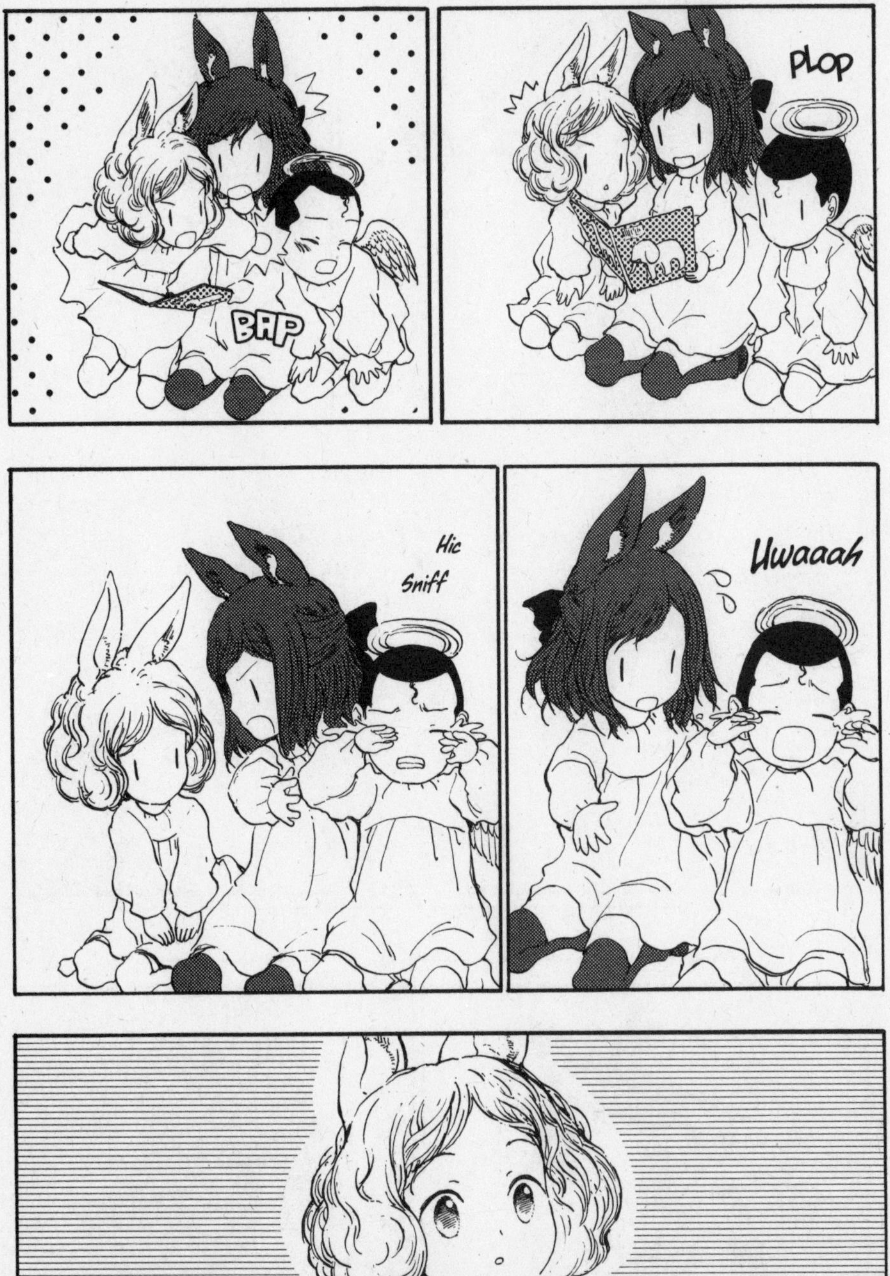
PLOP
BAP
Uwaaah
Hic
Sniff

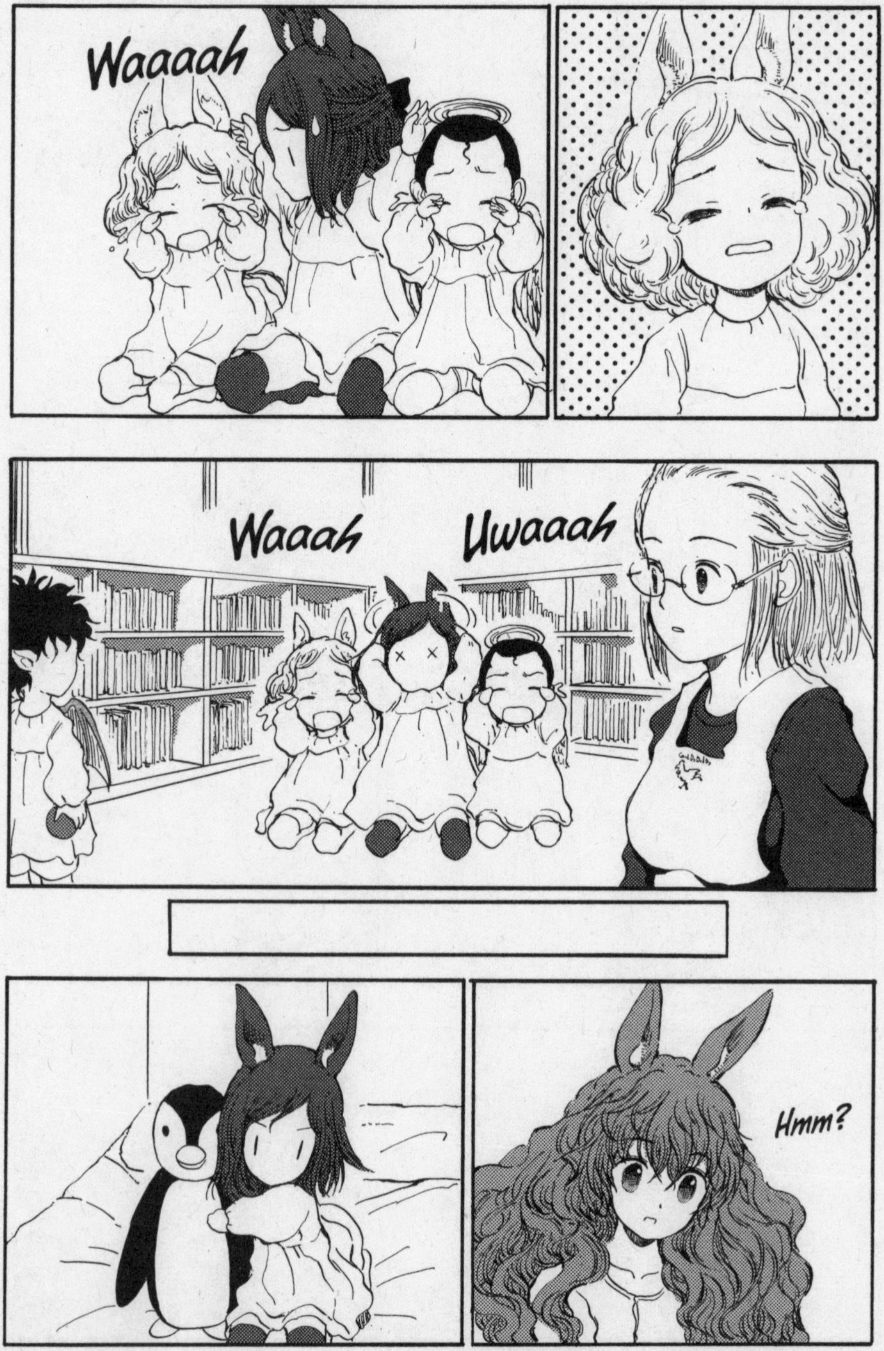
Waaaah
Uwaaah
Waaah
Hmm?

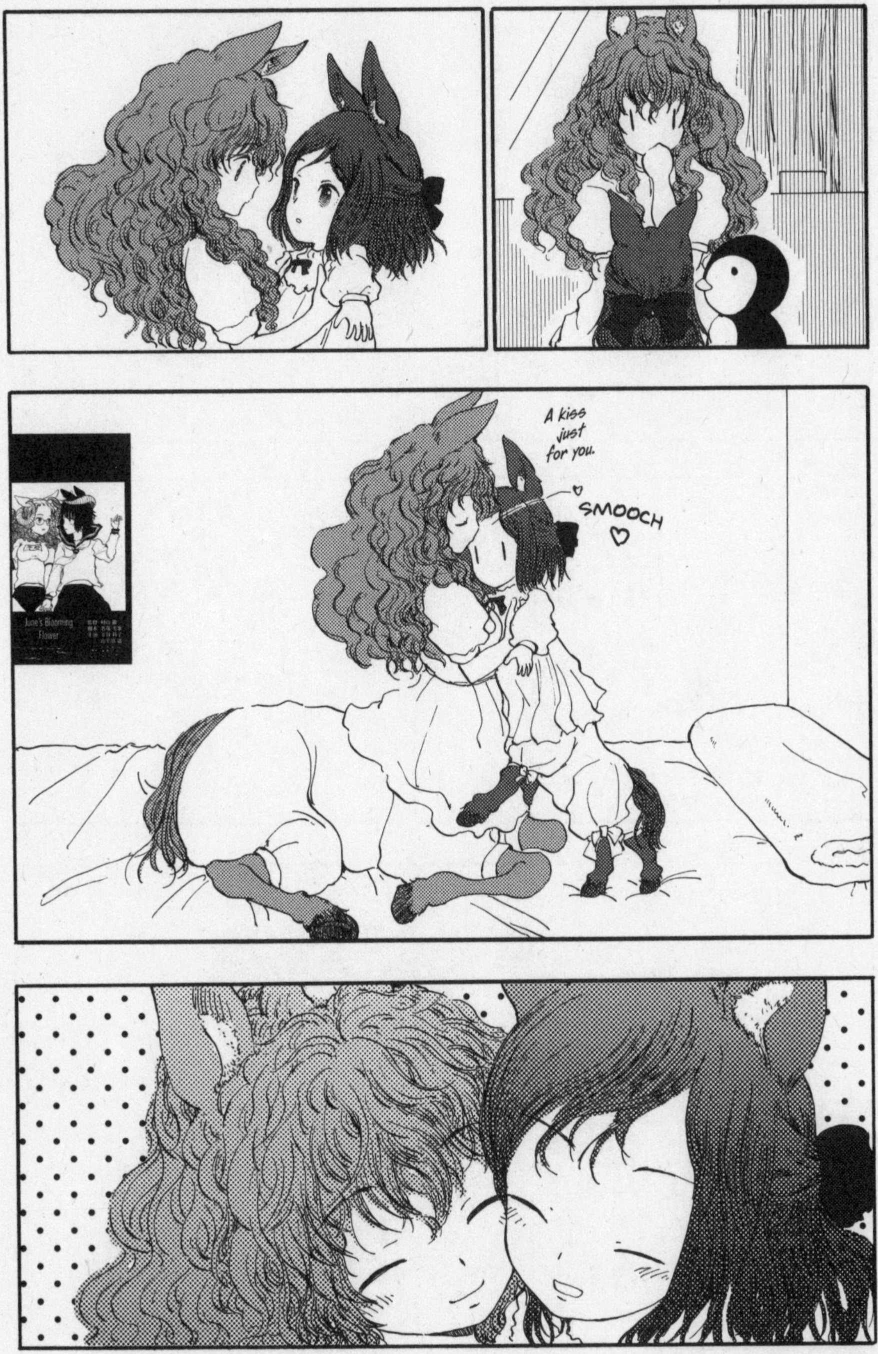
June's Blooming Flower
A kiss just for you.
SMOOCH

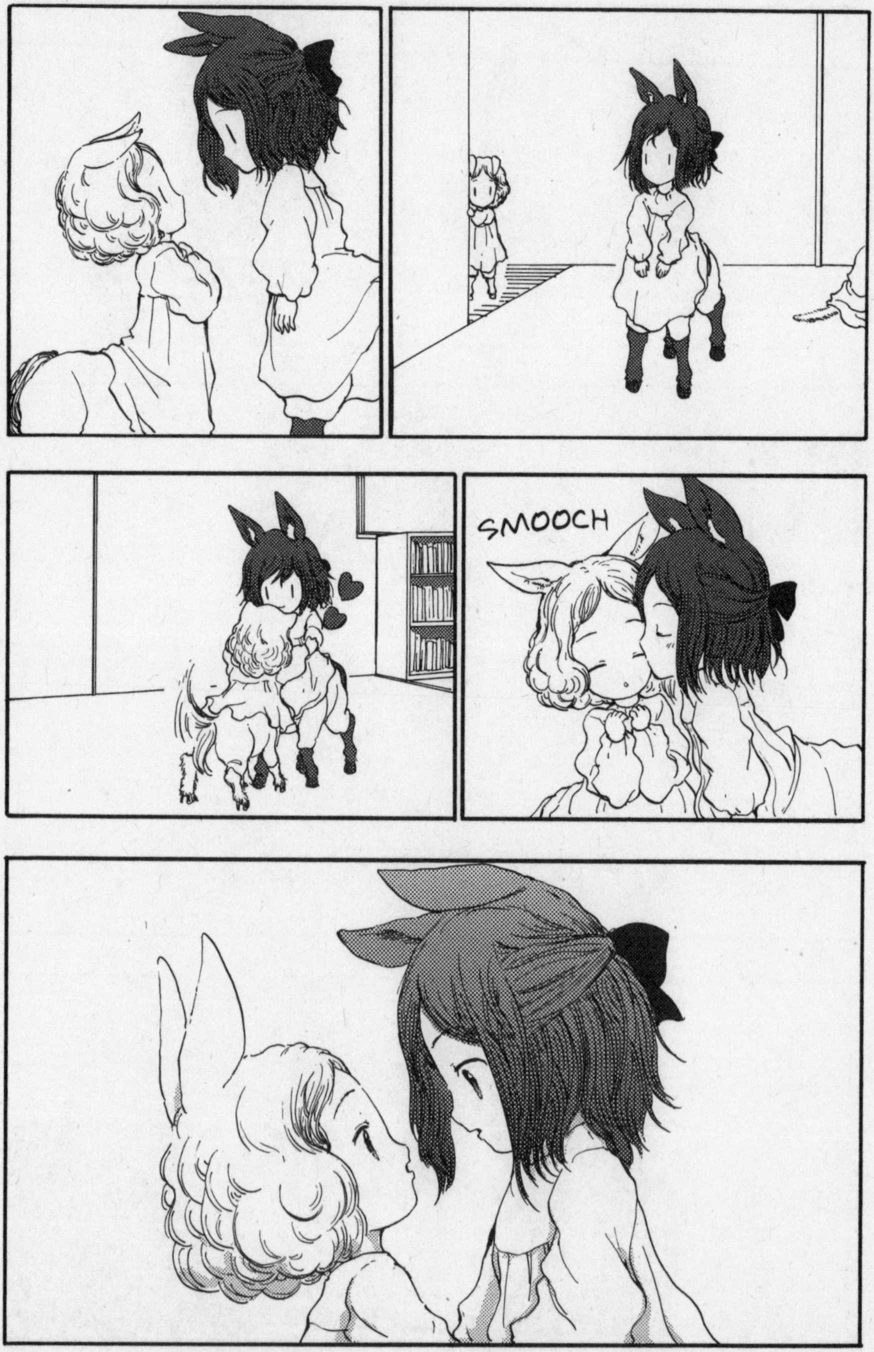
SMOOCH

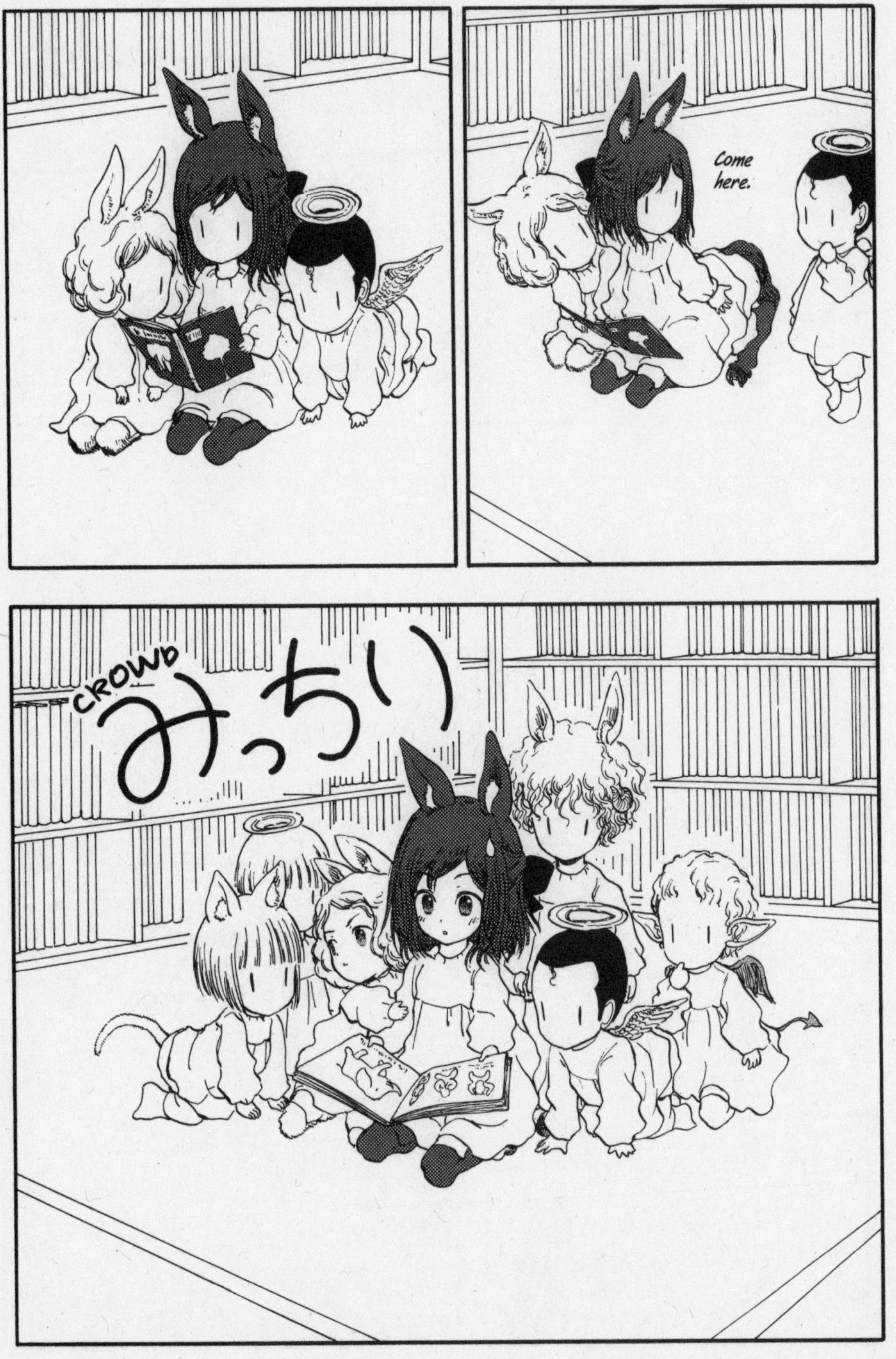
Come here.
CROWD
みっちり

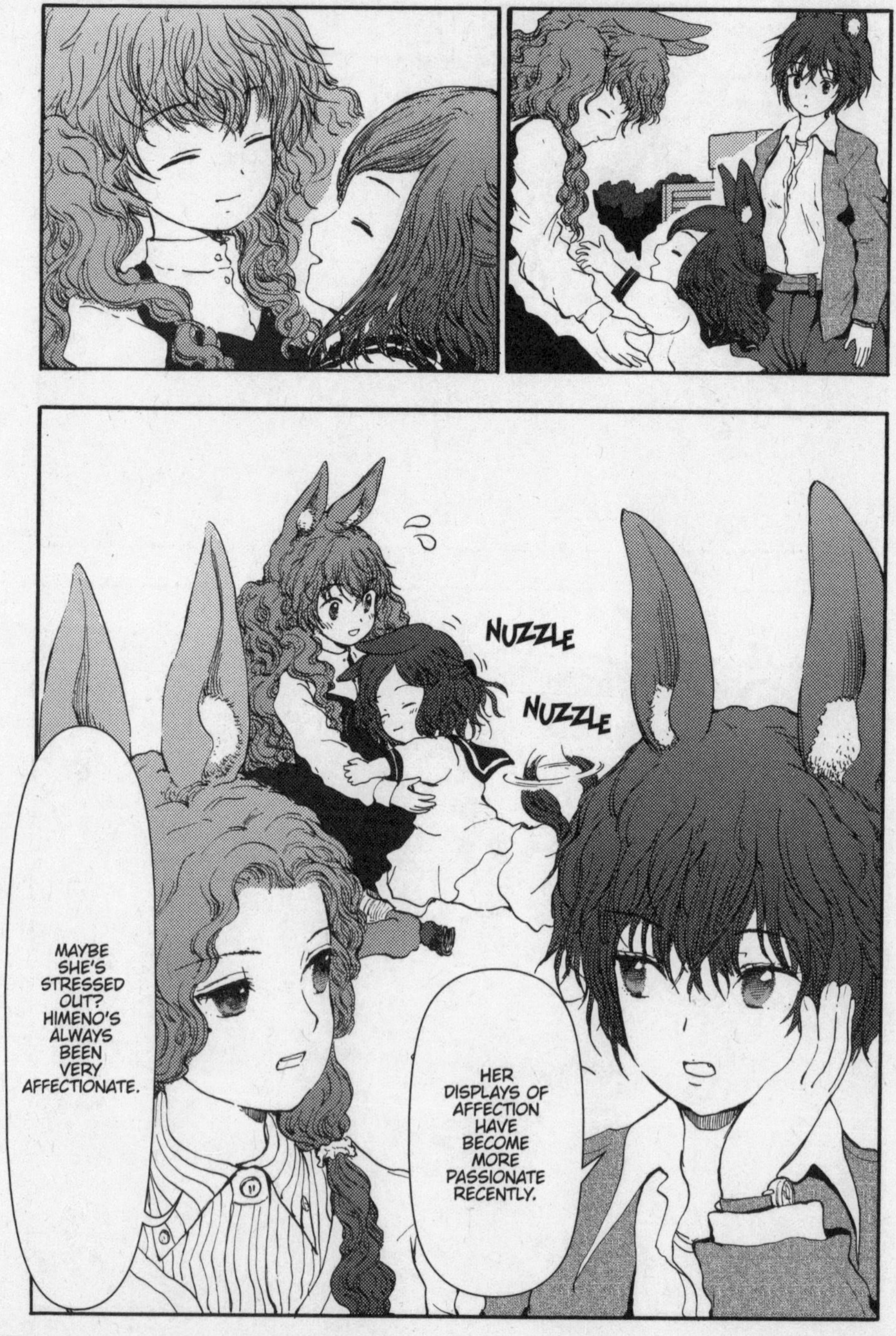
NUZZLE
NUZZLE
HER DISPLAYS OF AFFECTION HAVE BECOME MORE PASSIONATE RECENTLY.
MAYBE SHE'S STRESSED OUT? HIMENO'S ALWAYS BEEN VERY AFFECTIONATE.

A Centaur's Life

SUPERNATURAL BEINGS: DEMONS

AMONG SUPERNATURAL BEINGS, DEMONS PRESENT THE MOST DANGER TO HUMANS, ESPECIALLY WHEN IT COMES TO MORALITY AND TEMPTATION. THEY CAN APPEAR AS ANY MODERN RACE AND ARE ALMOST INDISTINGUISHABLE FROM THE MASSES, BUT THEY RETAIN SOME OF THE DANGEROUS PHYSICAL ADAPTATIONS OF THE ANIMAL KINGDOM, SUCH AS SHARP FANGS OR A BARBED TAIL. DEMONS ARE MORE LIMITED IN THEIR APPEARANCE THAN GODS, PROBABLY BECAUSE THEIR SPHERE OF INFLUENCE IS LIMITED TO THE MODERN HUMAN RACES.

THE DEMONIC CLASS OF SUPERNATURAL BEINGS DOES NOT INCLUDE MONSTERS AND SPIRITS. THOUGH MONSTERS AND SPIRITS CAN SOMETIMES CAUSE HARM TO HUMANS, THIS IS USUALLY INCIDENTAL RATHER THAN MALICIOUS. DEMONS ARE PURE FORCES OF EVIL AND ARE NOT COMMONLY DEPICTED OUTSIDE OF MONOTHEISTIC RELIGIONS WHERE THE GOD REPRESENTS A PURE FORCE OF GOOD. WHEN A LOCAL RELIGION IS ABSORBED BY A FOREIGN RELIGION, THE LOCAL GODS ARE OFTEN CONVERTED TO DEMONS BY THE FOREIGN FAITH.

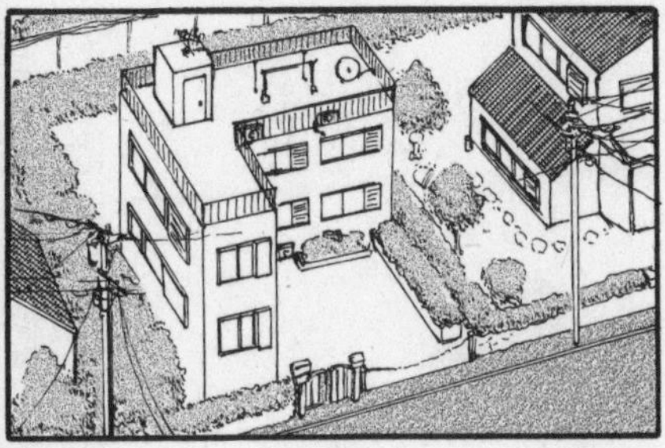

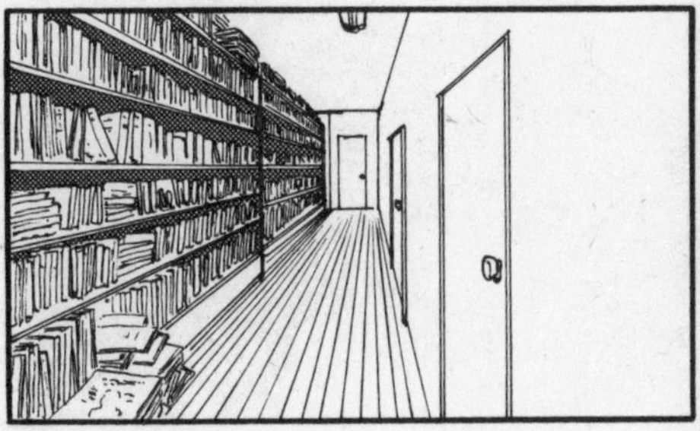

CHAPTER 11

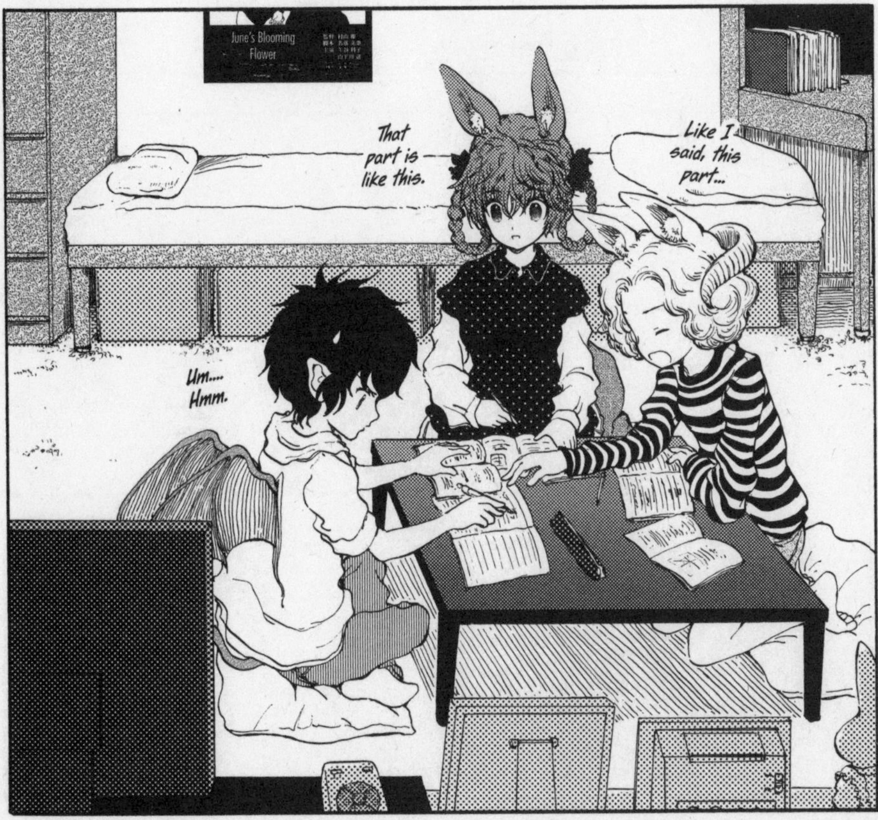
June's Blooming Flower
Like I said, this part...
That part is like this.
Um.... Hmm.

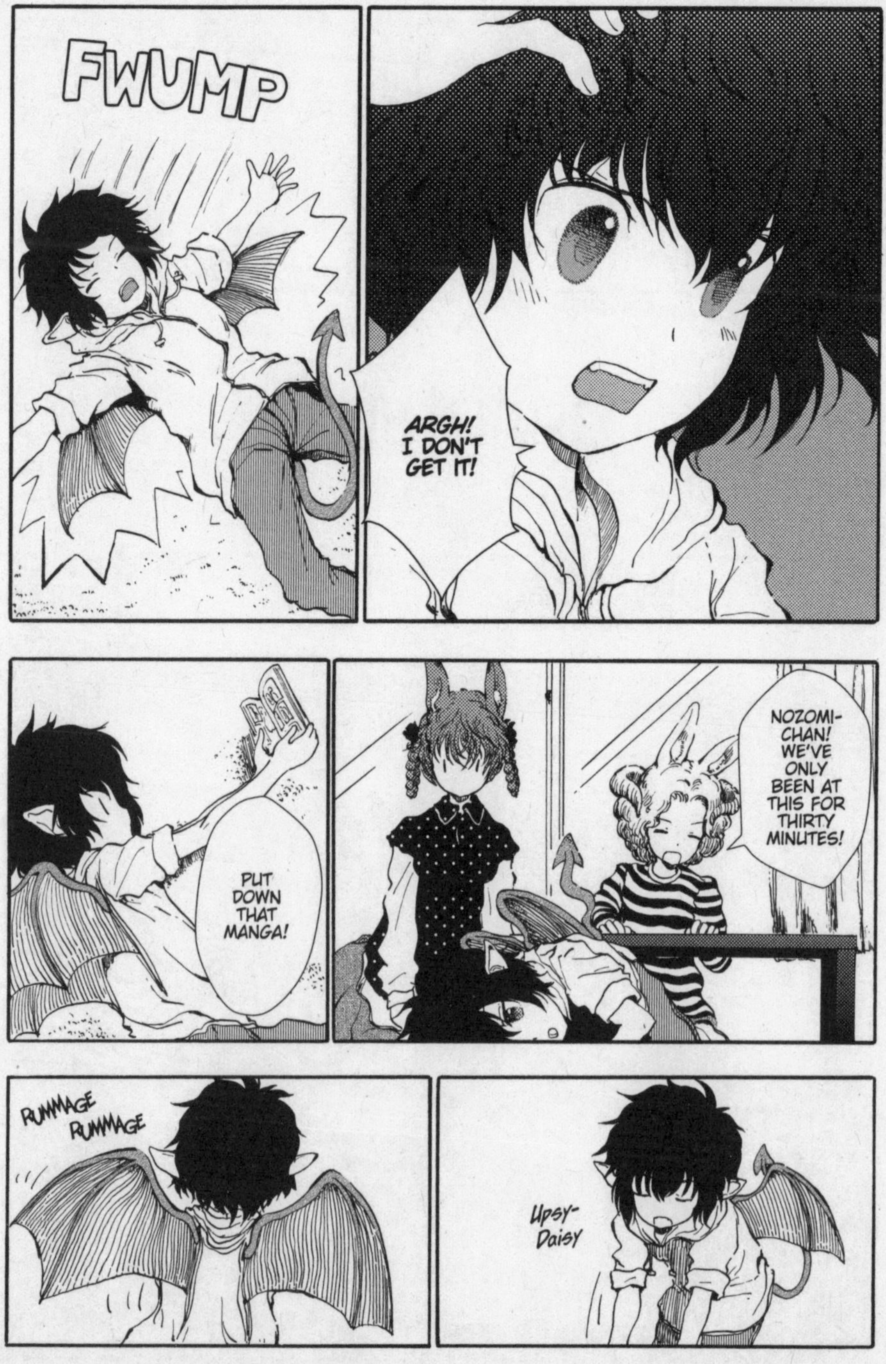
ARGH! I DON'T GET IT!
FWUMP
NOZOMI-CHAN! WE'VE ONLY BEEN AT THIS FOR THIRTY MINUTES!
PUT DOWN THAT MANGA!
Upsy-Daisy
RUMMAGE RUMMAGE

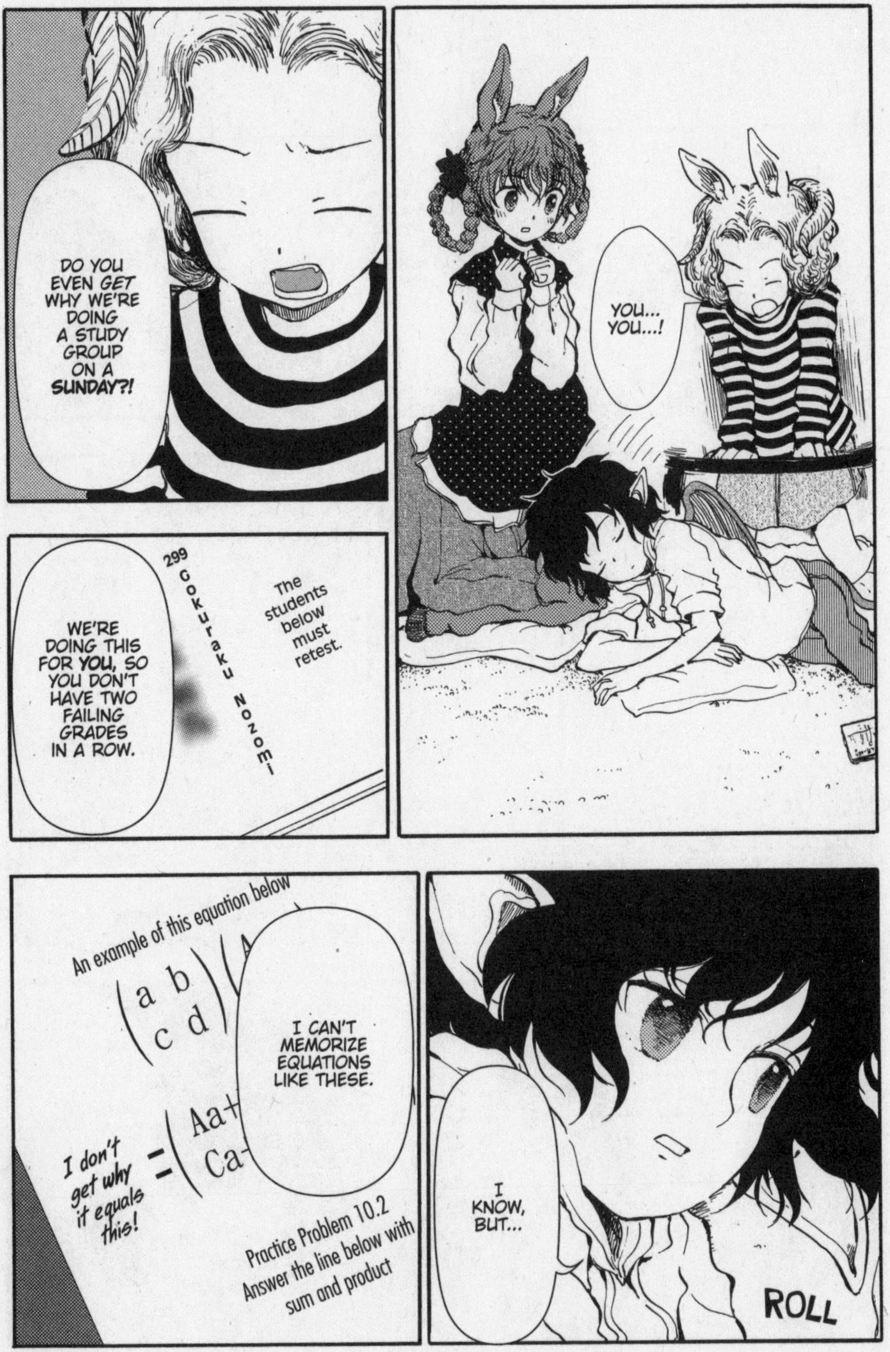
YOU... YOU...!
DO YOU EVEN GET WHY WE'RE DOING A STUDY GROUP ON A SUNDAY?!
The students below must retest.
299 Gokuraku Nozomi
WE'RE DOING THIS FOR YOU, SO YOU DON'T HAVE TWO FAILING GRADES IN A ROW.
I KNOW, BUT...
ROLL
I CAN'T MEMORIZE EQUATIONS LIKE THESE.
An example of this equation below
I don't get why it equals this!
Practice Problem 10.2 Answer the line below with sum and product

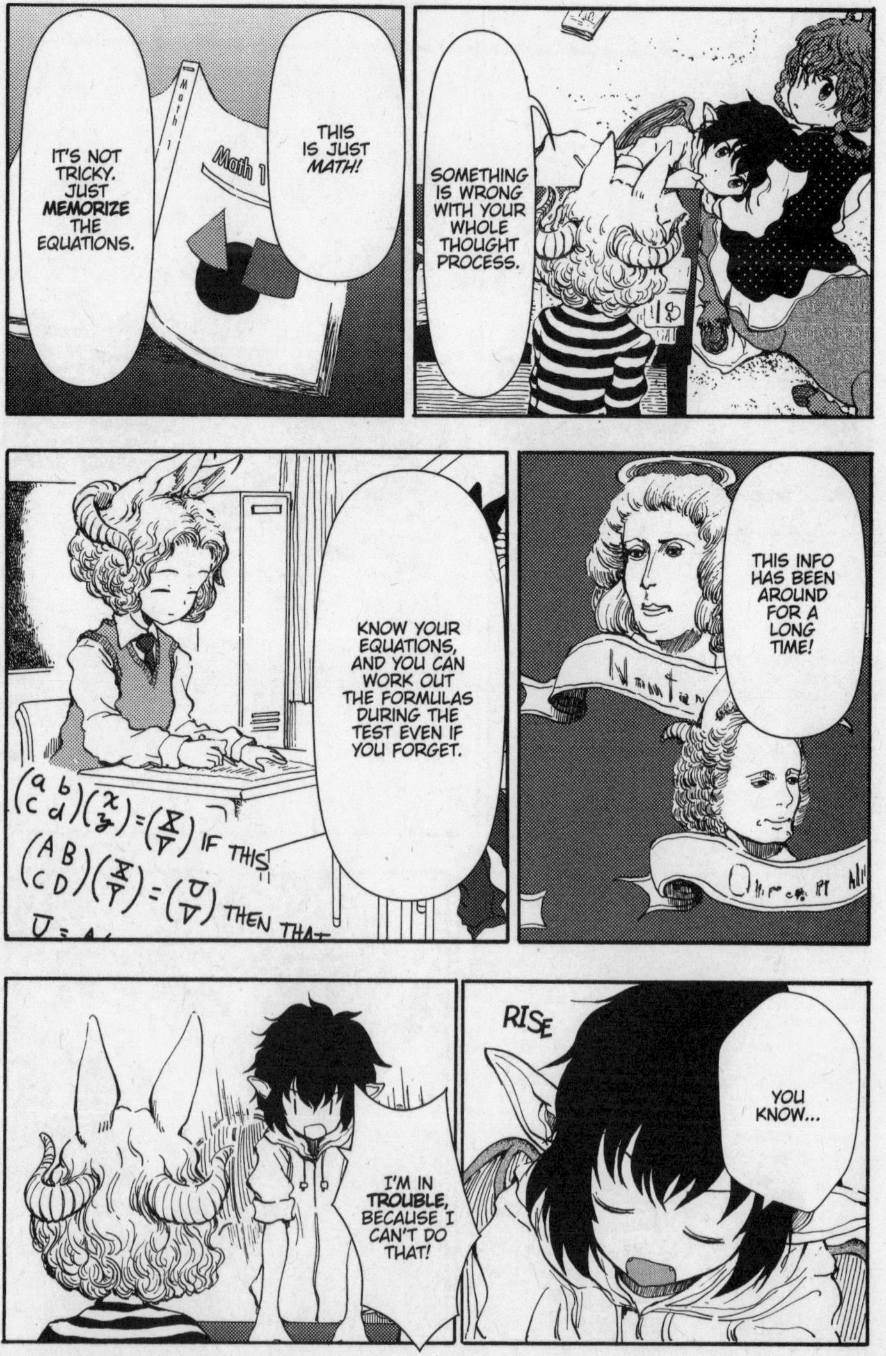
SOMETHING IS WRONG WITH YOUR WHOLE THOUGHT PROCESS.
THIS IS JUST *MATH!*
Math 1
IT'S NOT TRICKY. JUST **MEMORIZE** THE EQUATIONS.
THIS INFO HAS BEEN AROUND FOR A LONG TIME!
KNOW YOUR EQUATIONS, AND YOU CAN WORK OUT THE FORMULAS DURING THE TEST EVEN IF YOU FORGET.
IF THIS
THEN THAT
RISE
YOU KNOW...
I'M IN **TROUBLE,** BECAUSE I CAN'T DO THAT!

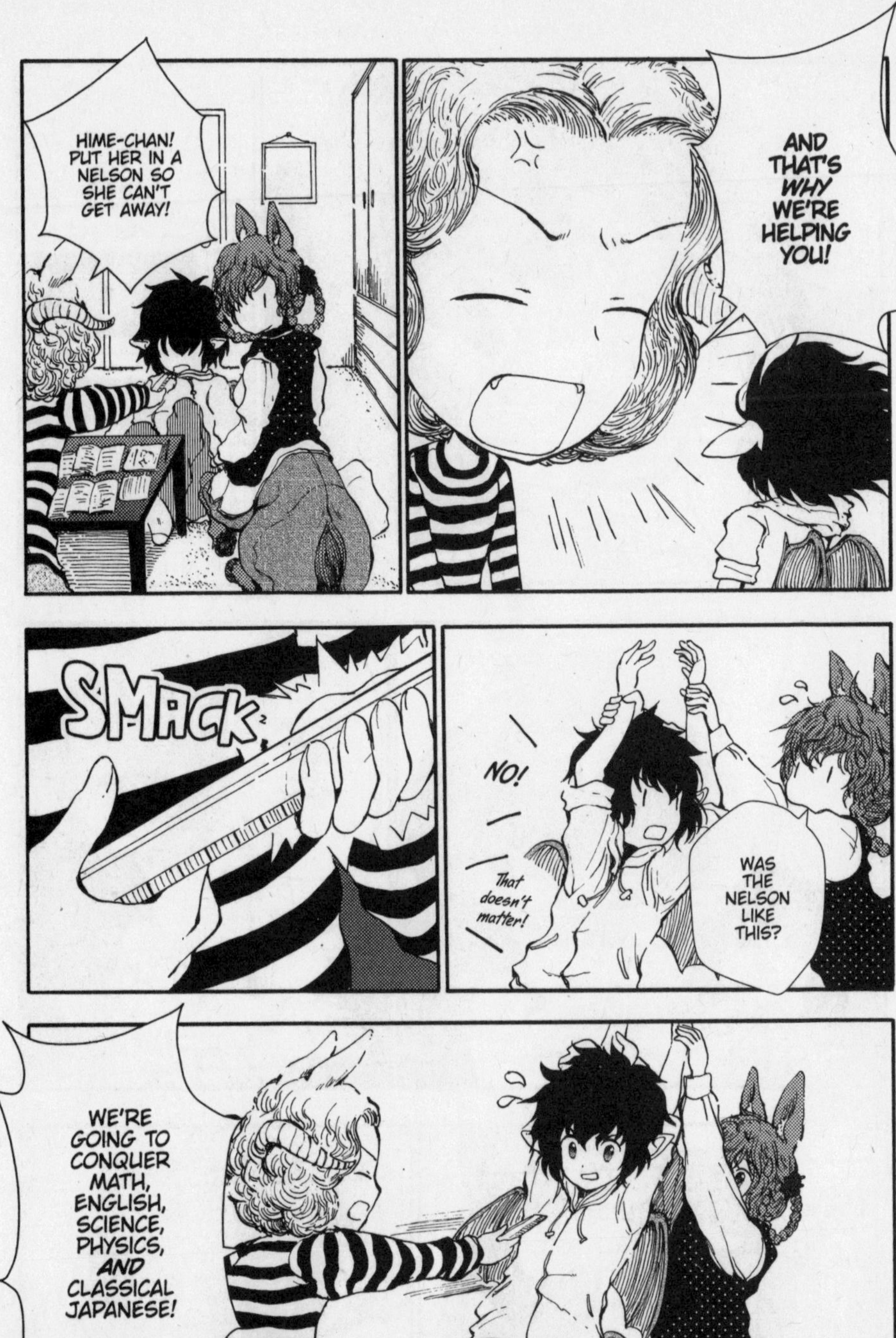
AND THAT'S *WHY* WE'RE HELPING YOU!
HIME-CHAN! PUT HER IN A NELSON SO SHE CAN'T GET AWAY!
WAS THE NELSON LIKE THIS?
NO!
That doesn't matter!
SMACK
WE'RE GOING TO CONQUER MATH, ENGLISH, SCIENCE, PHYSICS, ***AND*** CLASSICAL JAPANESE!

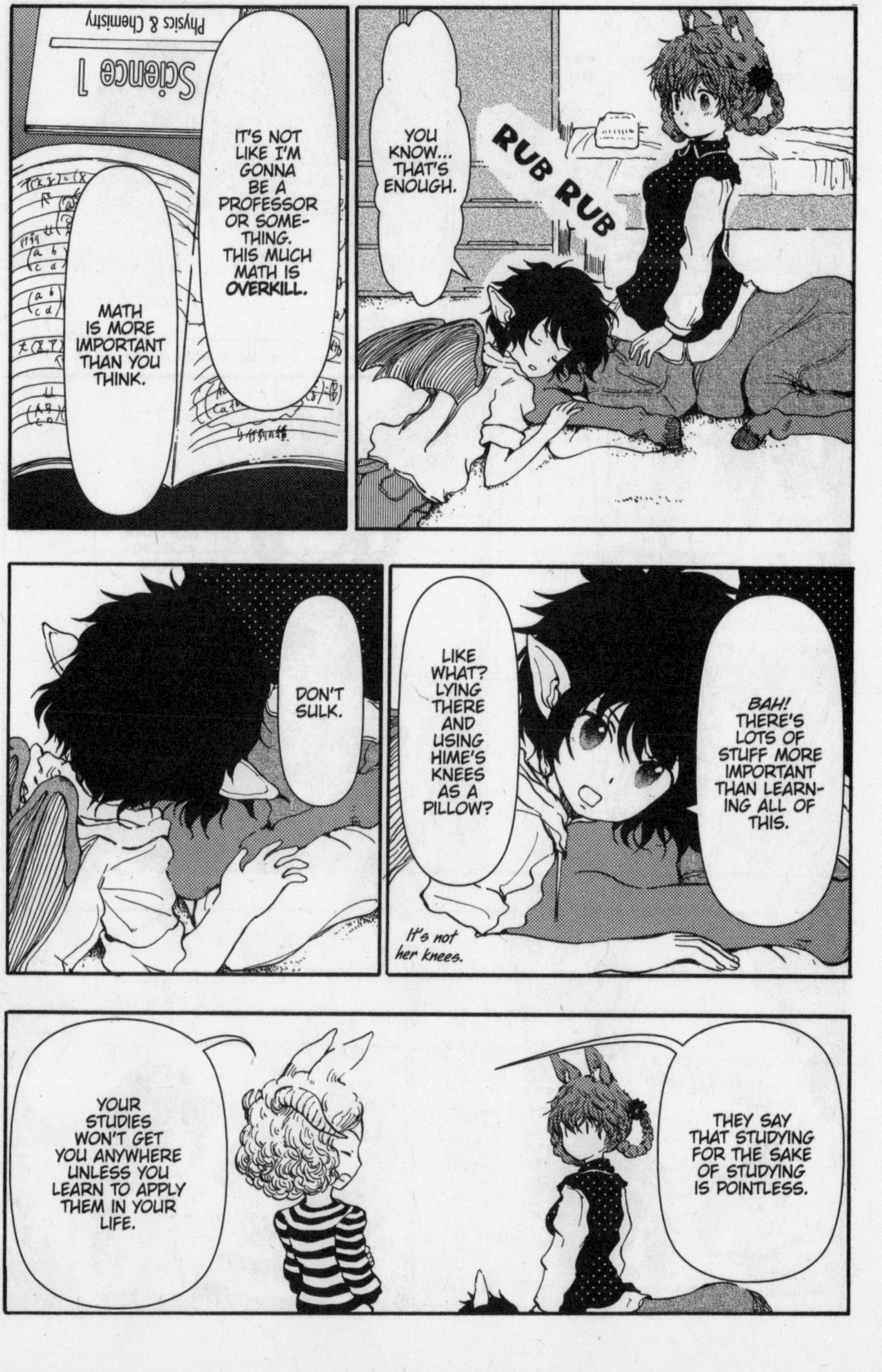
RUB RUB
YOU KNOW... THAT'S ENOUGH.
Science 1
Physics & Chemistry
IT'S NOT LIKE I'M GONNA BE A PROFESSOR OR SOMETHING. THIS MUCH MATH IS **OVERKILL.**
MATH IS MORE IMPORTANT THAN YOU THINK.
BAH! THERE'S LOTS OF STUFF MORE IMPORTANT THAN LEARNING ALL OF THIS.
LIKE WHAT? LYING THERE AND USING HIME'S KNEES AS A PILLOW?
It's not her knees.
DON'T SULK.
THEY SAY THAT STUDYING FOR THE SAKE OF STUDYING IS POINTLESS.
YOUR STUDIES WON'T GET YOU ANYWHERE UNLESS YOU LEARN TO APPLY THEM IN YOUR LIFE.

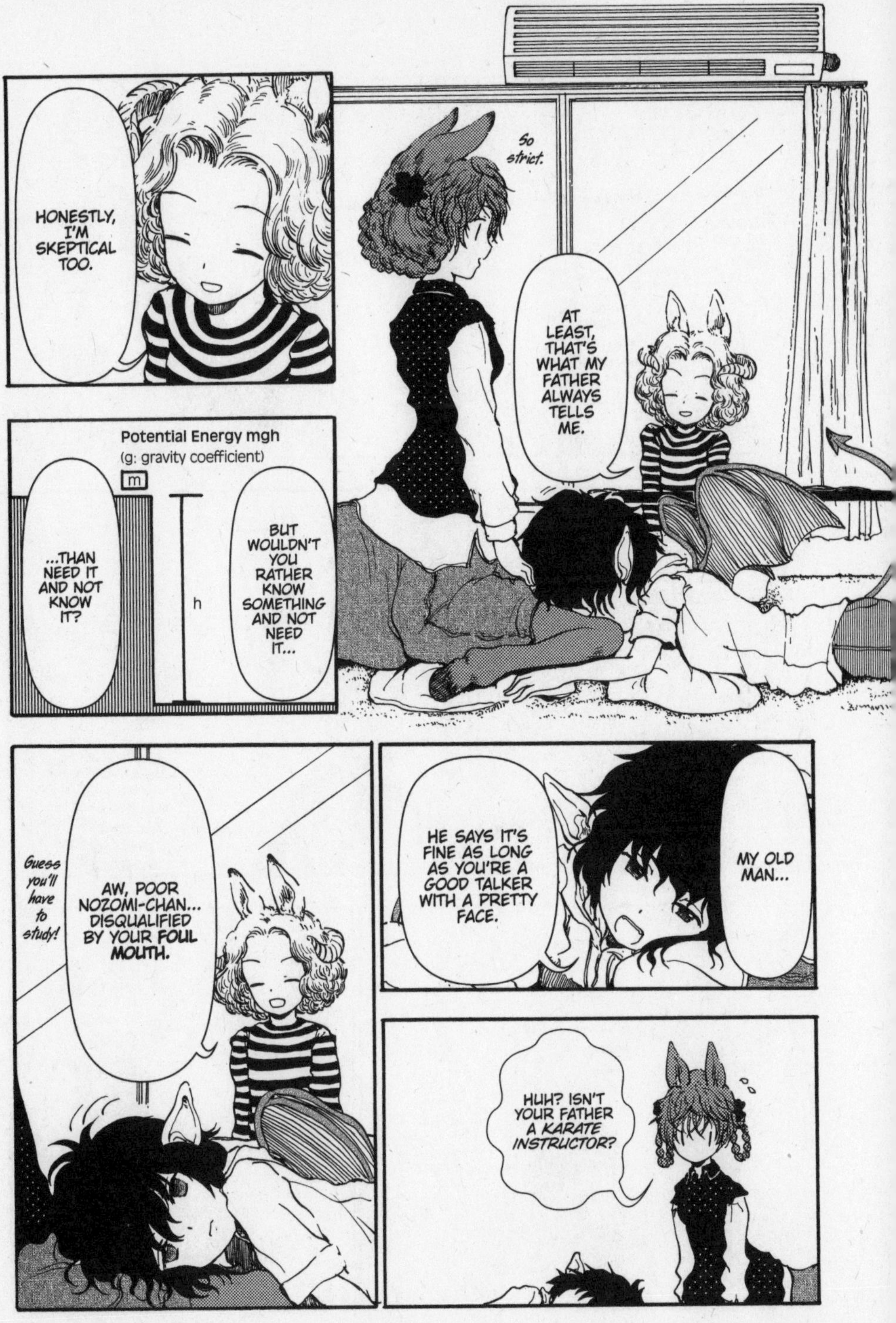
So strict.
AT LEAST, THAT'S WHAT MY FATHER ALWAYS TELLS ME.
HONESTLY, I'M SKEPTICAL TOO.
Potential Energy mgh
(g: gravity coefficient)
m
h
BUT WOULDN'T YOU RATHER KNOW SOMETHING AND NOT NEED IT...
...THAN NEED IT AND NOT KNOW IT?
MY OLD MAN...
HE SAYS IT'S FINE AS LONG AS YOU'RE A GOOD TALKER WITH A PRETTY FACE.
HUH? ISN'T YOUR FATHER A KARATE INSTRUCTOR?
AW, POOR NOZOMI-CHAN... DISQUALIFIED BY YOUR FOUL MOUTH.
Guess you'll have to study!

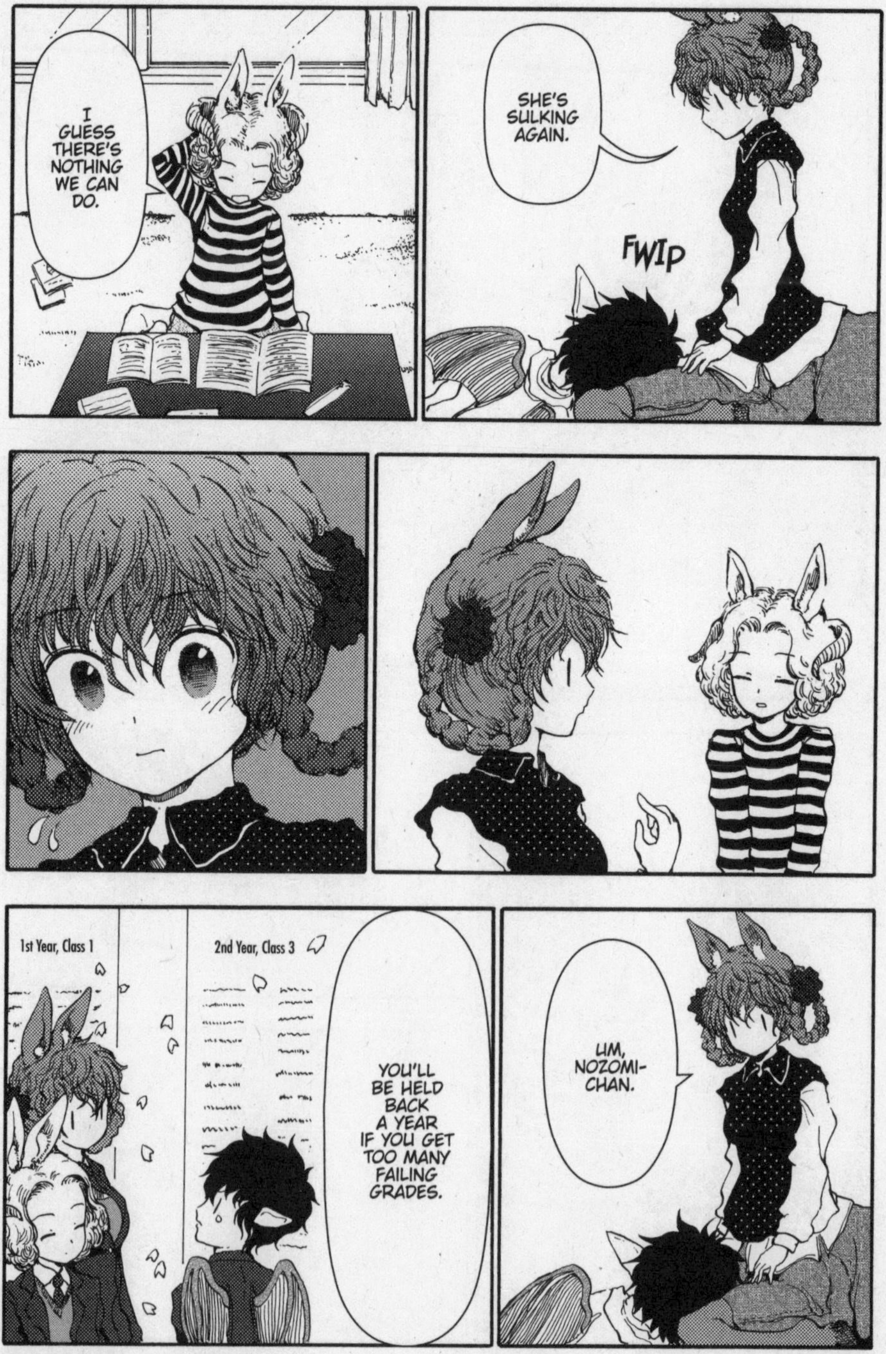
SHE'S SULKING AGAIN.
FWIP
I GUESS THERE'S NOTHING WE CAN DO.
UM, NOZOMI-CHAN.
YOU'LL BE HELD BACK A YEAR IF YOU GET TOO MANY FAILING GRADES.
2nd Year, Class 3
1st Year, Class 1

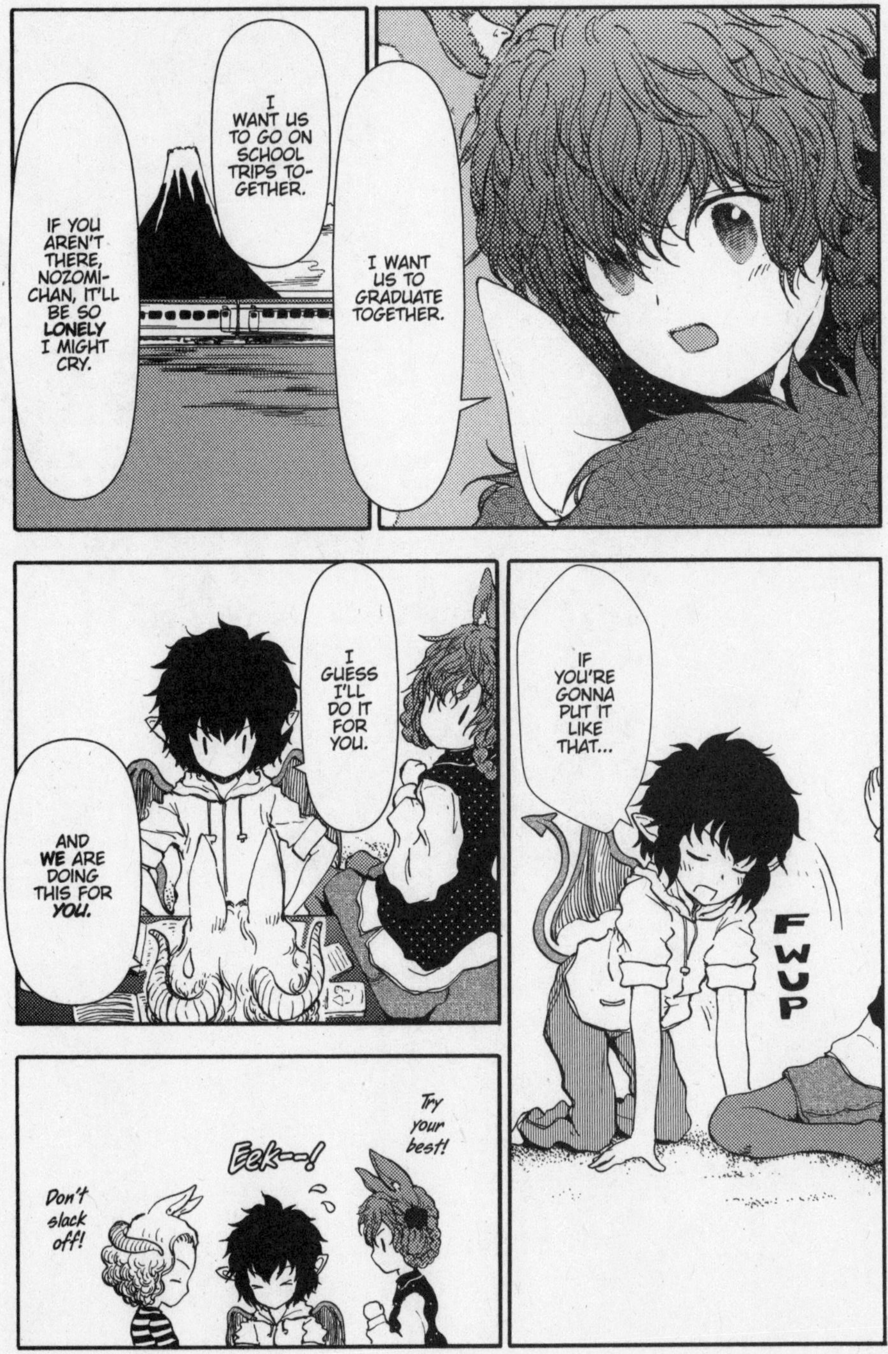
I WANT US TO GRADUATE TOGETHER.
I WANT US TO GO ON SCHOOL TRIPS TO-GETHER.
IF YOU AREN'T THERE, NOZOMI-CHAN, IT'LL BE SO **LONELY** I MIGHT CRY.
IF YOU'RE GONNA PUT IT LIKE THAT...
FWUP
I GUESS I'LL DO IT FOR YOU.
AND **WE** ARE DOING THIS FOR ***YOU.***
Try your best!
Eek--!
Don't slack off!

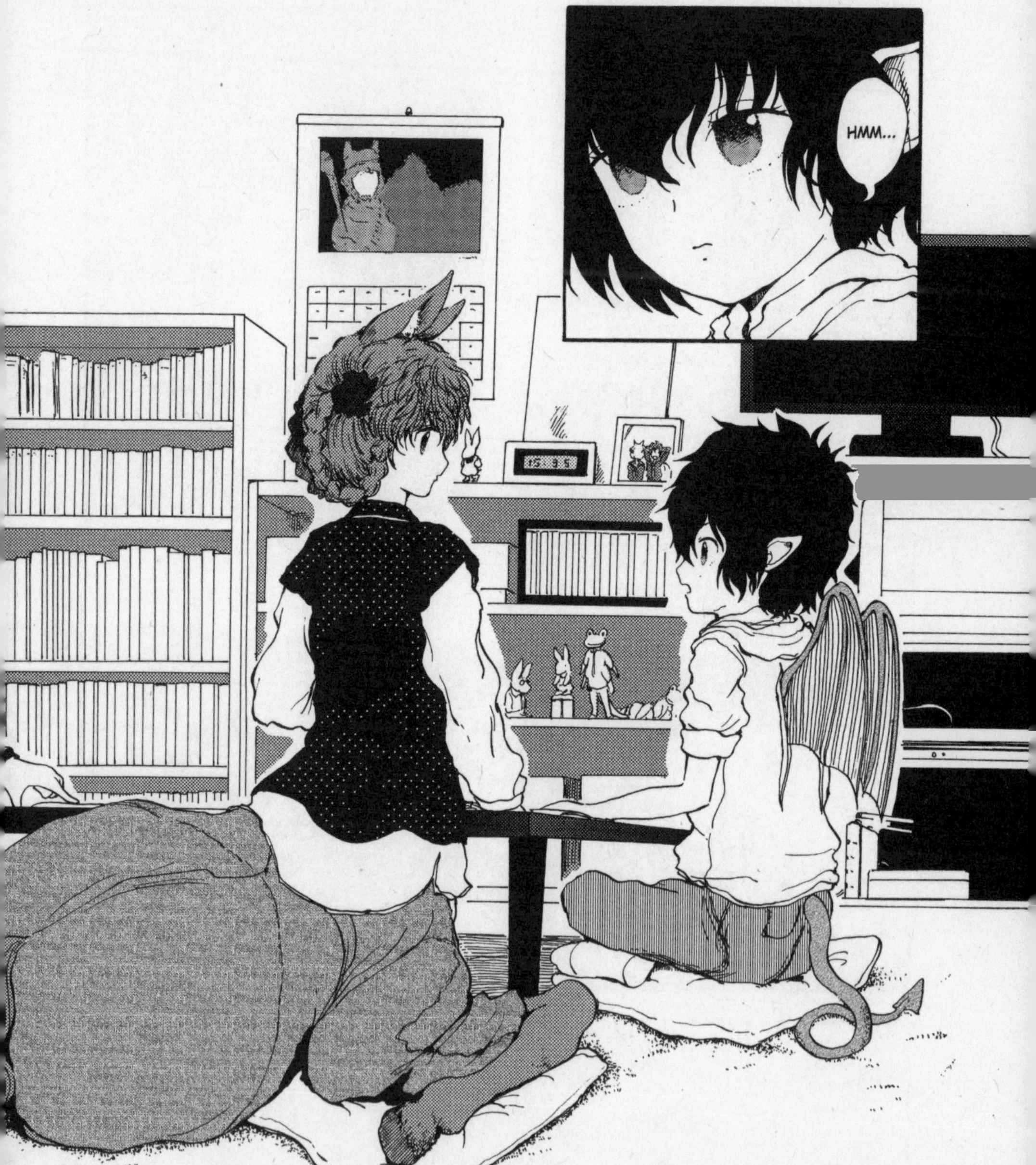
HMM...

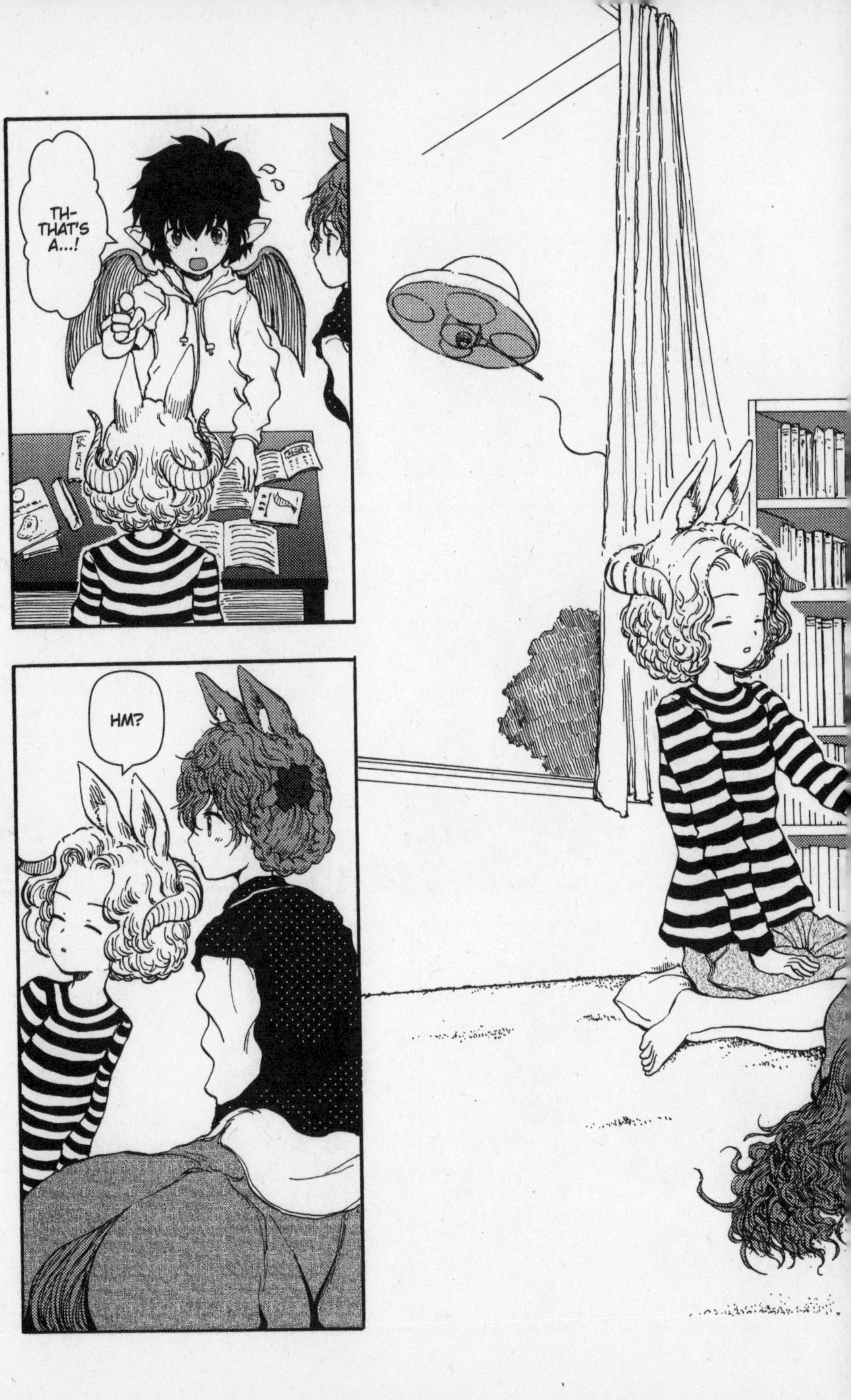
TH-THAT'S A...!
HM?

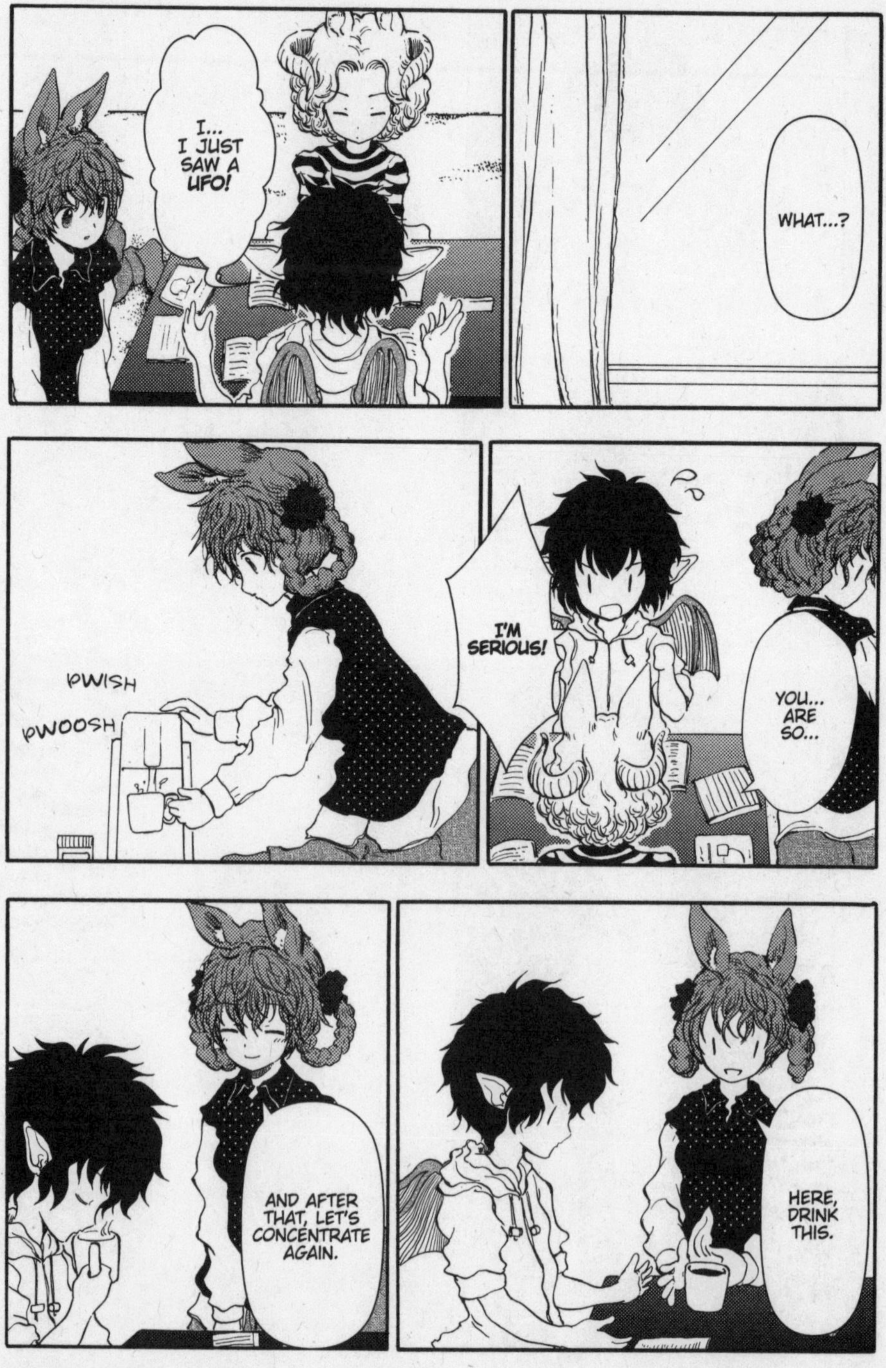
WHAT...?
I... I JUST SAW A UFO!
YOU... ARE SO...
I'M SERIOUS!
PWISH
PWOOSH
HERE, DRINK THIS.
AND AFTER THAT, LET'S CONCENTRATE AGAIN.

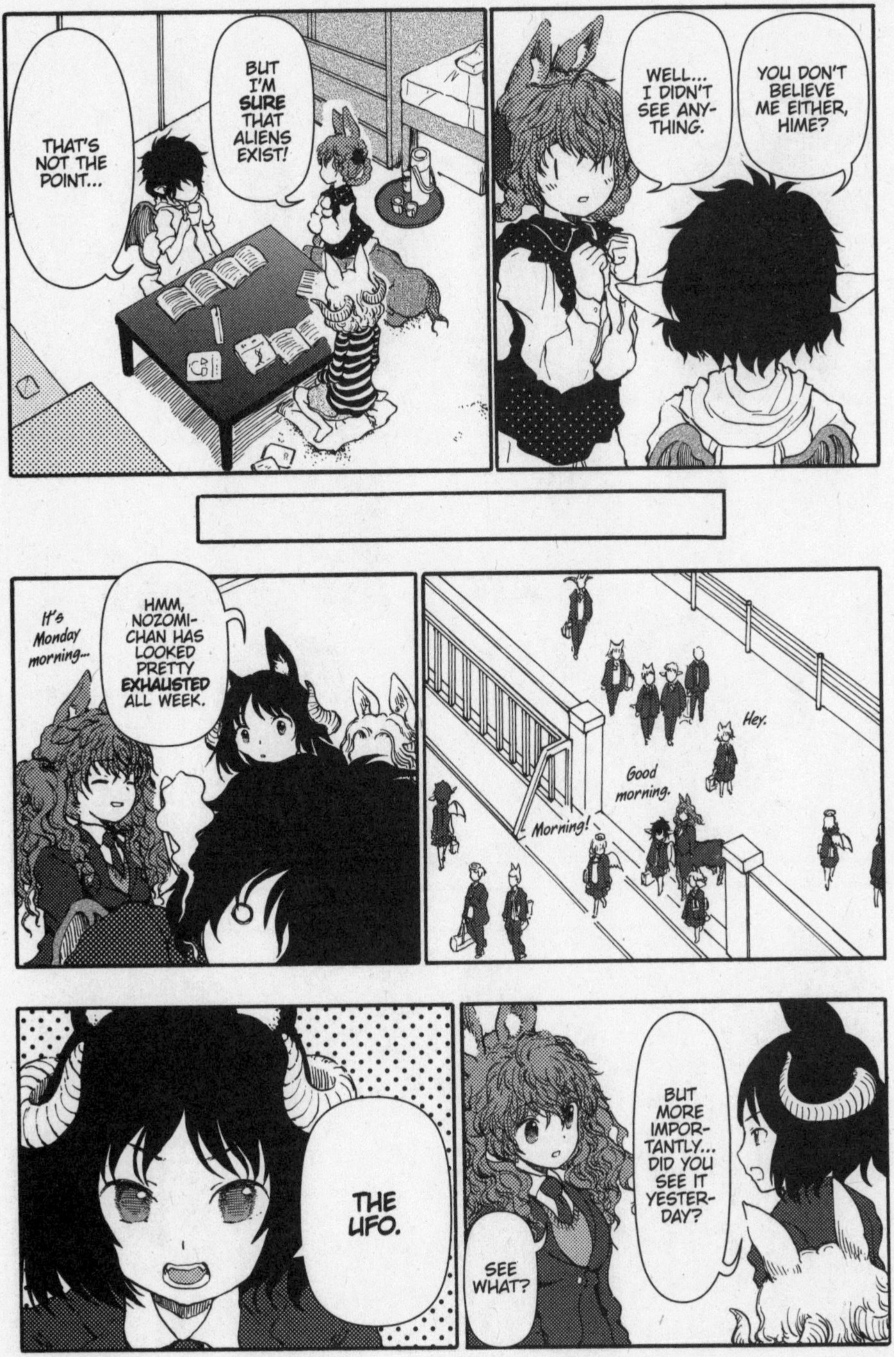
YOU DON'T BELIEVE ME EITHER, HIME?
WELL... I DIDN'T SEE ANY-THING.
BUT I'M **SURE** THAT ALIENS EXIST!
THAT'S NOT THE POINT...
Hey.
Good morning.
Morning!
HMM, NOZOMI-CHAN HAS LOOKED PRETTY **EXHAUSTED** ALL WEEK.
It's Monday morning...
BUT MORE IMPOR-TANTLY... DID YOU SEE IT YESTER-DAY?
SEE WHAT?
THE UFO.

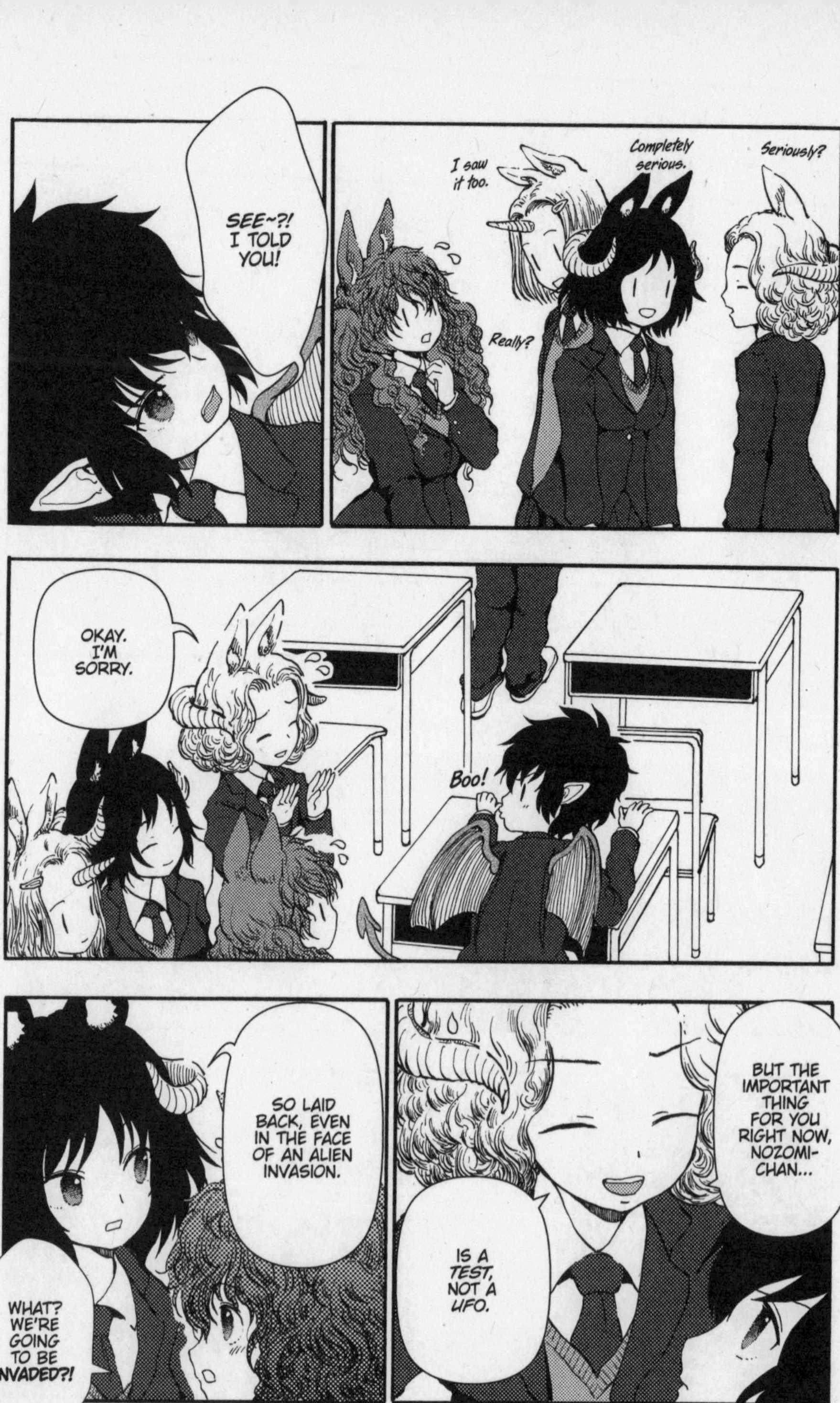
Seriously?
Completely serious.
I saw it too.
Really?
SEE~?! I TOLD YOU!
OKAY. I'M SORRY.
Boo!
BUT THE IMPORTANT THING FOR YOU RIGHT NOW, NOZOMI-CHAN...
IS A TEST, NOT A UFO.
SO LAID BACK, EVEN IN THE FACE OF AN ALIEN INVASION.
WHAT? WE'RE GOING TO BE INVADED?!

A Centaur's Life

SUPERNATURAL BEINGS:
FRANKENSTEIN'S MONSTER

ALL SUPERNATURAL CREATURES ARE CREATIONS OF HUMAN IMAGINATION, AND THE STORY OF FRANKENSTEIN'S MONSTER AND ITS CREATOR ARE KNOWN THROUGHOUT THE WORLD. *FRANKENSTEIN* THE NOVEL INSPIRED COUNTLESS MOVIES AND COMICS. IT IS ONE OF THE TRUE ICONS OF HORROR.

THE ORIGINAL DESCRIPTION BY AUTHOR MARY SHELLEY, HOWEVER, WAS NOT OF A GIANT WINGED MAN WITH A FLAT HEAD AND BOLTS ON THE SIDES OF HIS NECK. THAT VERSION OF THE MONSTER STEMS FROM THE MAKE-UP THAT ACTOR BORIS KARLOFF WORE IN THE ORIGINAL *FRANKENSTEIN* FILM. PEOPLE COMMONLY (AND MISTAKENLY!) REFER TO THE MONSTER AS "FRANKENSTEIN," BUT IN THE STORY, THAT NAME ACTUALLY BELONGS TO THE DOCTOR WHO CREATED THE MONSTER. THE MONSTER DOES NOT HAVE ITS OWN NAME.

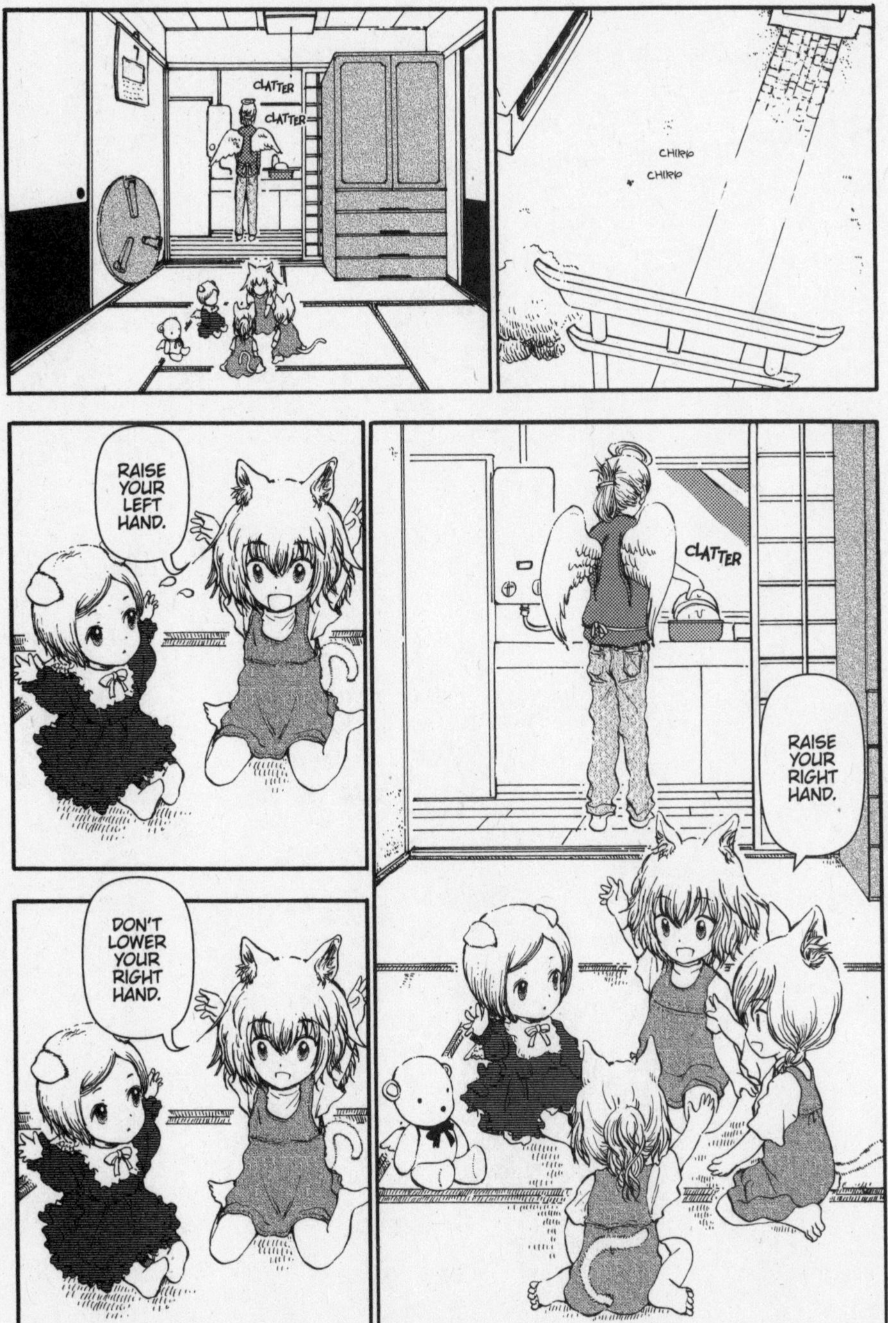
CHIRP
CHIRP
CLATTER
CLATTER
CLATTER
RAISE YOUR RIGHT HAND.
RAISE YOUR LEFT HAND.
DON'T LOWER YOUR RIGHT HAND.

CHAPTER 12

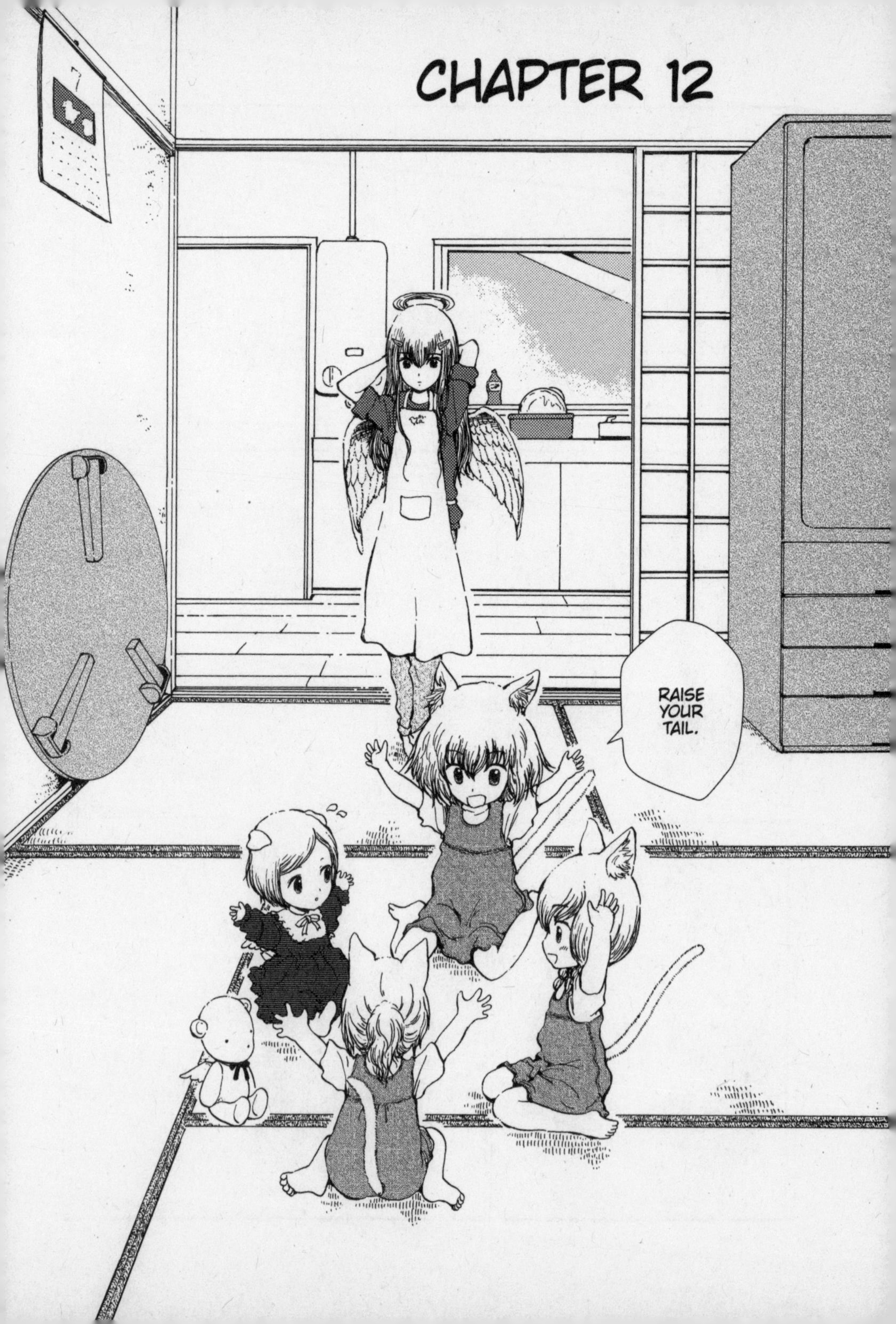
RAISE YOUR TAIL.

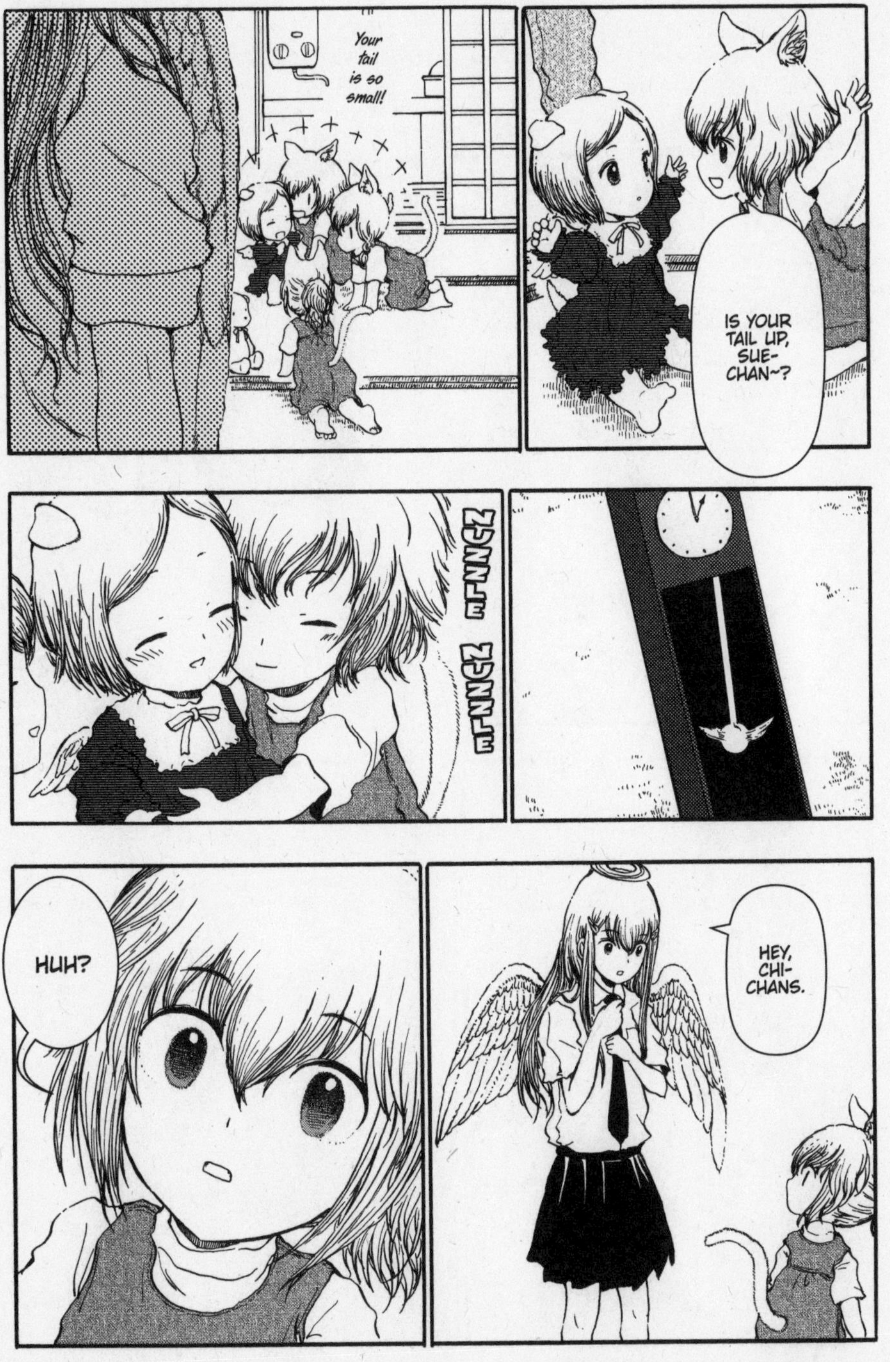
IS YOUR TAIL UP, SUE-CHAN~?
Your tail is so small!
NUZZLE NUZZLE
HEY, CHI-CHANS.
HUH?

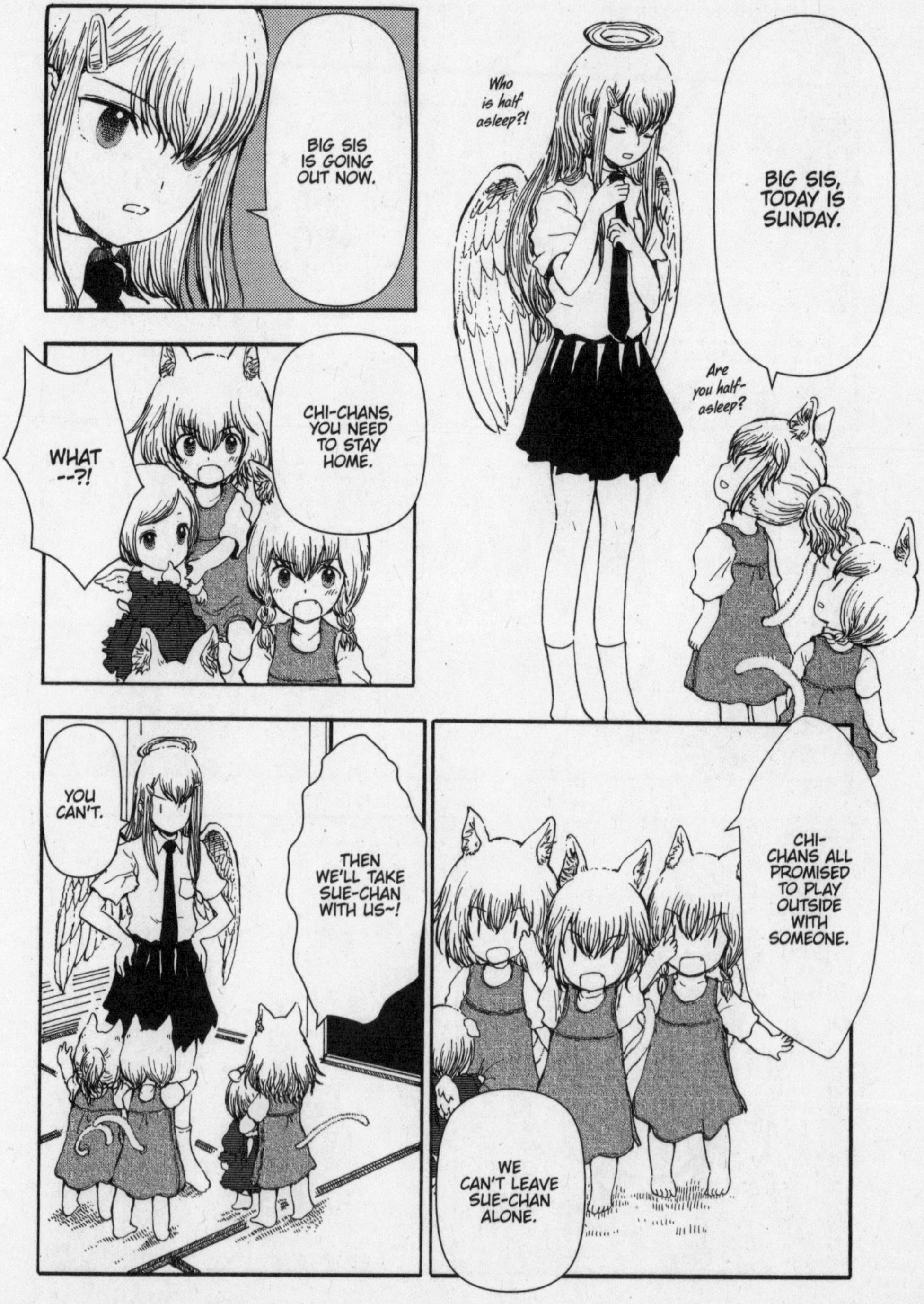
BIG SIS IS GOING OUT NOW.
BIG SIS, TODAY IS SUNDAY.
Are you half-asleep?
Who is half asleep?!
CHI-CHANS, YOU NEED TO STAY HOME.
WHAT--?!
CHI-CHANS ALL PROMISED TO PLAY OUTSIDE WITH SOMEONE.
WE CAN'T LEAVE SUE-CHAN ALONE.
THEN WE'LL TAKE SUE-CHAN WITH US~!
YOU CAN'T.

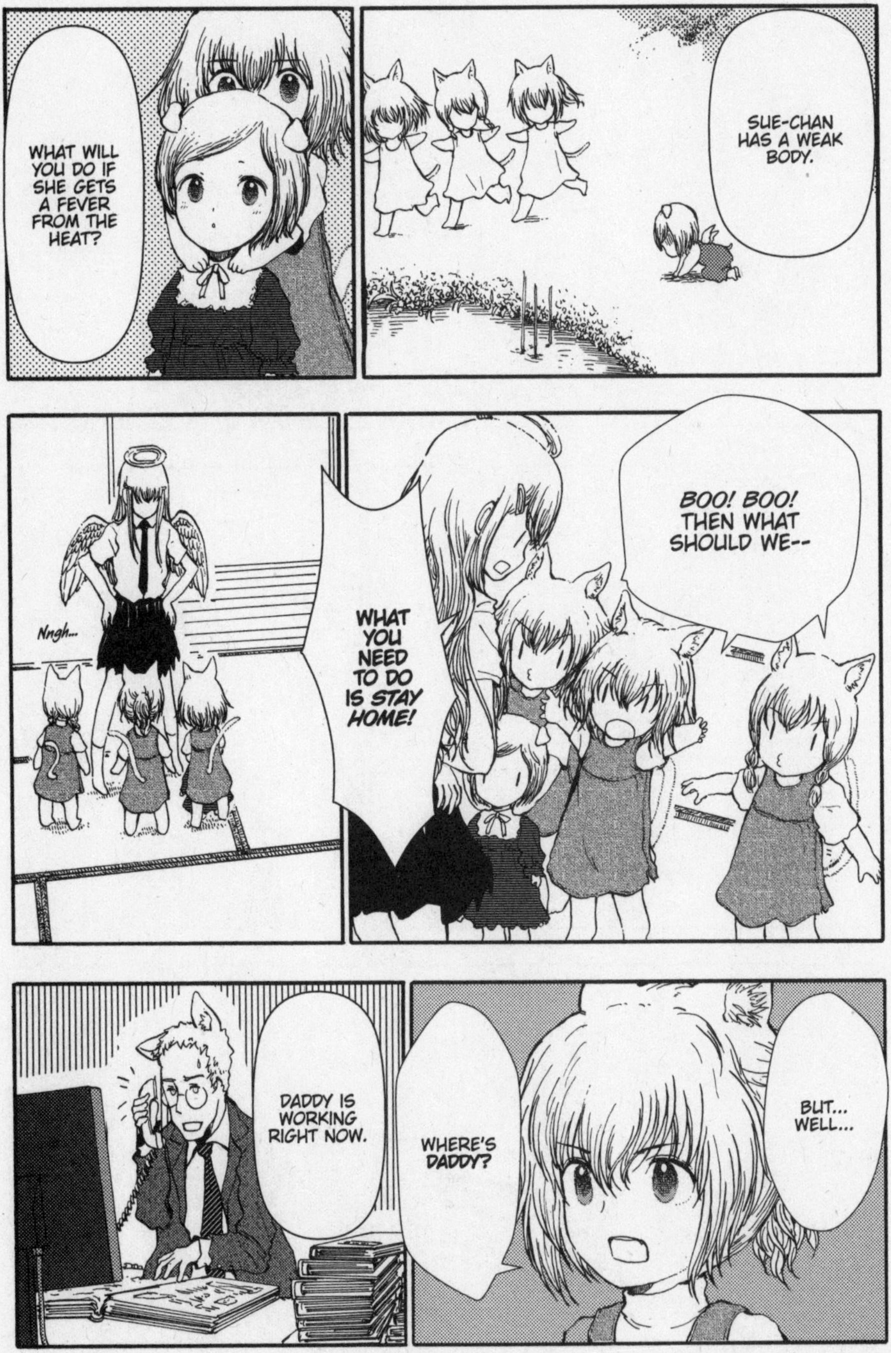
SUE-CHAN HAS A WEAK BODY.
WHAT WILL YOU DO IF SHE GETS A FEVER FROM THE HEAT?
BOO! BOO! THEN WHAT SHOULD WE--
WHAT YOU NEED TO DO IS STAY HOME!
Nngh...
BUT... WELL...
WHERE'S DADDY?
DADDY IS WORKING RIGHT NOW.

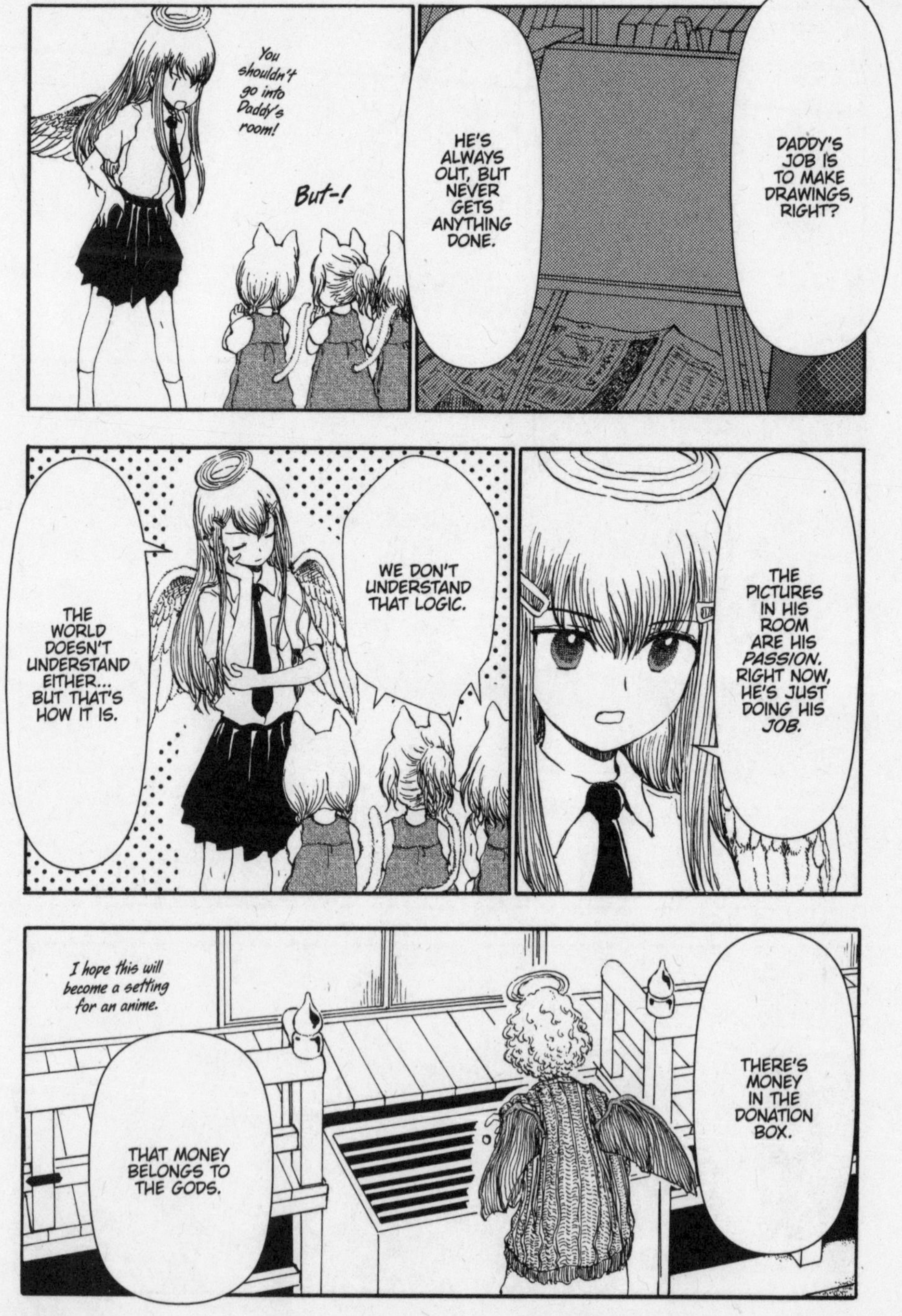
DADDY'S JOB IS TO MAKE DRAWINGS, RIGHT?
HE'S ALWAYS OUT, BUT NEVER GETS ANYTHING DONE.
You shouldn't go into Daddy's room!
But-!
THE PICTURES IN HIS ROOM ARE HIS *PASSION*. RIGHT NOW, HE'S JUST DOING HIS *JOB*.
WE DON'T UNDERSTAND THAT LOGIC.
THE WORLD DOESN'T UNDERSTAND EITHER... BUT THAT'S HOW IT IS.
THERE'S MONEY IN THE DONATION BOX.
THAT MONEY BELONGS TO THE GODS.
I hope this will become a setting for an anime.

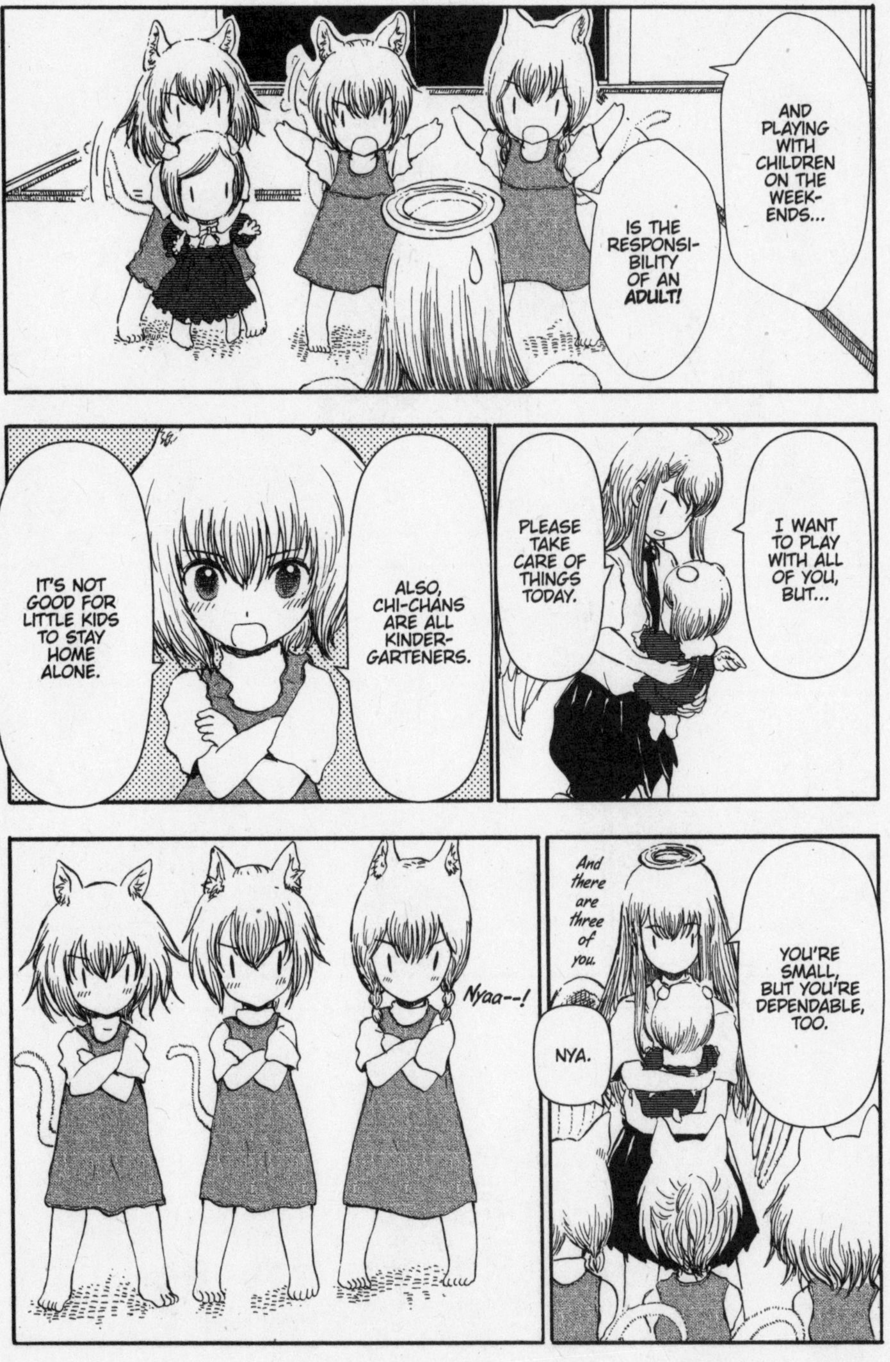
AND PLAYING WITH CHILDREN ON THE WEEKENDS...
IS THE RESPONSIBILITY OF AN **ADULT!**
I WANT TO PLAY WITH ALL OF YOU, BUT...
PLEASE TAKE CARE OF THINGS TODAY.
ALSO, CHI-CHANS ARE ALL KINDERGARTENERS.
IT'S NOT GOOD FOR LITTLE KIDS TO STAY HOME ALONE.
YOU'RE SMALL, BUT YOU'RE DEPENDABLE, TOO.
And there are three of you.
NYA.
Nyaa--!

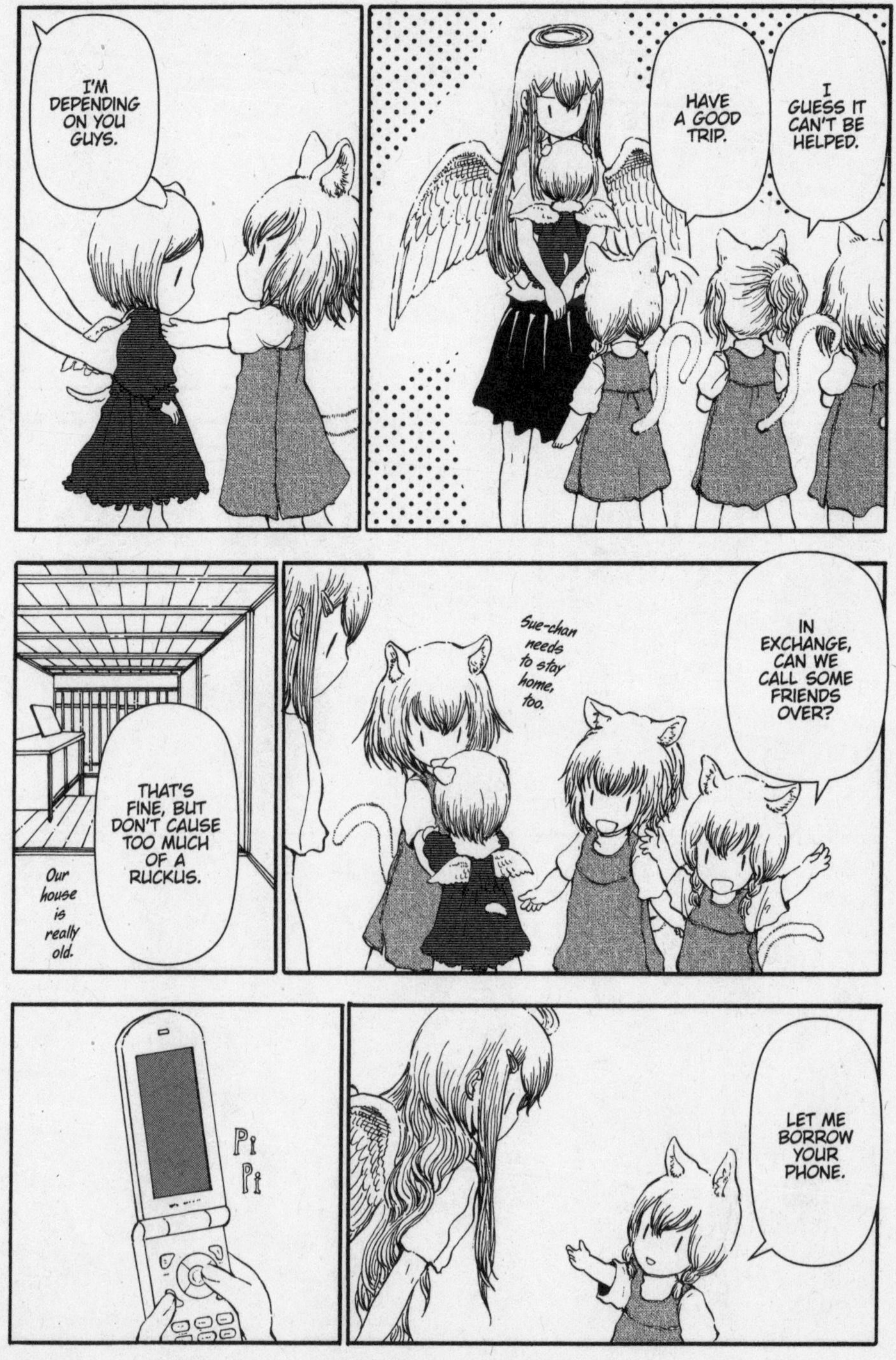
I GUESS IT CAN'T BE HELPED.
HAVE A GOOD TRIP.
I'M DEPENDING ON YOU GUYS.
IN EXCHANGE, CAN WE CALL SOME FRIENDS OVER?
Sue-chan needs to stay home, too.
THAT'S FINE, BUT DON'T CAUSE TOO MUCH OF A RUCKUS.
Our house is really old.
LET ME BORROW YOUR PHONE.
Pi Pi

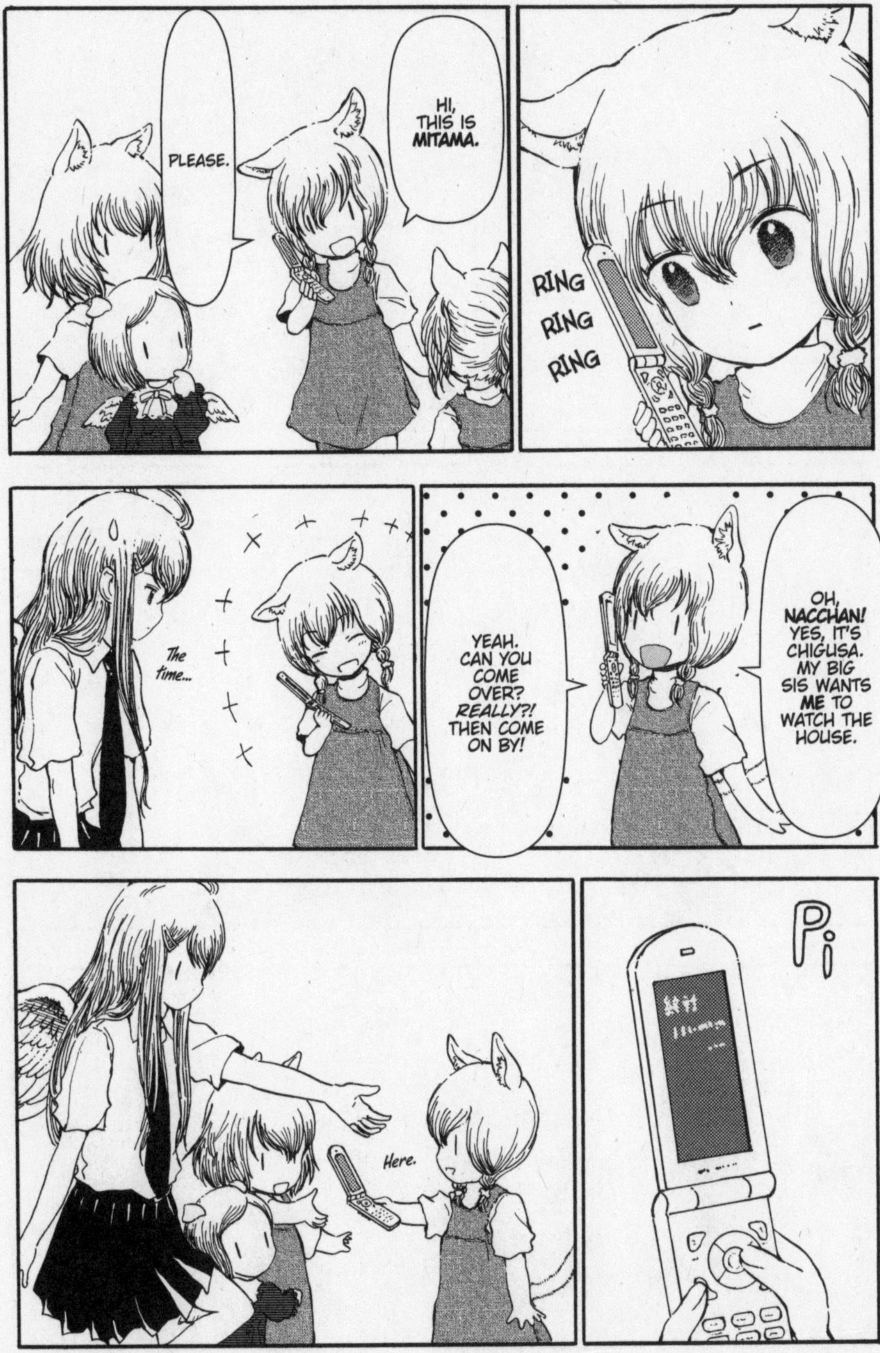
RING
RING
RING
HI, THIS IS **MITAMA.**
PLEASE.
OH, **NACCHAN!** YES, IT'S CHIGUSA. MY BIG SIS WANTS **ME** TO WATCH THE HOUSE.
YEAH. CAN YOU COME OVER? *REALLY?!* THEN COME ON BY!
The time...
Pi
Here.

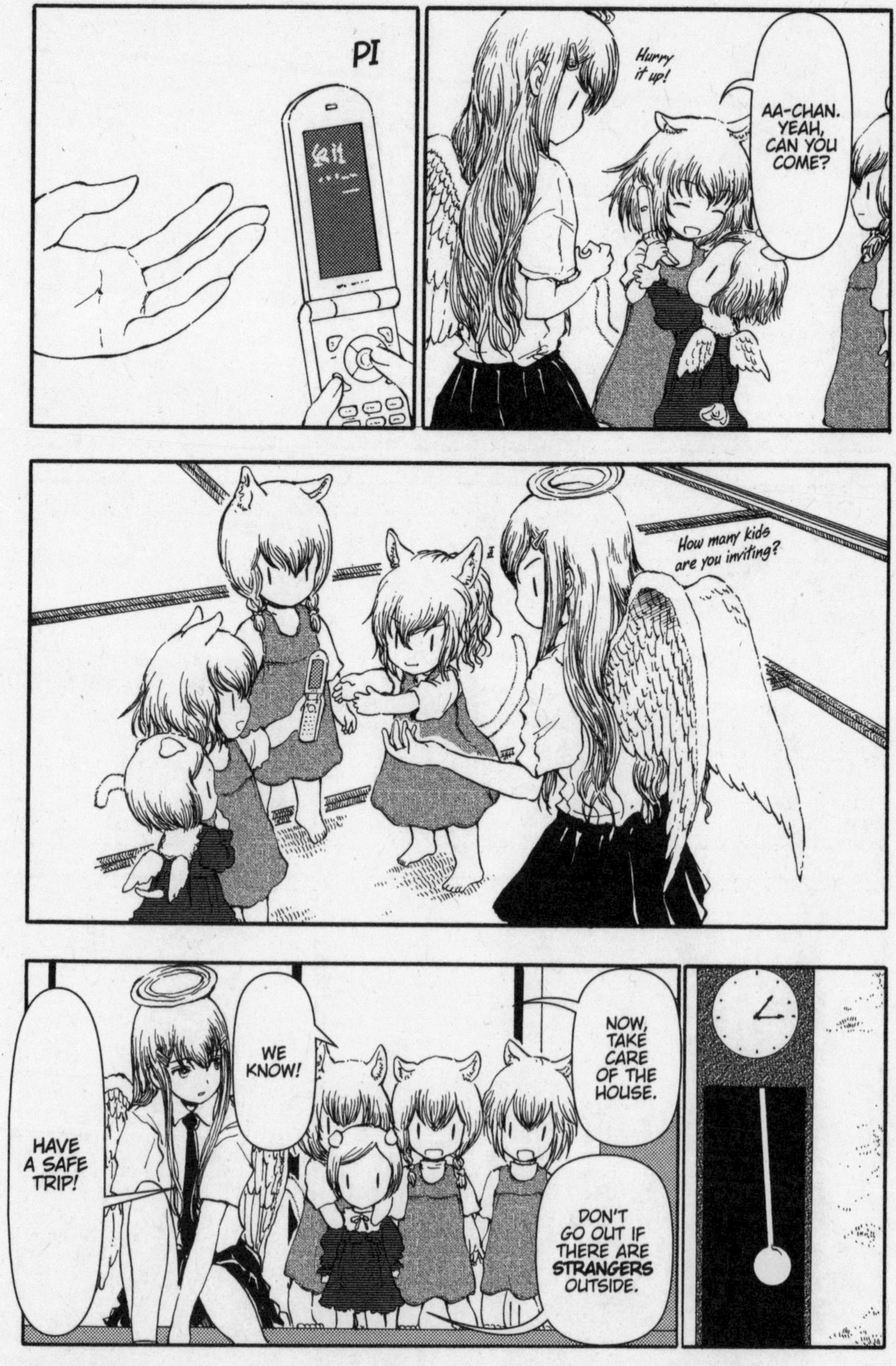
AA-CHAN. YEAH, CAN YOU COME?
Hurry it up!
PI
How many kids are you inviting?
NOW, TAKE CARE OF THE HOUSE.
DON'T GO OUT IF THERE ARE STRANGERS OUTSIDE.
WE KNOW!
HAVE A SAFE TRIP!

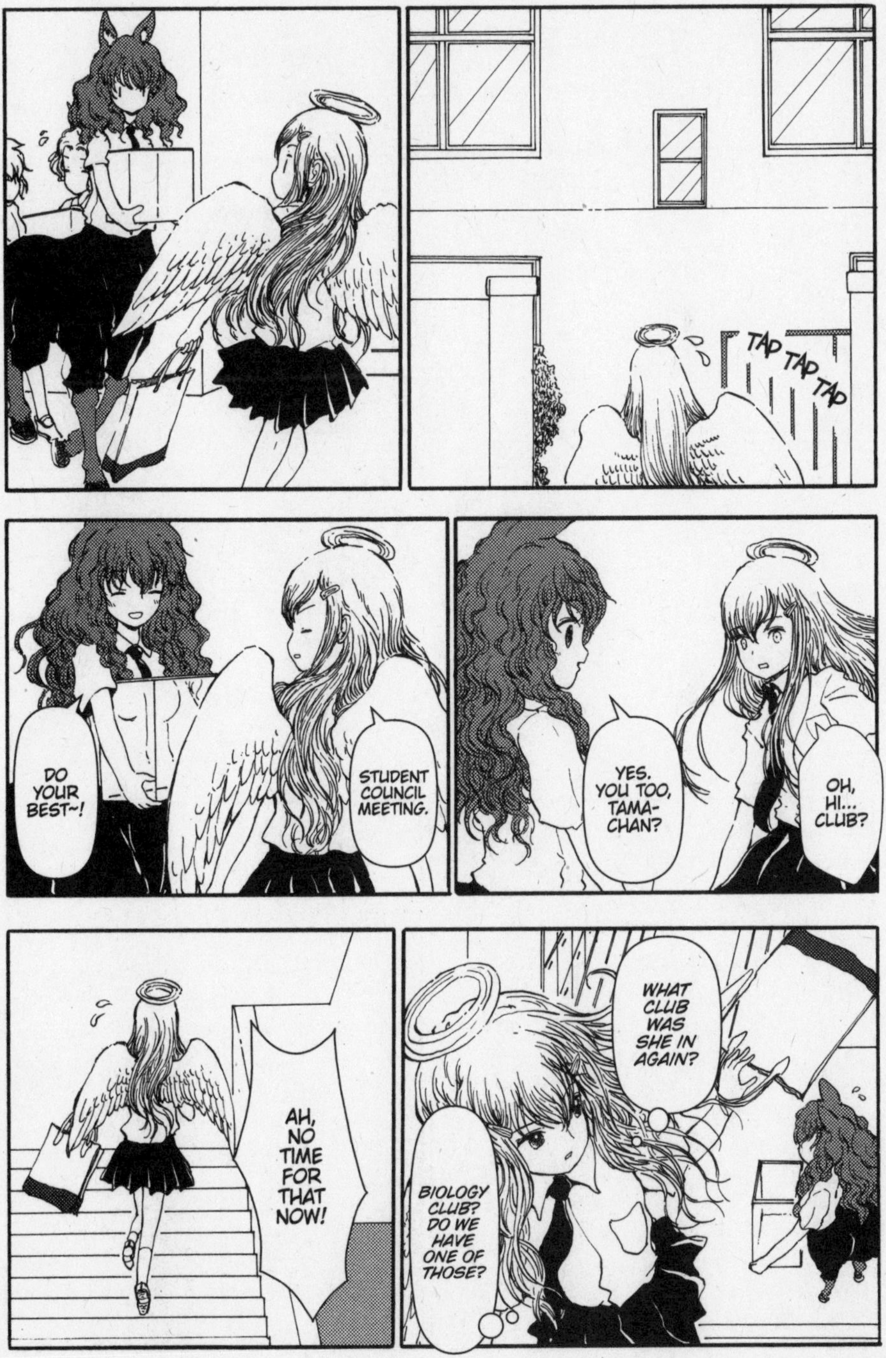
TAP TAP TAP
OH, HI... CLUB?
YES. YOU TOO, TAMA-CHAN?
STUDENT COUNCIL MEETING.
DO YOUR BEST~!
WHAT CLUB WAS SHE IN AGAIN?
BIOLOGY CLUB? DO WE HAVE ONE OF THOSE?
AH, NO TIME FOR THAT NOW!

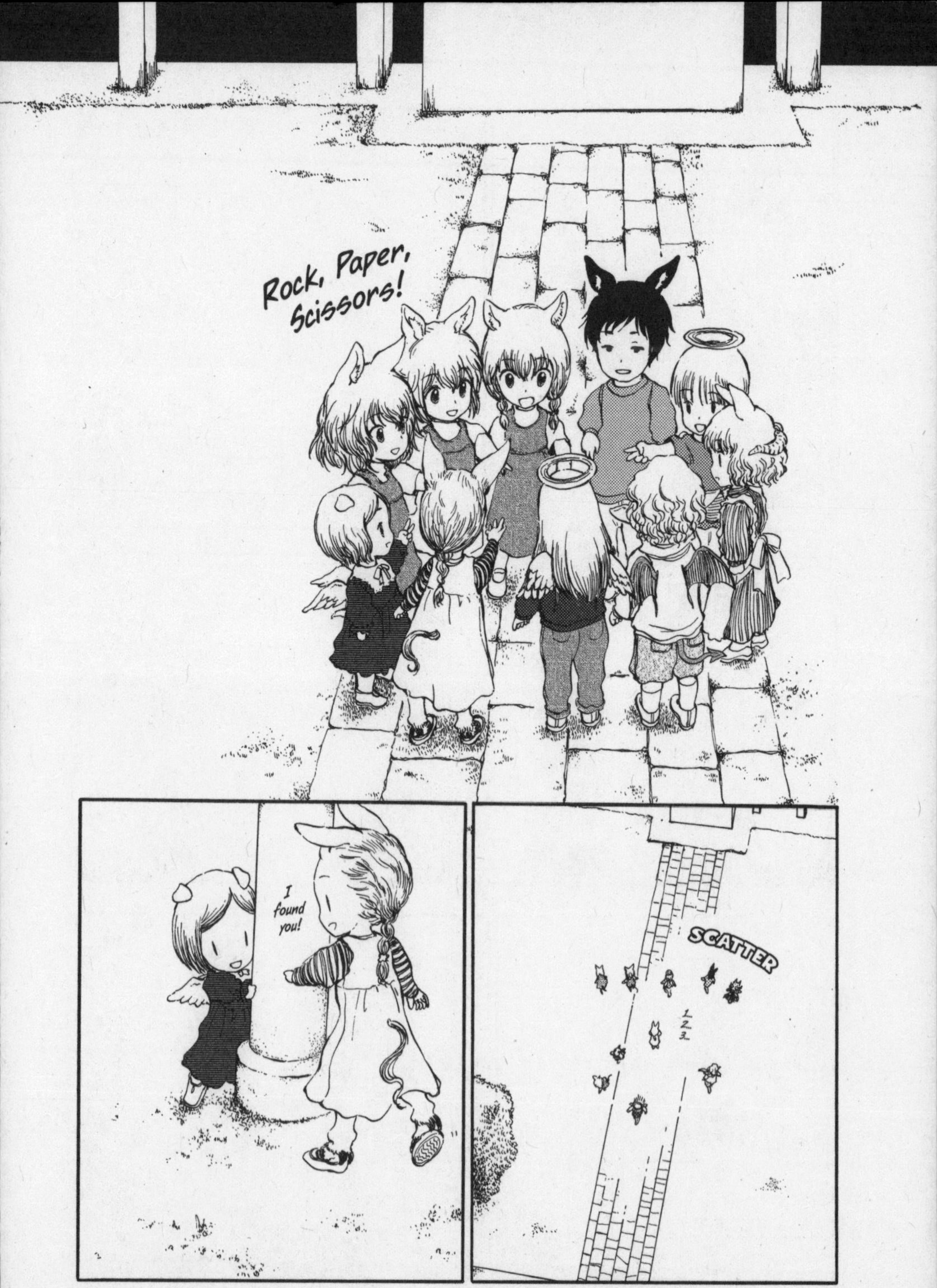
Rock, Paper, Scissors!
SCATTER
1 2 3
I found you!

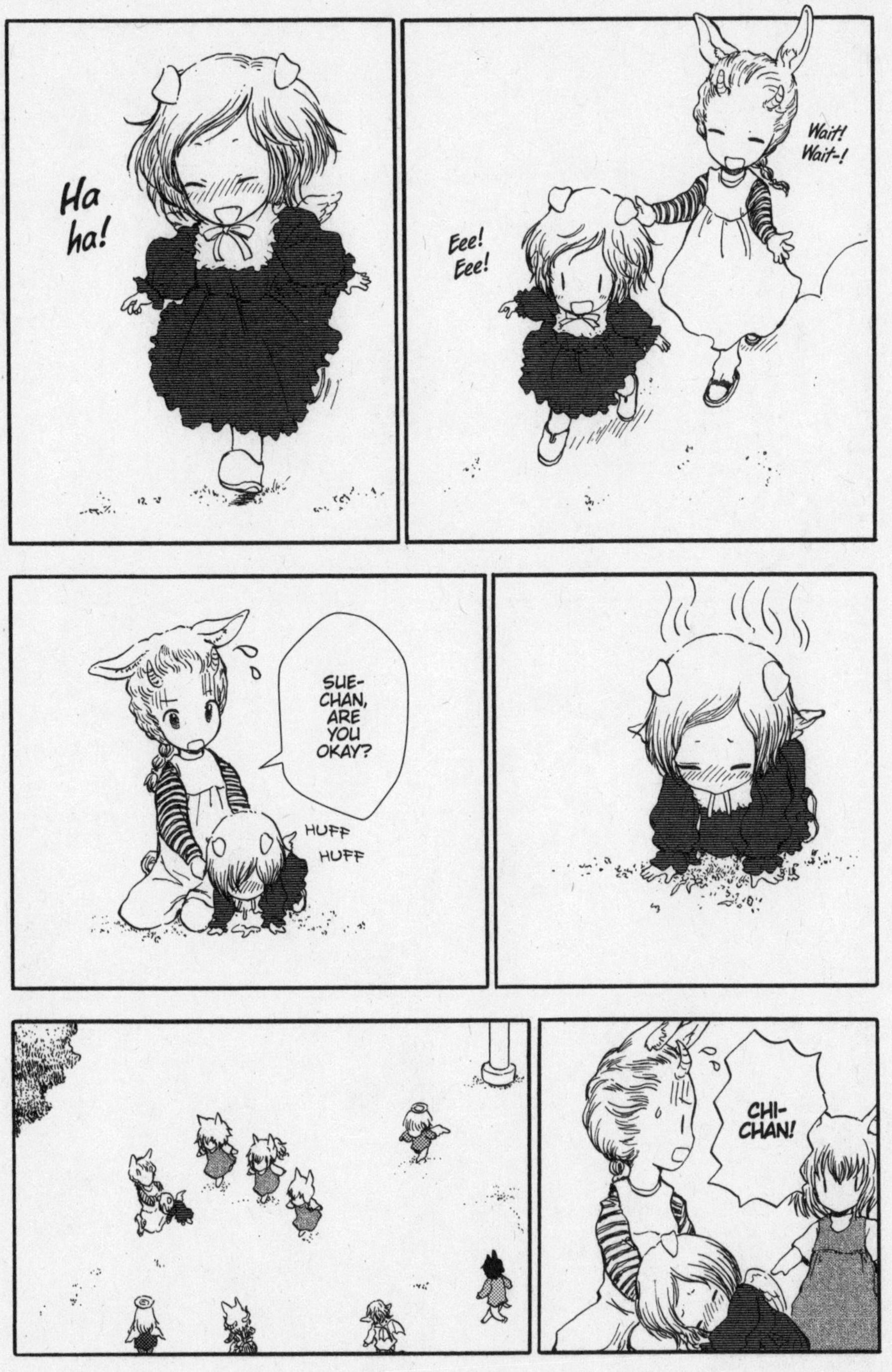
Wait! Wait-!
Eee! Eee!
Ha ha!
SUE-CHAN, ARE YOU OKAY?
HUFF HUFF
CHI-CHAN!

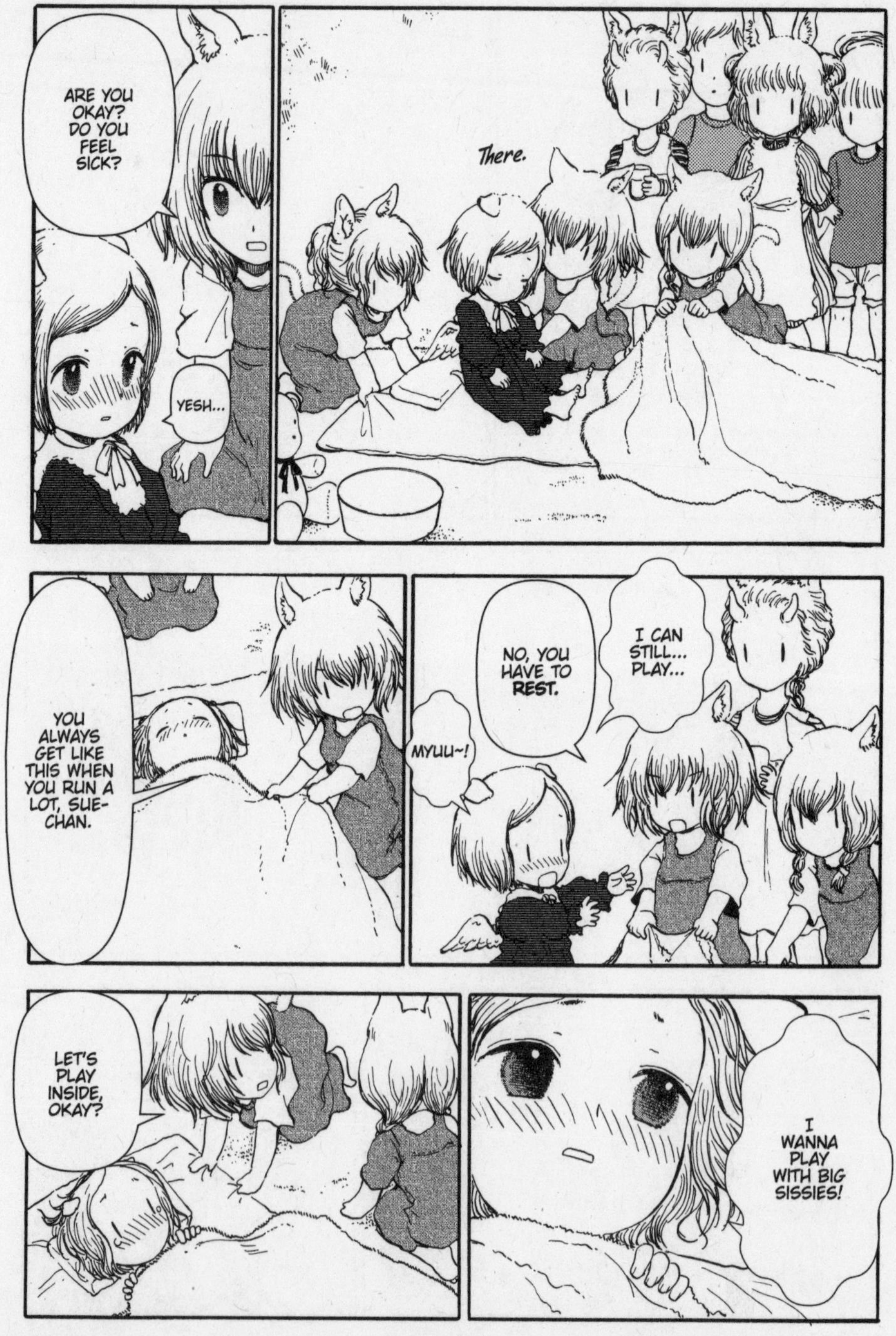
There.
ARE YOU OKAY? DO YOU FEEL SICK?
YESH...
I CAN STILL... PLAY...
NO, YOU HAVE TO REST.
MYUU~!
YOU ALWAYS GET LIKE THIS WHEN YOU RUN A LOT, SUE-CHAN.
I WANNA PLAY WITH BIG SISSIES!
LET'S PLAY INSIDE, OKAY?

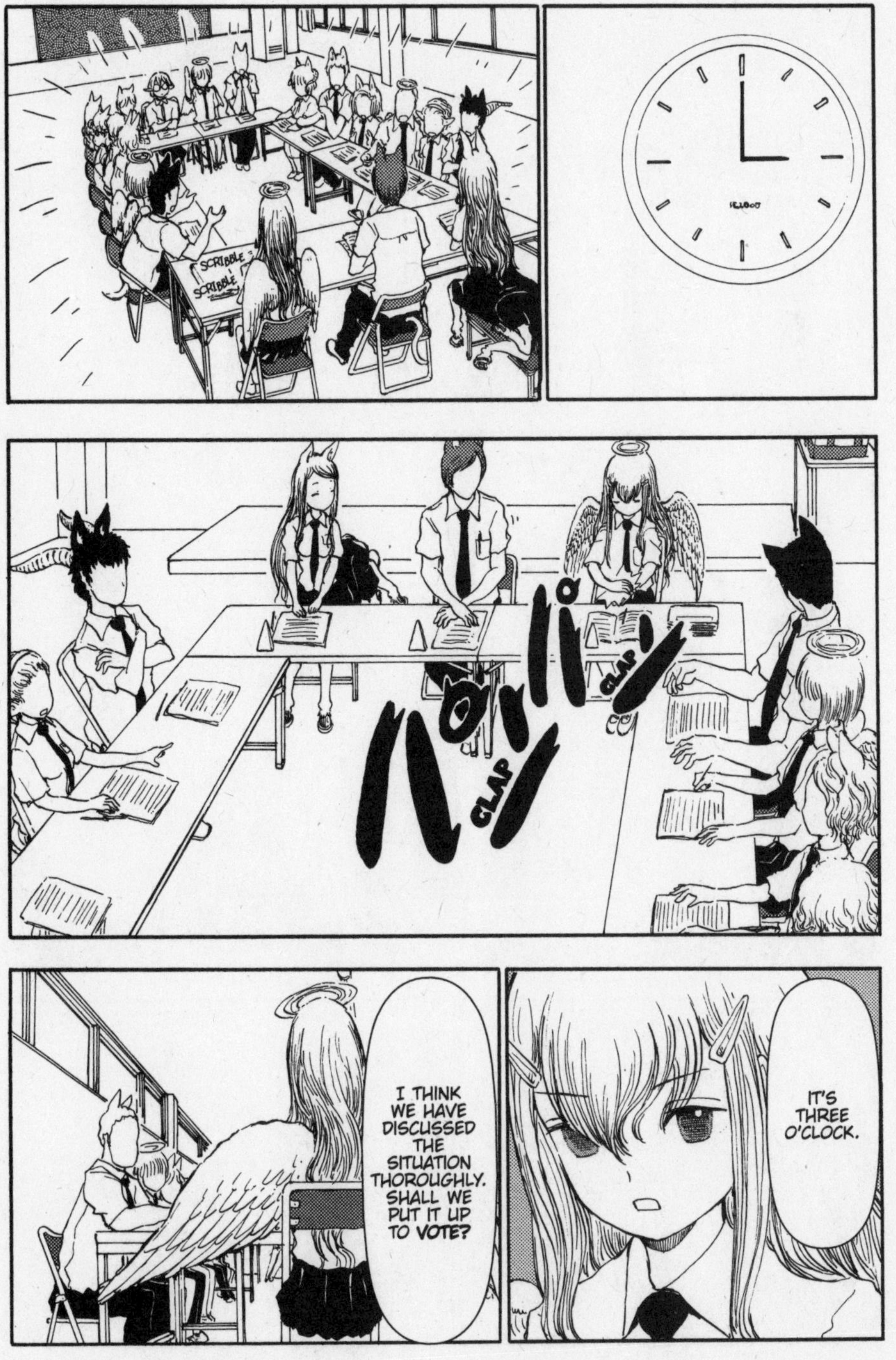
SCRIBBLE
SCRIBBLE
CLAP
CLAP
IT'S THREE O'CLOCK.
I THINK WE HAVE DISCUSSED THE SITUATION THOROUGHLY. SHALL WE PUT IT UP TO VOTE?

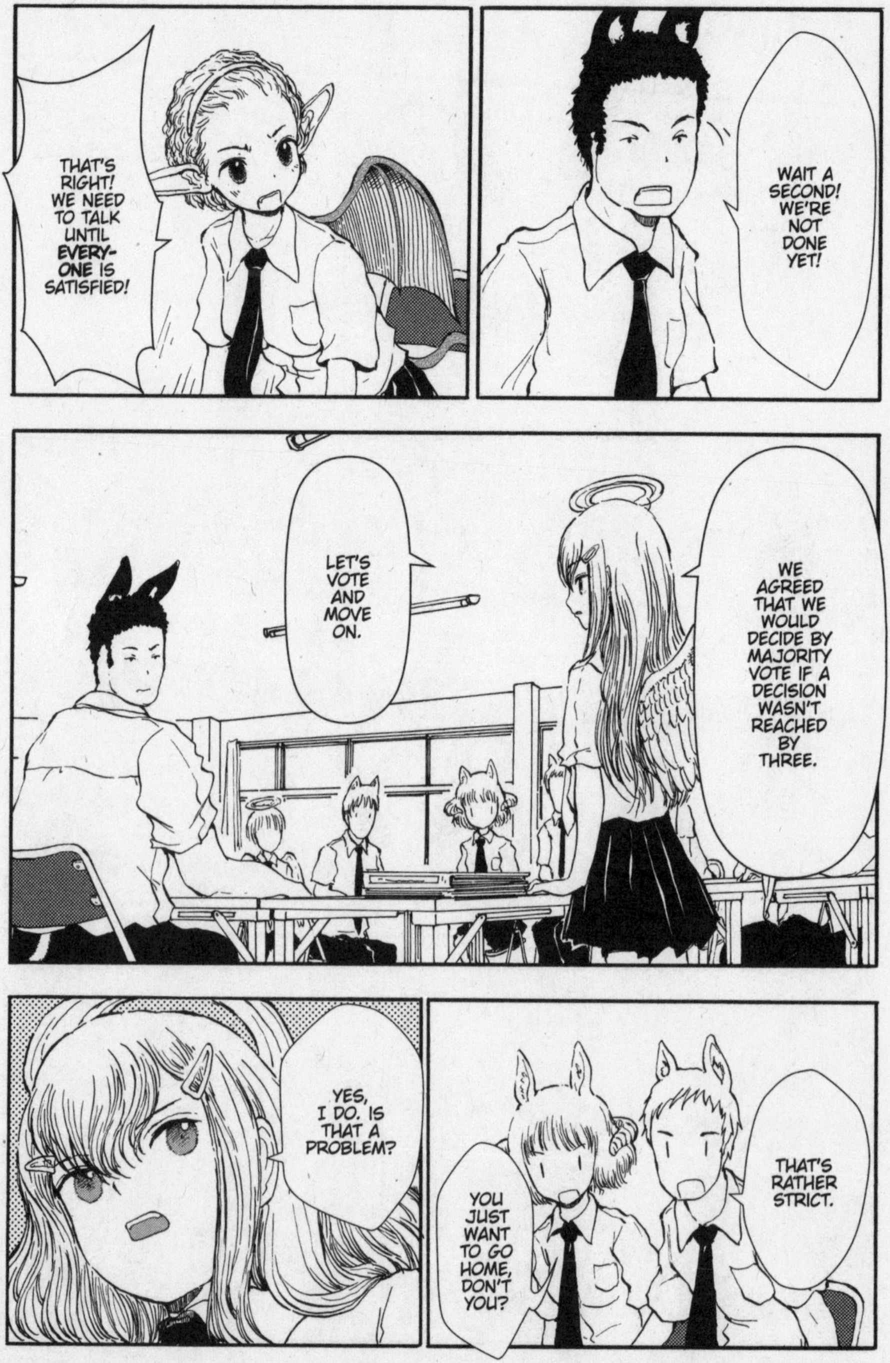
WAIT A SECOND! WE'RE NOT DONE YET!
THAT'S RIGHT! WE NEED TO TALK UNTIL EVERYONE IS SATISFIED!
WE AGREED THAT WE WOULD DECIDE BY MAJORITY VOTE IF A DECISION WASN'T REACHED BY THREE.
LET'S VOTE AND MOVE ON.
THAT'S RATHER STRICT.
YOU JUST WANT TO GO HOME, DON'T YOU?
YES, I DO. IS THAT A PROBLEM?

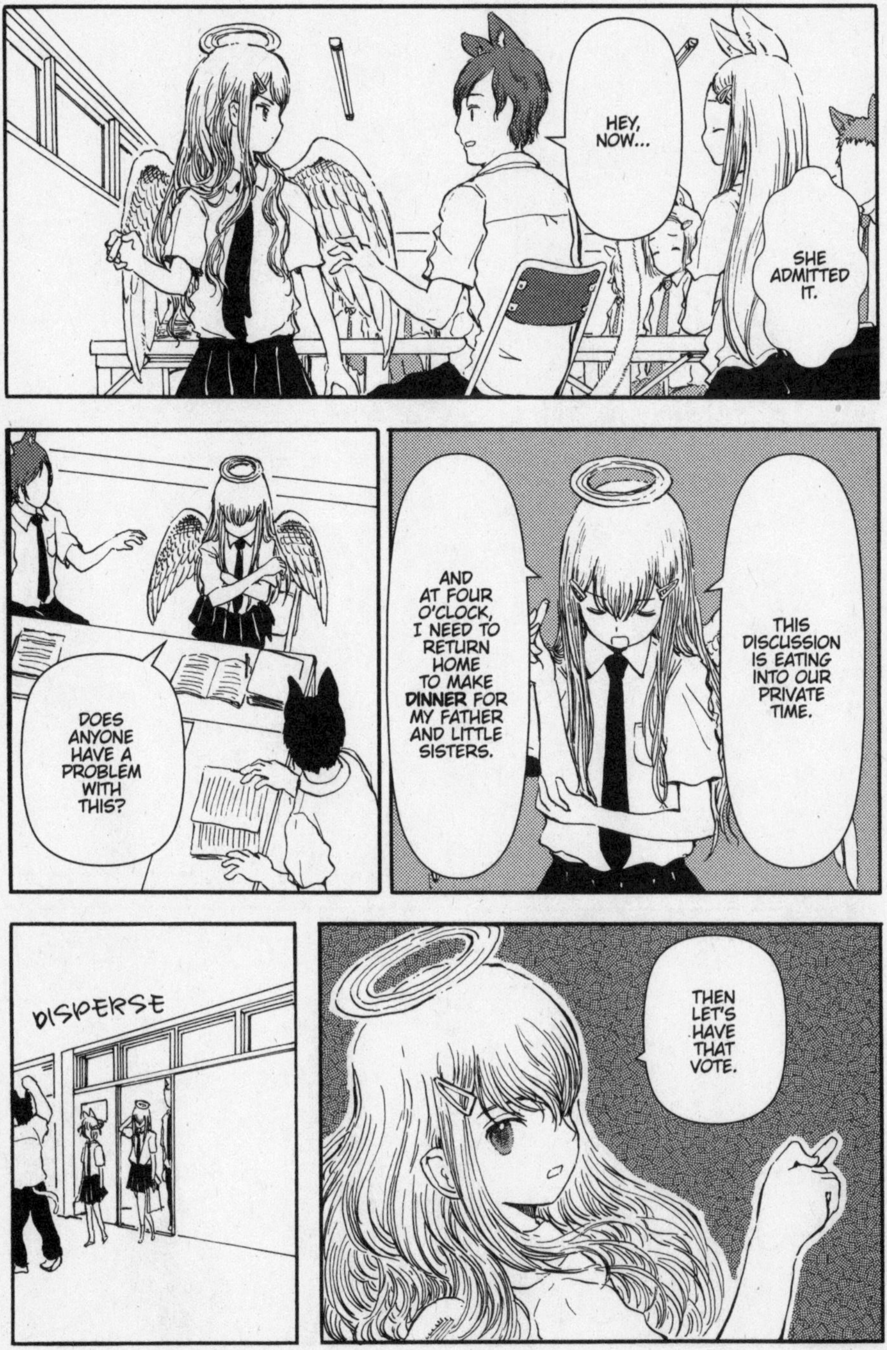
SHE ADMITTED IT.
HEY, NOW...
THIS DISCUSSION IS EATING INTO OUR PRIVATE TIME.
AND AT FOUR O'CLOCK, I NEED TO RETURN HOME TO MAKE DINNER FOR MY FATHER AND LITTLE SISTERS.
DOES ANYONE HAVE A PROBLEM WITH THIS?
THEN LET'S HAVE THAT VOTE.
DISPERSE

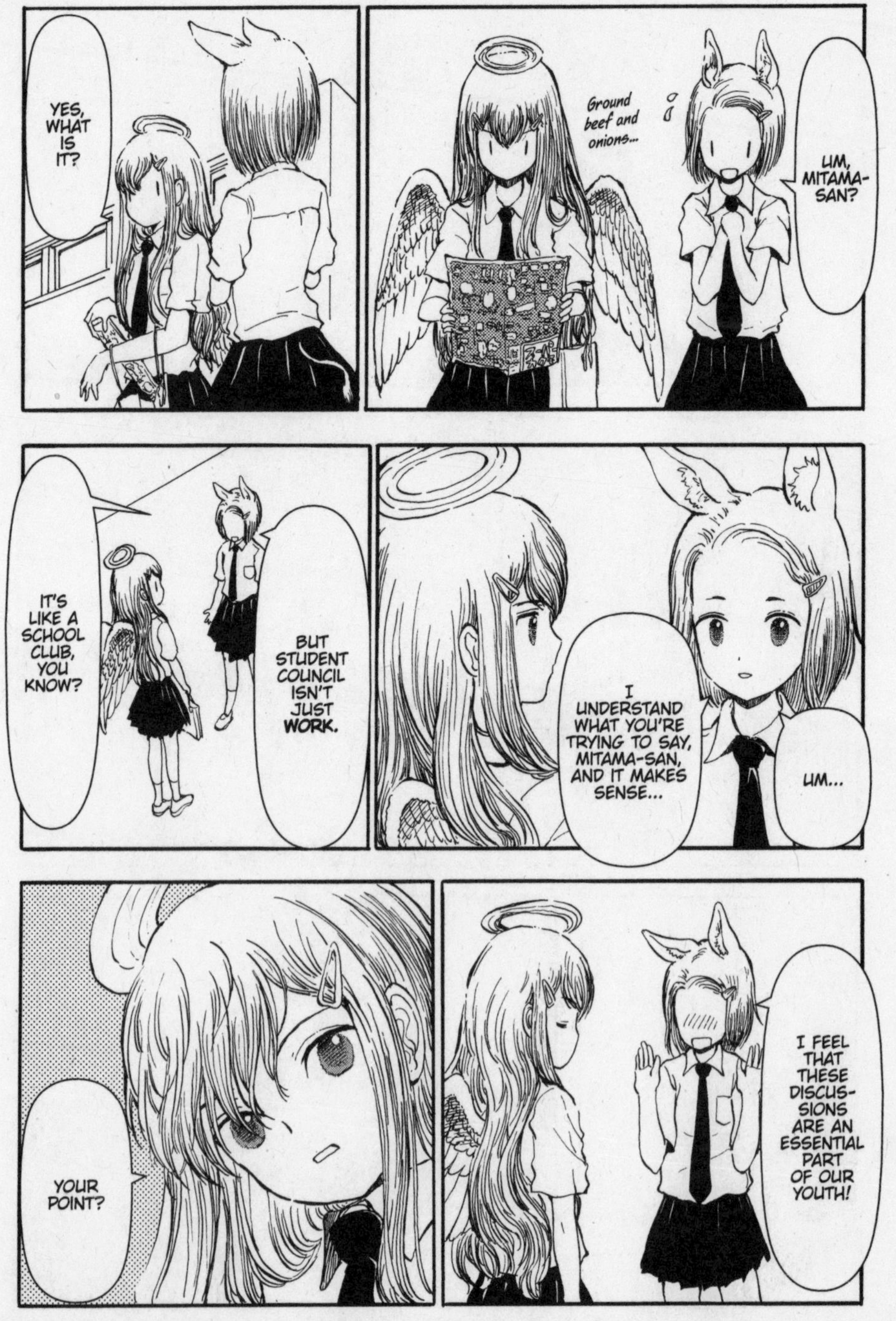
UM, MITAMA-SAN?
Ground beef and onions...
YES, WHAT IS IT?
UM...
I UNDERSTAND WHAT YOU'RE TRYING TO SAY, MITAMA-SAN, AND IT MAKES SENSE...
BUT STUDENT COUNCIL ISN'T JUST **WORK.**
IT'S LIKE A SCHOOL CLUB, YOU KNOW?
I FEEL THAT THESE DISCUSSIONS ARE AN ESSENTIAL PART OF OUR YOUTH!
YOUR POINT?

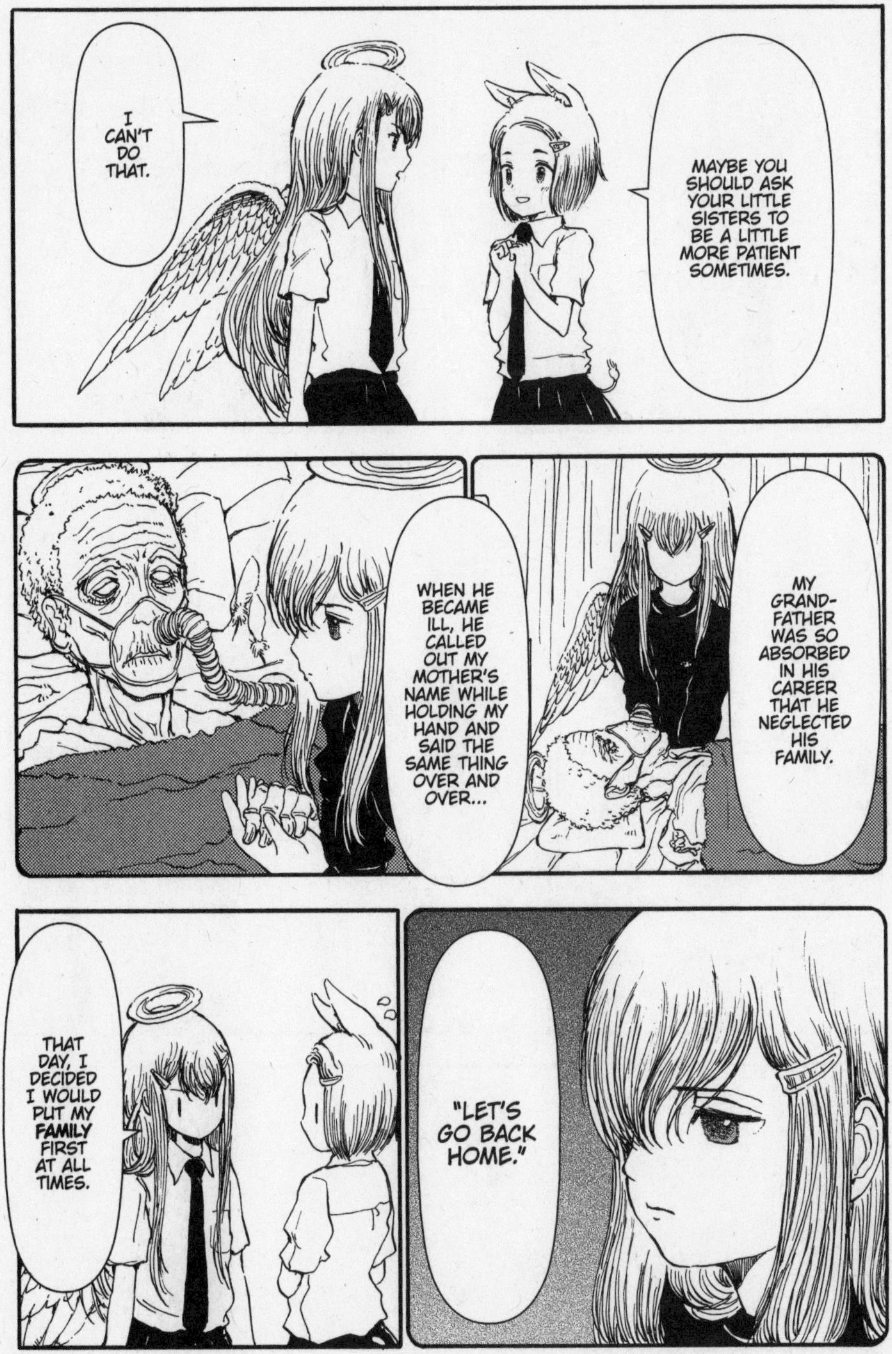
MAYBE YOU SHOULD ASK YOUR LITTLE SISTERS TO BE A LITTLE MORE PATIENT SOMETIMES.
I CAN'T DO THAT.
MY GRAND-FATHER WAS SO ABSORBED IN HIS CAREER THAT HE NEGLECTED HIS FAMILY.
WHEN HE BECAME ILL, HE CALLED OUT MY MOTHER'S NAME WHILE HOLDING MY HAND AND SAID THE SAME THING OVER AND OVER...
"LET'S GO BACK HOME."
THAT DAY, I DECIDED I WOULD PUT MY **FAMILY** FIRST AT ALL TIMES.

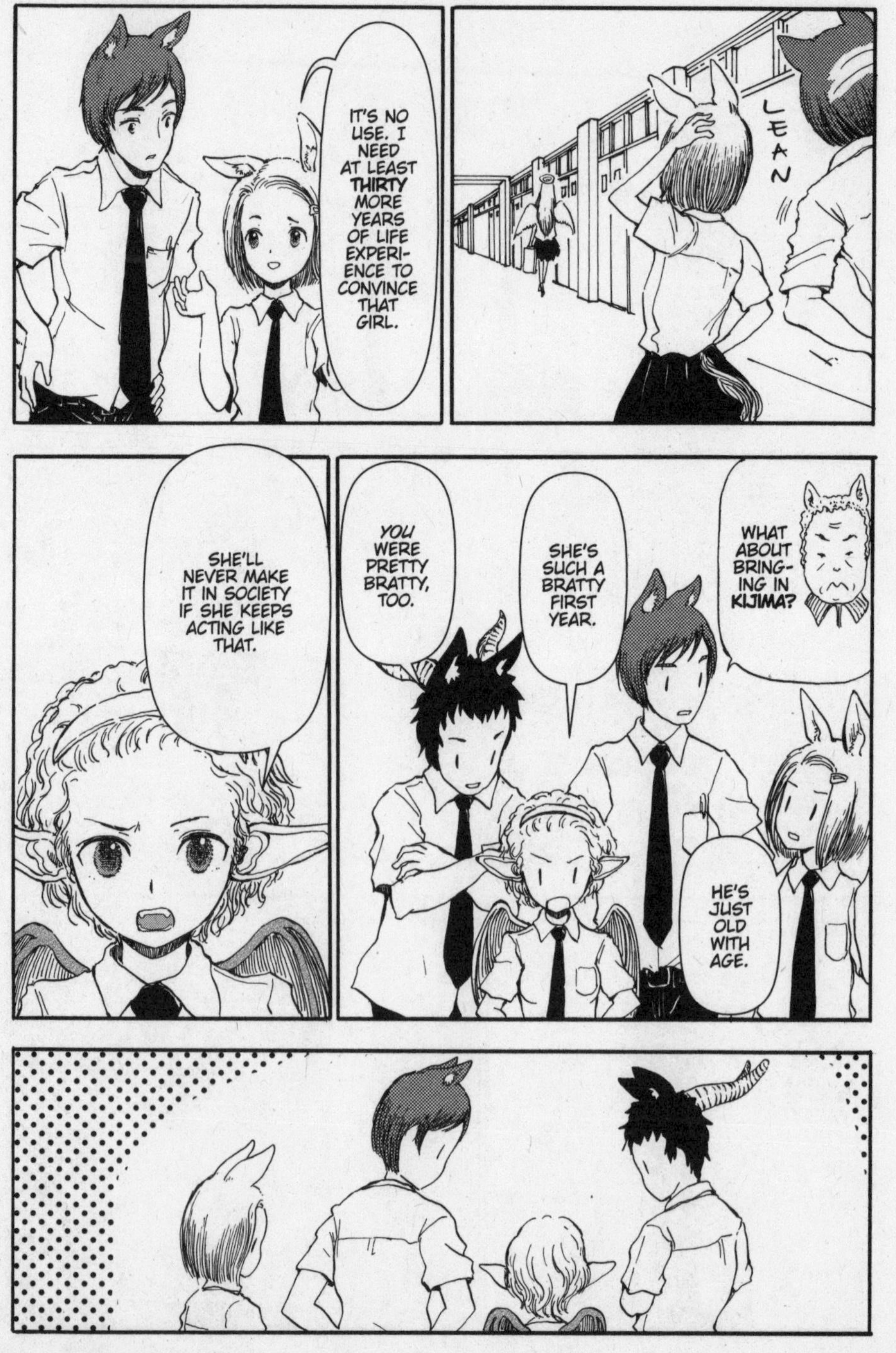
LEAN
IT'S NO USE. I NEED AT LEAST THIRTY MORE YEARS OF LIFE EXPERIENCE TO CONVINCE THAT GIRL.
WHAT ABOUT BRINGING IN KIJIMA?
HE'S JUST OLD WITH AGE.
SHE'S SUCH A BRATTY FIRST YEAR.
YOU WERE PRETTY BRATTY, TOO.
SHE'LL NEVER MAKE IT IN SOCIETY IF SHE KEEPS ACTING LIKE THAT.

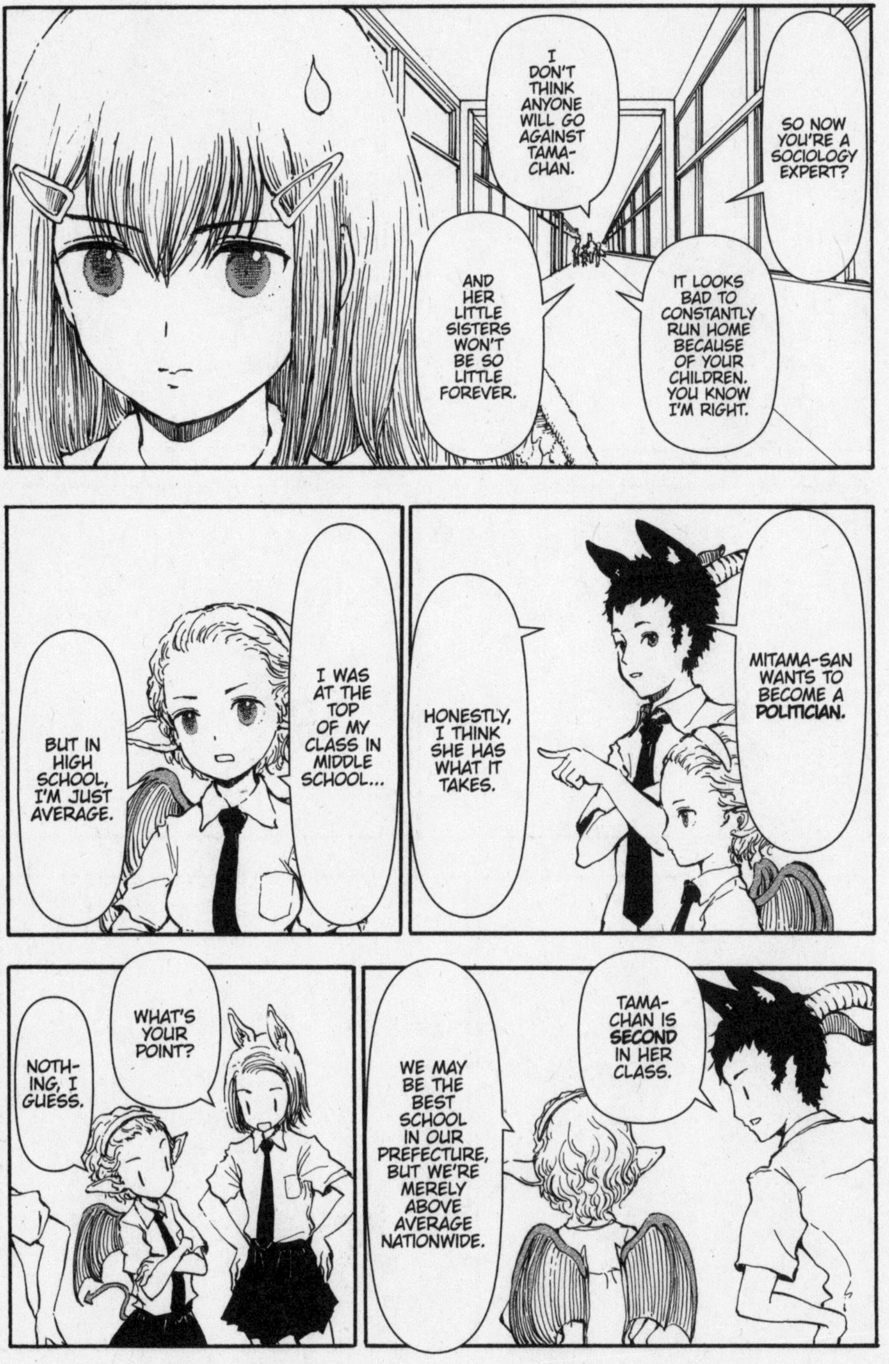
SO NOW YOU'RE A SOCIOLOGY EXPERT?
I DON'T THINK ANYONE WILL GO AGAINST TAMA-CHAN.
IT LOOKS BAD TO CONSTANTLY RUN HOME BECAUSE OF YOUR CHILDREN. YOU KNOW I'M RIGHT.
AND HER LITTLE SISTERS WON'T BE SO LITTLE FOREVER.
MITAMA-SAN WANTS TO BECOME A **POLITICIAN.**
HONESTLY, I THINK SHE HAS WHAT IT TAKES.
I WAS AT THE TOP OF MY CLASS IN MIDDLE SCHOOL...
BUT IN HIGH SCHOOL, I'M JUST AVERAGE.
TAMA-CHAN IS **SECOND** IN HER CLASS.
WE MAY BE THE BEST SCHOOL IN OUR PREFECTURE, BUT WE'RE MERELY ABOVE AVERAGE NATIONWIDE.
WHAT'S YOUR POINT?
NOTH-ING, I GUESS.

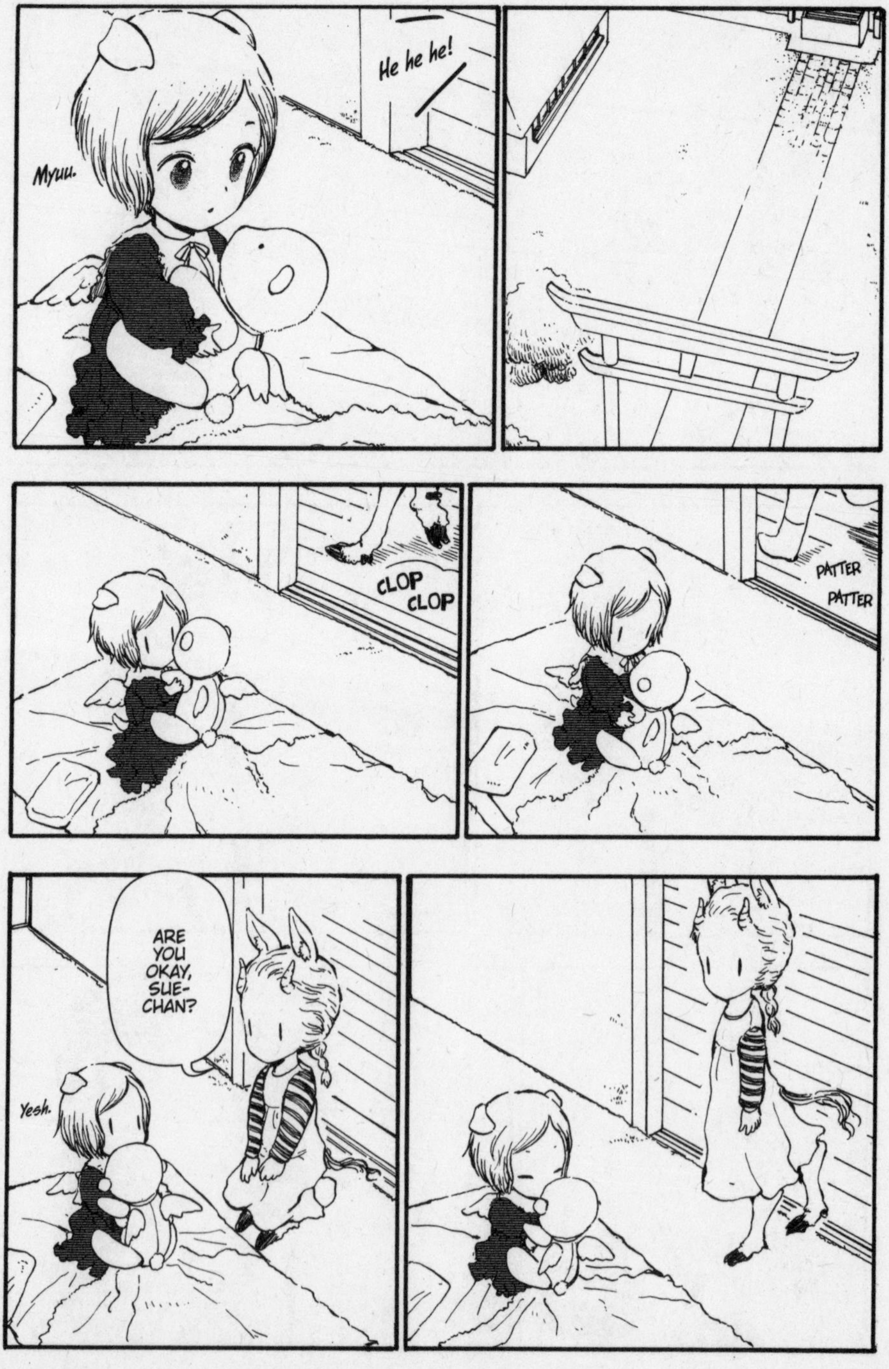
He he he!
Myuu.
PATTER
PATTER
CLOP
CLOP
ARE YOU OKAY, SUE-CHAN?
Yesh.

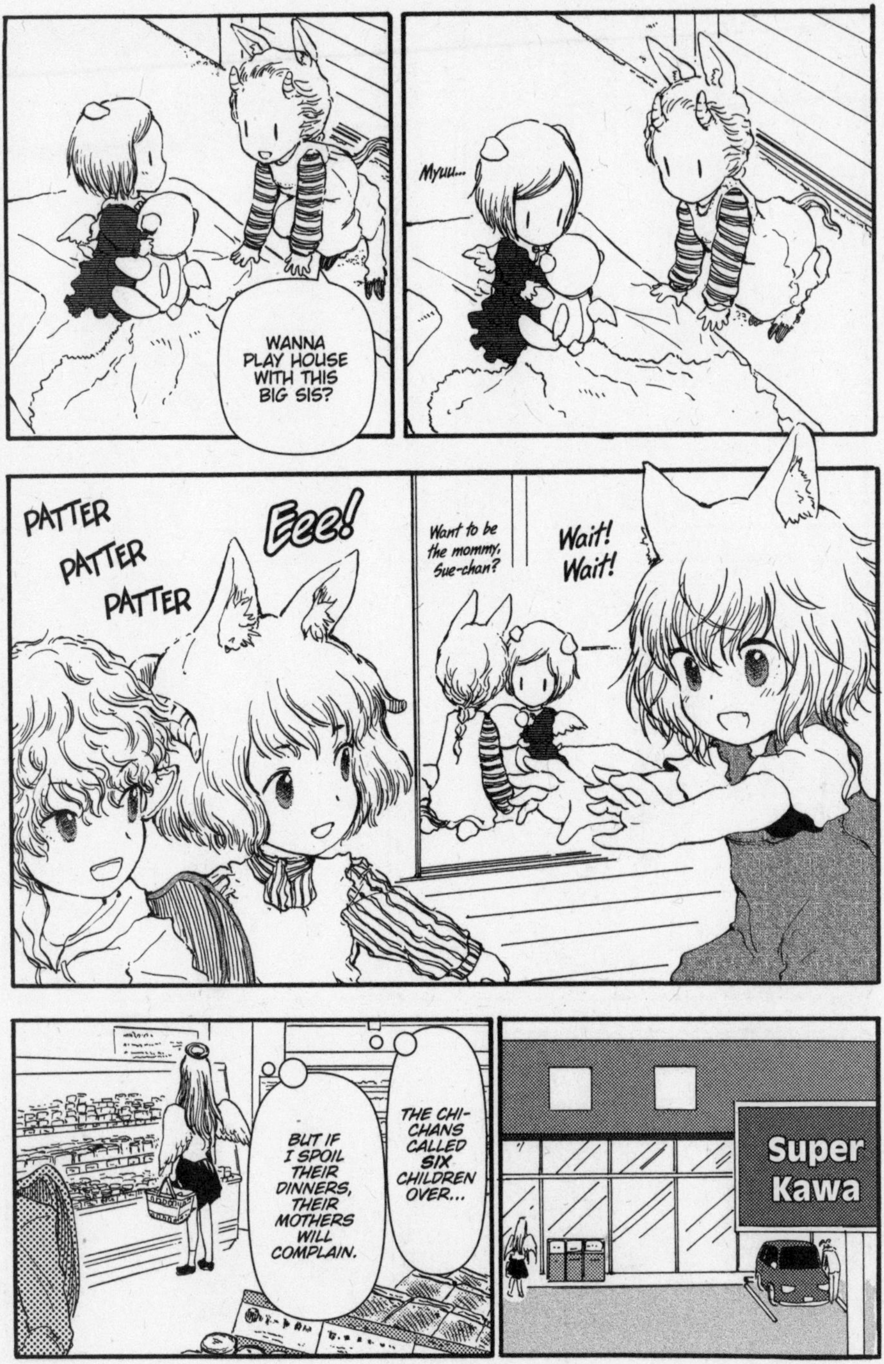
Myuu...
WANNA PLAY HOUSE WITH THIS BIG SIS?
Wait! Wait!
Want to be the mommy, Sue-chan?
Eee!
PATTER PATTER PATTER
Super Kawa
THE CHI-CHANS CALLED SIX CHILDREN OVER...
BUT IF I SPOIL THEIR DINNERS, THEIR MOTHERS WILL COMPLAIN.

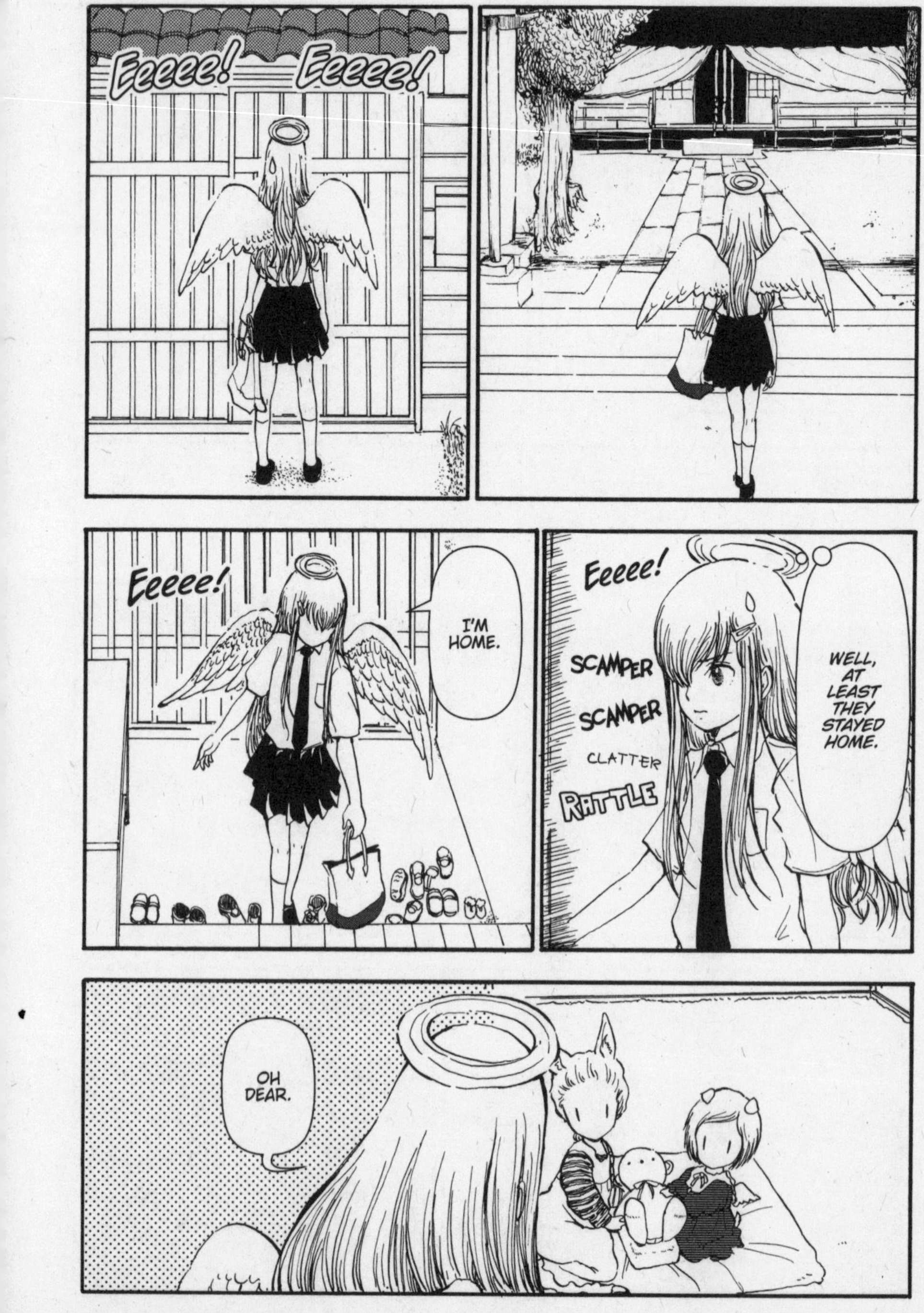
Eeeee! Eeeee!
WELL, AT LEAST THEY STAYED HOME.
Eeeee!
SCAMPER
SCAMPER
CLATTER
RATTLE
I'M HOME.
Eeeee!
OH DEAR.

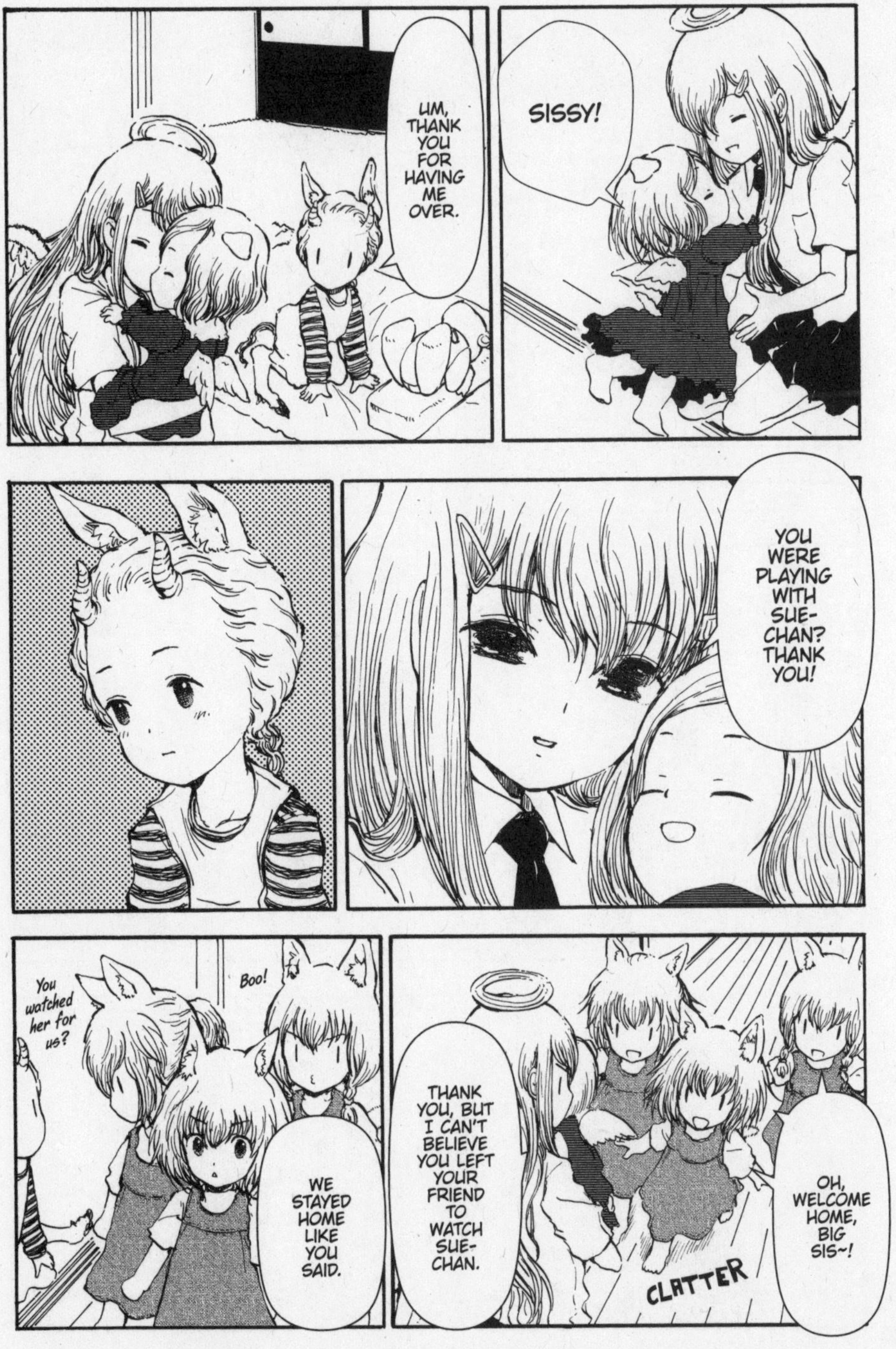
SISSY!
UM, THANK YOU FOR HAVING ME OVER.
YOU WERE PLAYING WITH SUE-CHAN? THANK YOU!
OH, WELCOME HOME, BIG SIS~!
CLATTER
THANK YOU, BUT I CAN'T BELIEVE YOU LEFT YOUR FRIEND TO WATCH SUE-CHAN.
Boo!
You watched her for us?
WE STAYED HOME LIKE YOU SAID.

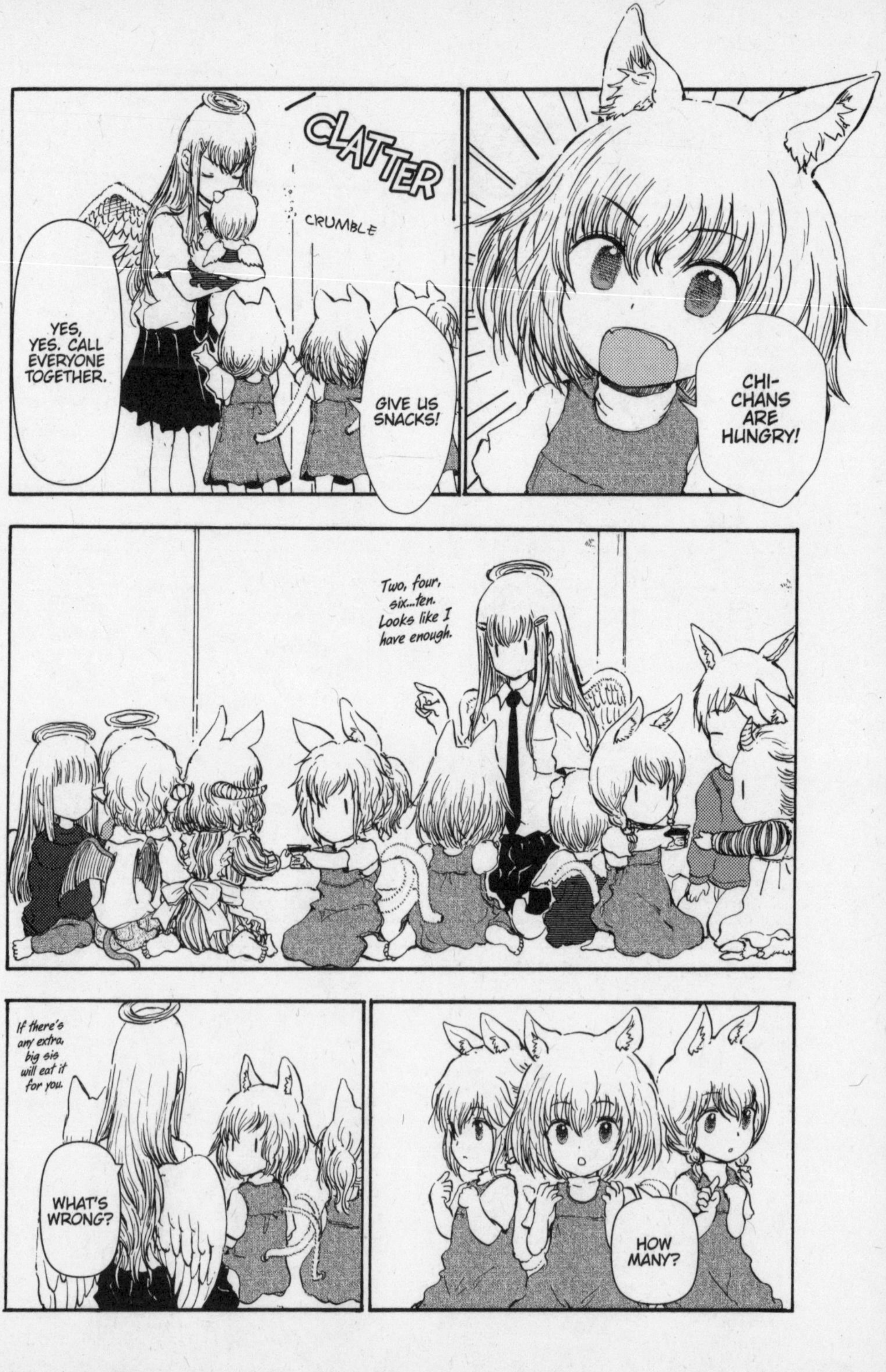
CHI-CHANS ARE HUNGRY!
CLATTER
CRUMBLE
GIVE US SNACKS!
YES, YES. CALL EVERYONE TOGETHER.
Two, four, six...ten. Looks like I have enough.
HOW MANY?
If there's any extra, big sis will eat it for you.
WHAT'S WRONG?

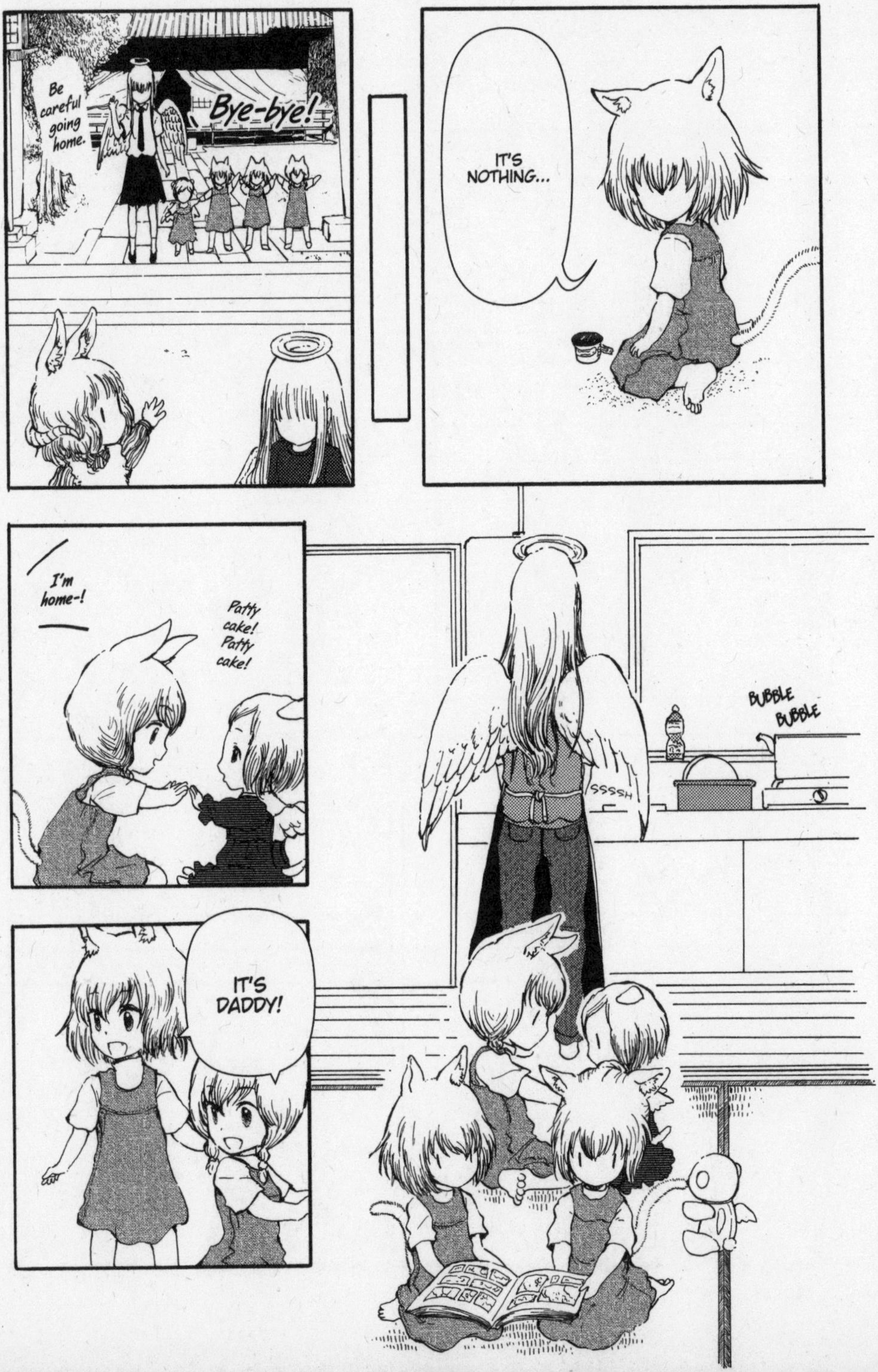
IT'S NOTHING...
Bye-bye!
Be careful going home.
BUBBLE BUBBLE
SSSSH
Patty cake! Patty cake!
I'm home-!
IT'S DADDY!

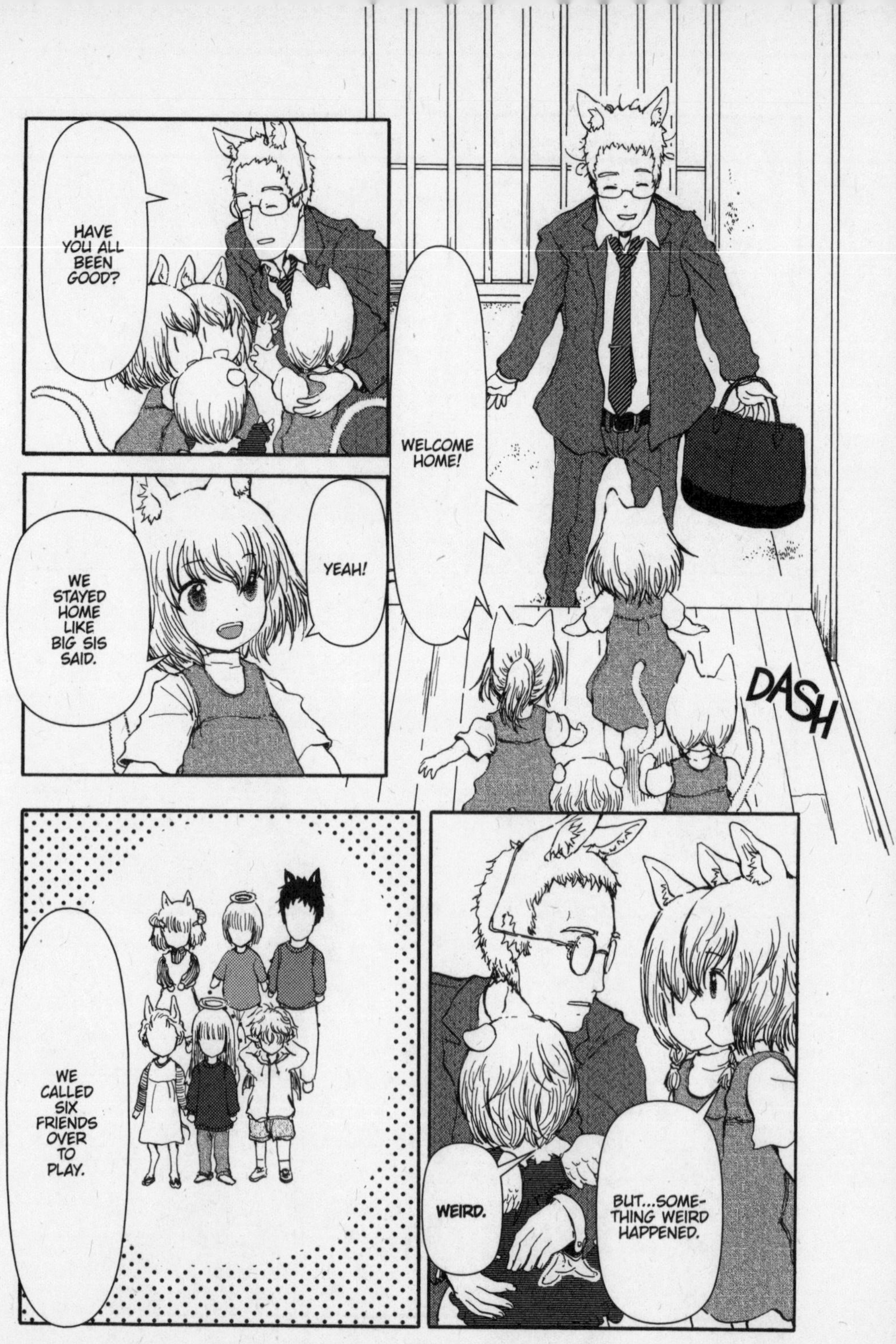
WELCOME HOME!
DASH
HAVE YOU ALL BEEN GOOD?
YEAH!
WE STAYED HOME LIKE BIG SIS SAID.
BUT...SOME-THING WEIRD HAPPENED.
WEIRD.
WE CALLED SIX FRIENDS OVER TO PLAY.

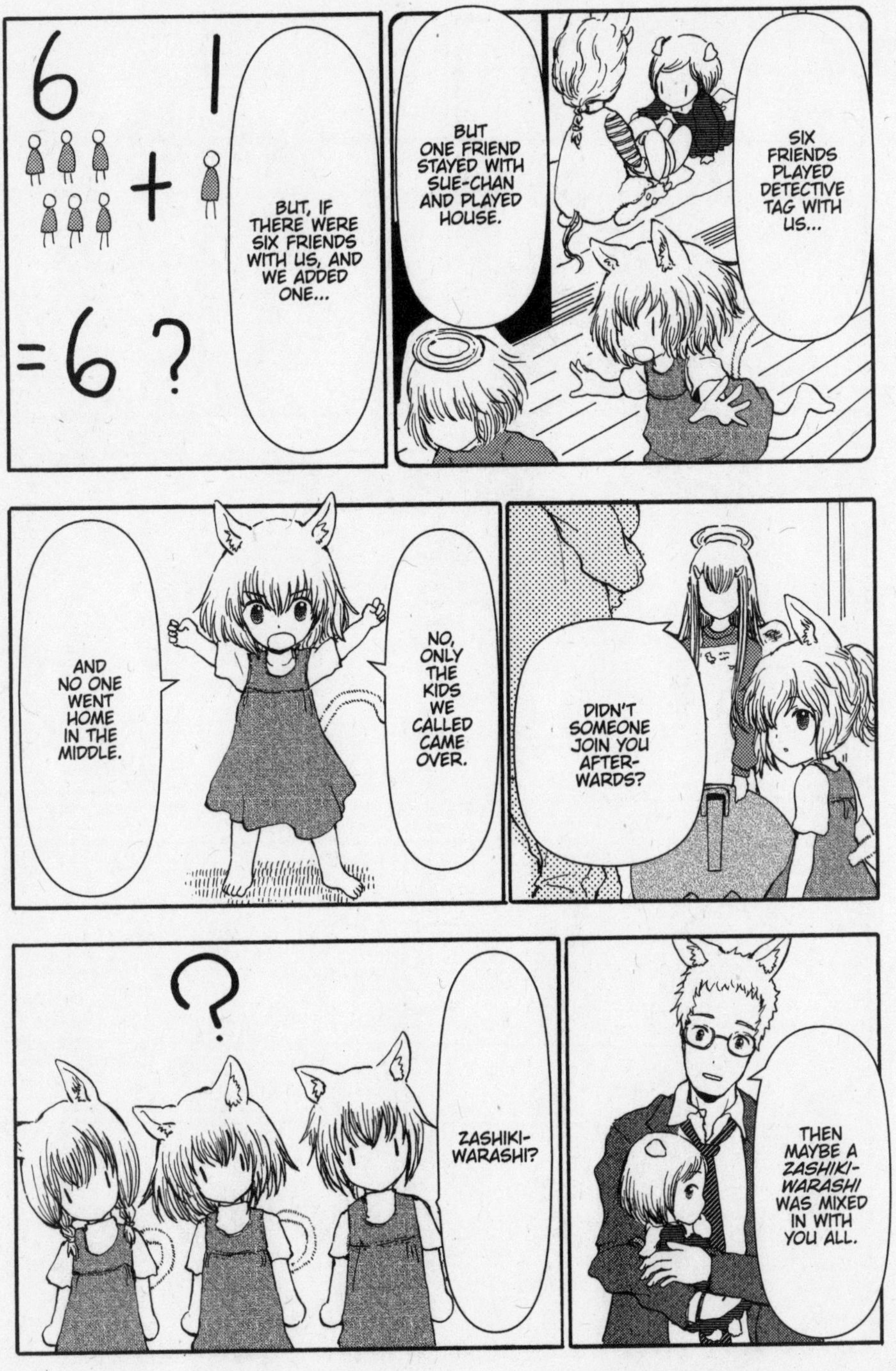
SIX FRIENDS PLAYED DETECTIVE TAG WITH US...
BUT ONE FRIEND STAYED WITH SUE-CHAN AND PLAYED HOUSE.
BUT, IF THERE WERE SIX FRIENDS WITH US, AND WE ADDED ONE...
6 + 1
=6 ?
DIDN'T SOMEONE JOIN YOU AFTER-WARDS?
NO, ONLY THE KIDS WE CALLED CAME OVER.
AND NO ONE WENT HOME IN THE MIDDLE.
THEN MAYBE A ZASHIKI-WARASHI WAS MIXED IN WITH YOU ALL.
ZASHIKI-WARASHI?
?

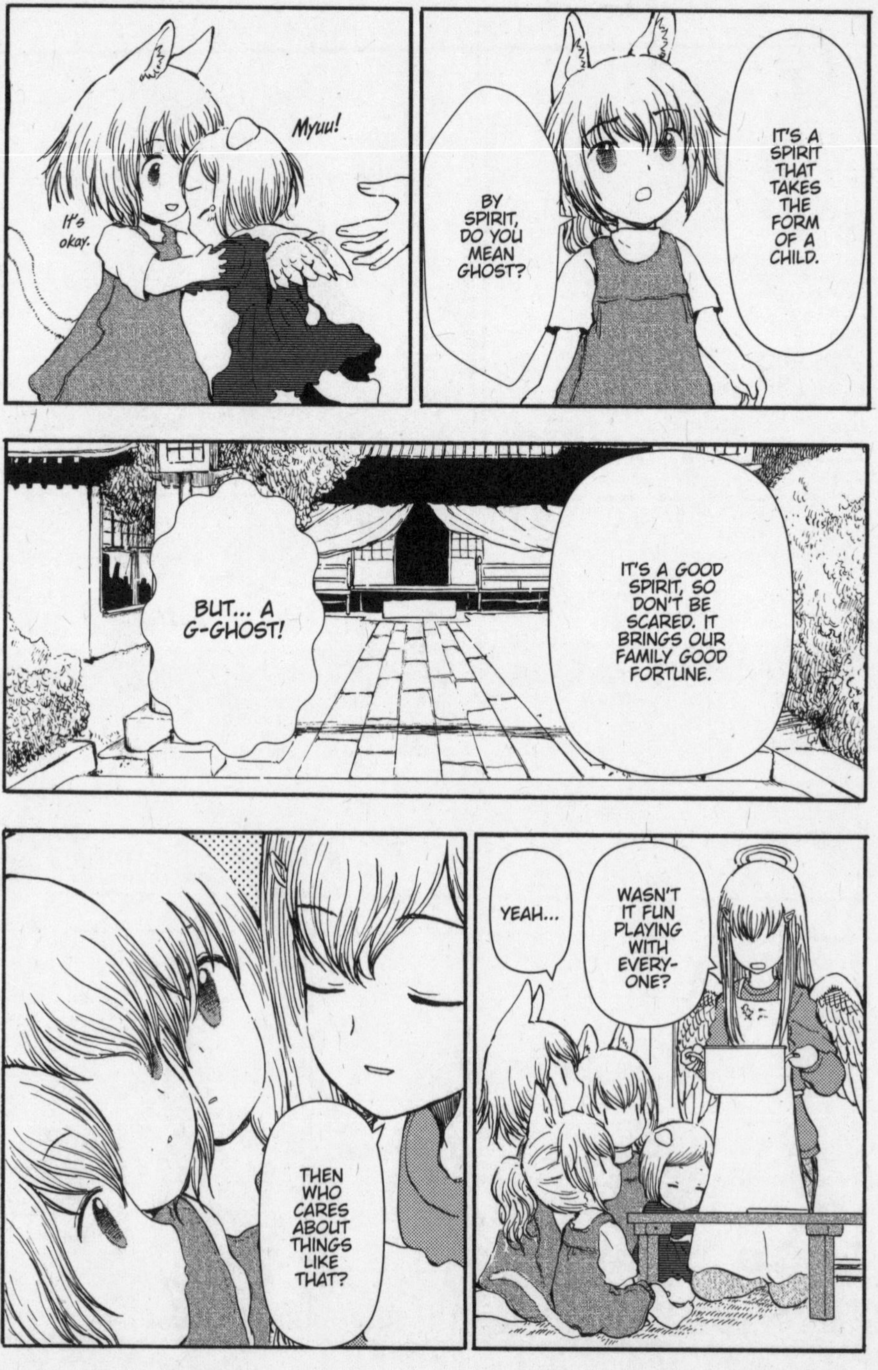
IT'S A SPIRIT THAT TAKES THE FORM OF A CHILD.
BY SPIRIT, DO YOU MEAN GHOST?
Myuu!
It's okay.
IT'S A GOOD SPIRIT, SO DON'T BE SCARED. IT BRINGS OUR FAMILY GOOD FORTUNE.
BUT... A G-GHOST!
WASN'T IT FUN PLAYING WITH EVERY-ONE?
YEAH...
THEN WHO CARES ABOUT THINGS LIKE THAT?

CHAPTER 12 TRANSLATION NOTE:
A ZASHIKI-WARASHI IS A CREATURE FABLED TO LIVE IN SOME TATAMI ROOMS THAT BRINGS GOOD FORTUNE TO THE FAMILY WHILE IT STAYS IN THE HOUSE AND BAD FORTUNE IF IT LEAVES.

SUPERNATURAL BEINGS: VAMPIRES

SUPERNATURAL BEINGS THAT DRINK HUMAN BLOOD ARE FOUND IN FOLKLORE ALL OVER THE WORLD, BUT THE ICONIC IMAGE OF VAMPIRES COMES FROM THE NOVEL *DRACULA*, WRITTEN BY BRAM STOKER. THE VAMPIRE'S WEAKNESS TO LIGHT, GARLIC, AND THE CROSS, AS WELL AS THE ABILITY TO TURN INTO A BAT, ARE ALL TRAITS THAT WERE POPULARIZED IN THE BOOK.

VAMPIRES ARE OFTEN DEPICTED TO BE DRAGONFOLK WITH ARISTOCRATIC SPEECH, PULLED-BACK HAIR, AND A CAPE AS BLACK AS NIGHT. THIS DEPICTION ORIGINATED FROM THE DRAGONFOLK THAT DRESSED AS DRACULA ON THE STAGE AND IN EARLY MOVIES. THE FIRST ACTOR TO PORTRAY DRACULA FOR A MASS AUDIENCE, BELA LUGOSI, BECAME THE ARCHETYPE FOR THE VAMPIRE CHARACTER. DRACULA WAS BASED ON THE ACTUAL TRANSYLVANIAN RULER VLAD THE IMPALER. THIS CREATURE IS EVERY BIT AS ICONIC AS FRANKENSTEIN'S MONSTER.

CHAPTER 13

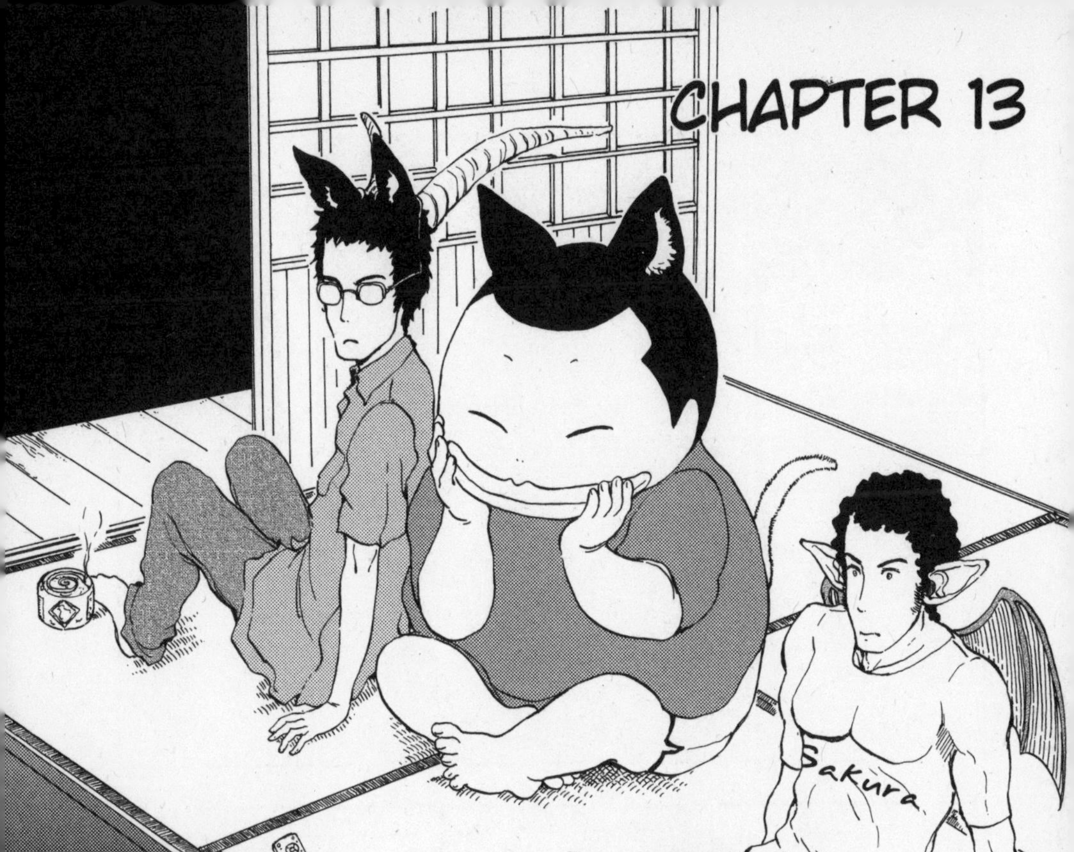
Sakura

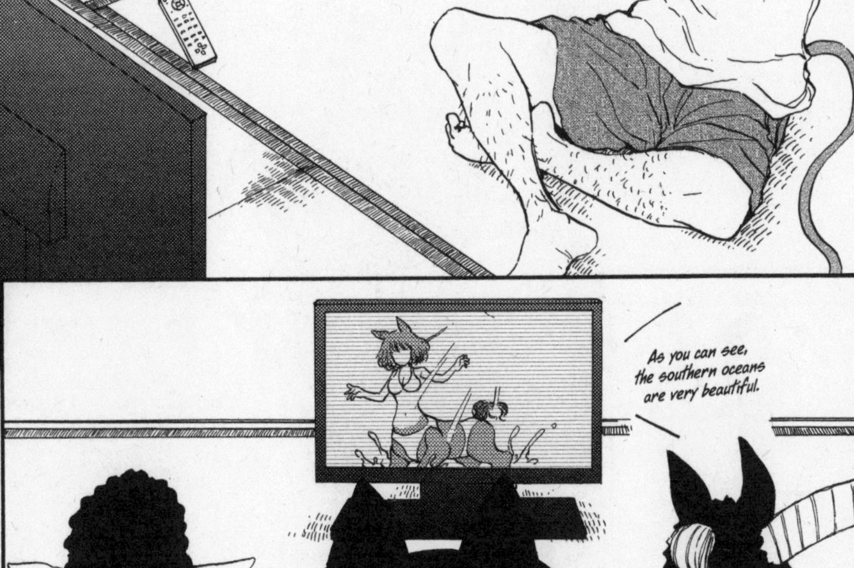
As you can see, the southern oceans are very beautiful.

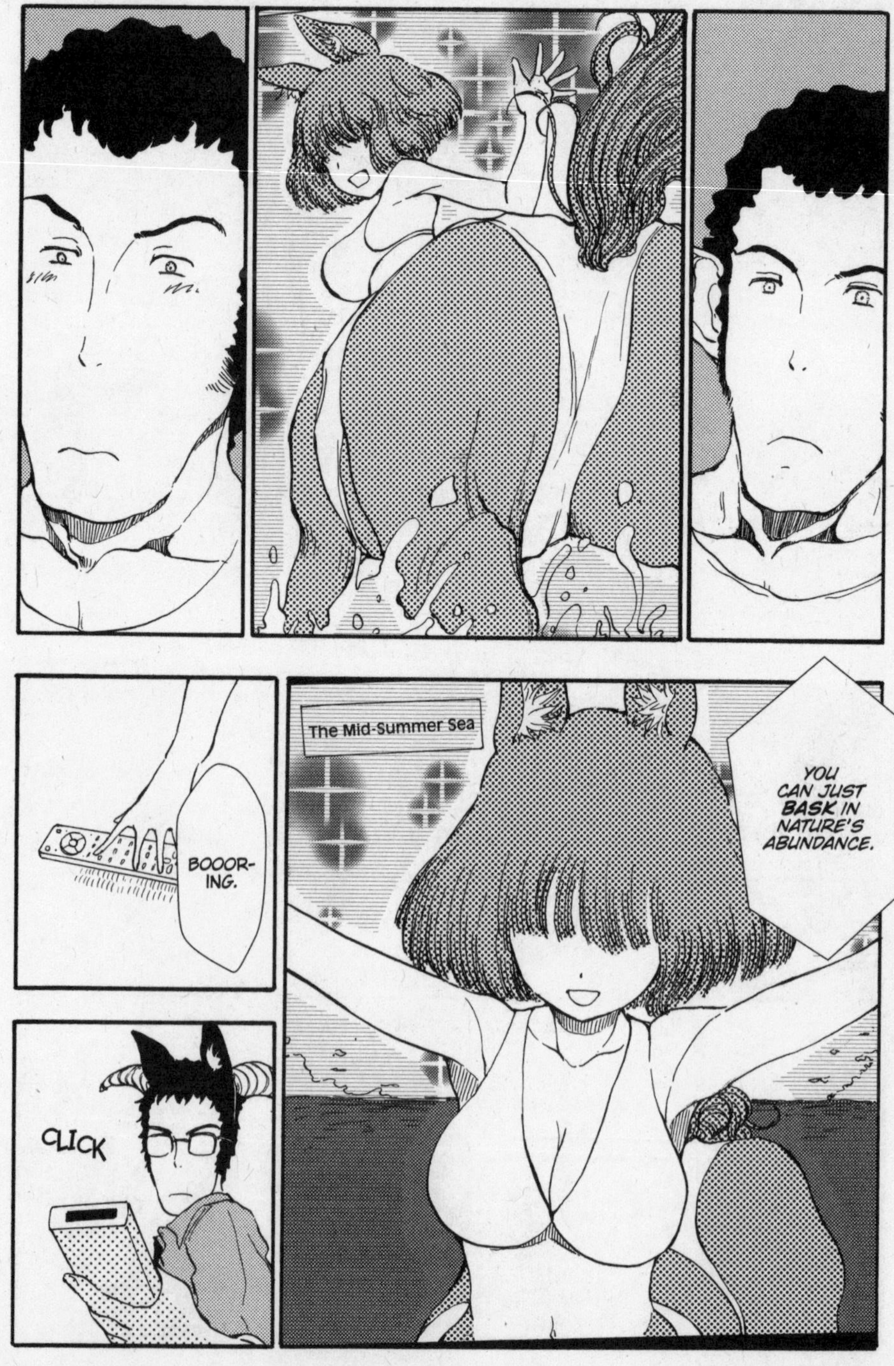
YOU CAN JUST BASK IN NATURE'S ABUNDANCE.
The Mid-Summer Sea
BOOOR-ING.
CLICK

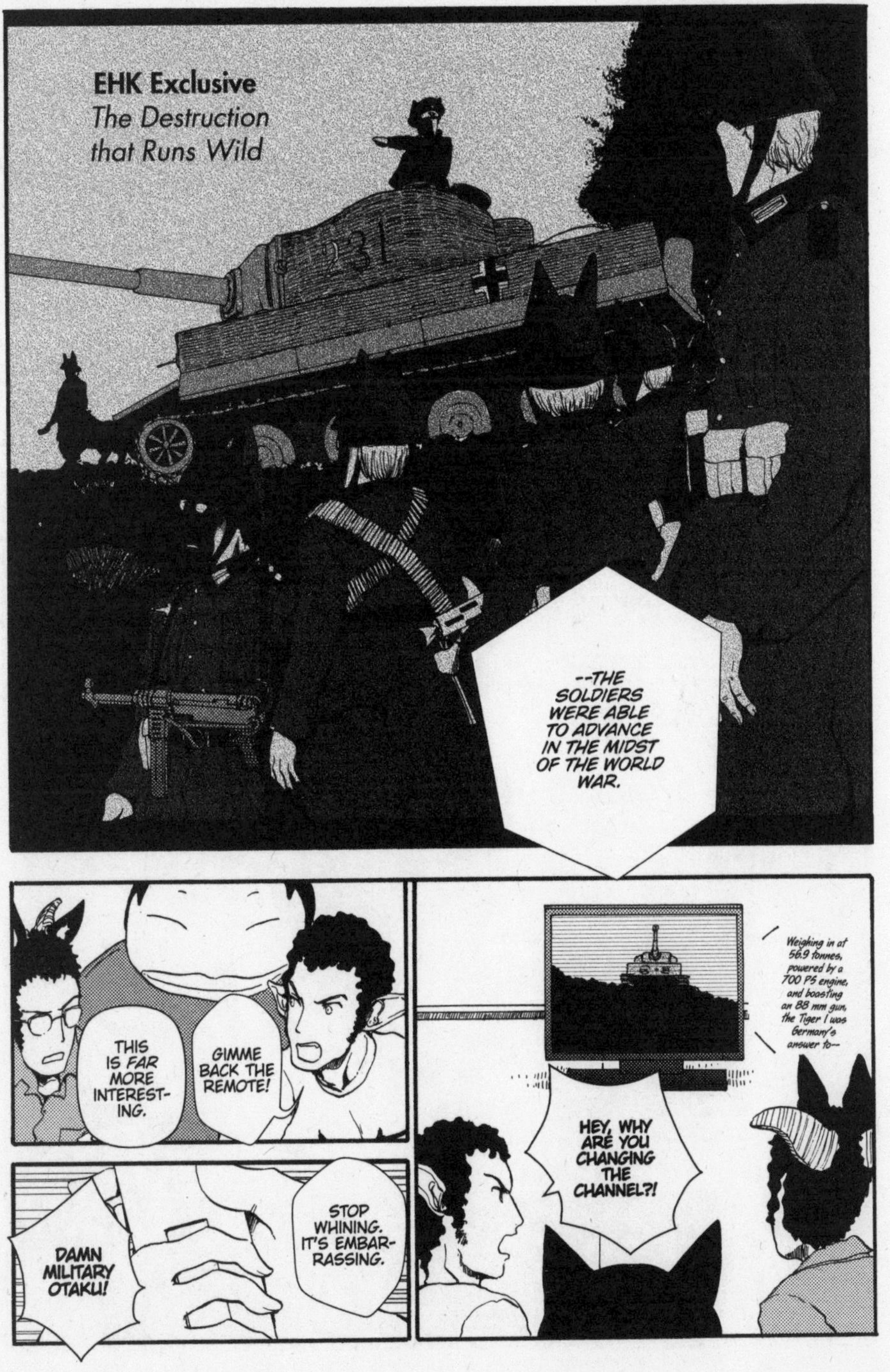
EHK Exclusive
The Destruction that Runs Wild
--THE SOLDIERS WERE ABLE TO ADVANCE IN THE MIDST OF THE WORLD WAR.
Weighing in at 56.9 tonnes, powered by a 700 PS engine, and boosting an 88 mm gun, the Tiger I was Germany's answer to--
HEY, WHY ARE YOU CHANGING THE CHANNEL?!
GIMME BACK THE REMOTE!
THIS IS FAR MORE INTERESTING.
STOP WHINING. IT'S EMBARRASSING.
DAMN MILITARY OTAKU!

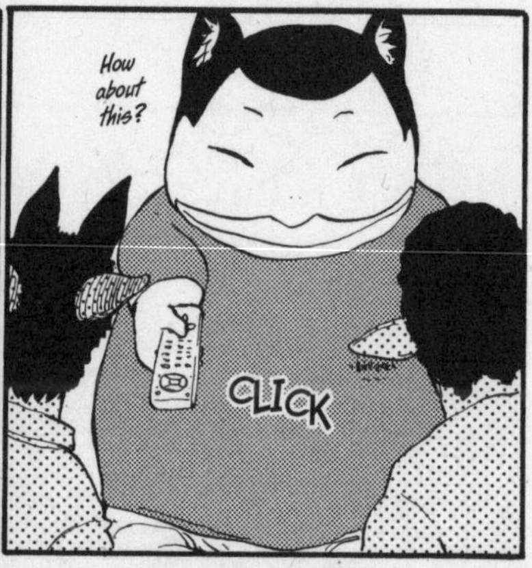
How about this?
CLICK

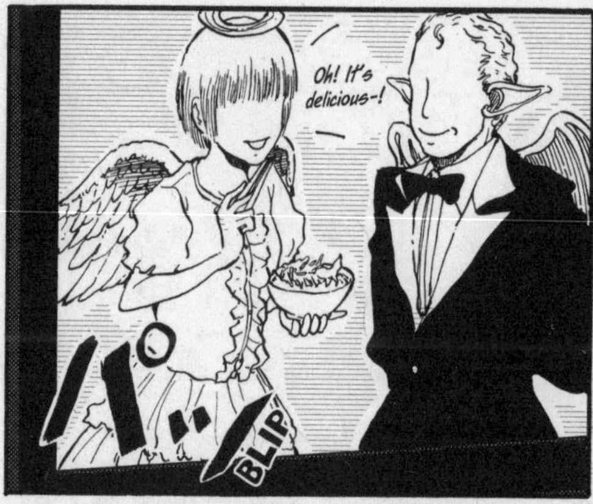
Oh! It's delicious-!
BLIP

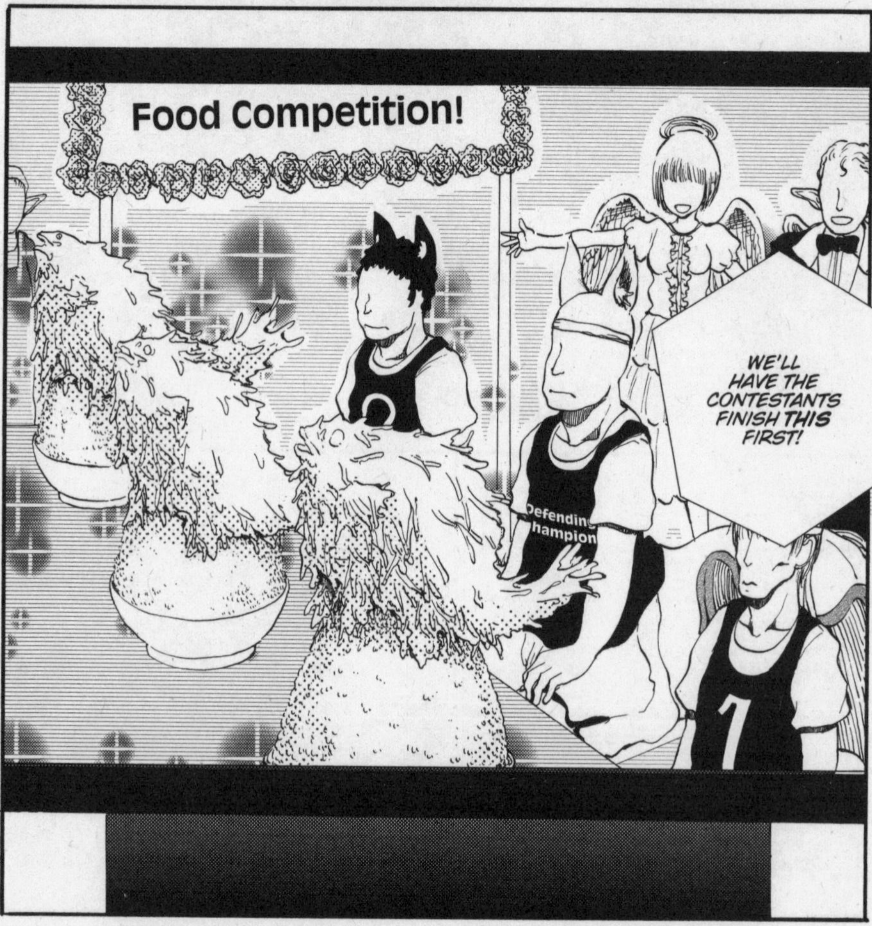
Food Competition!
WE'LL HAVE THE CONTESTANTS FINISH THIS FIRST!
Defending
hampion

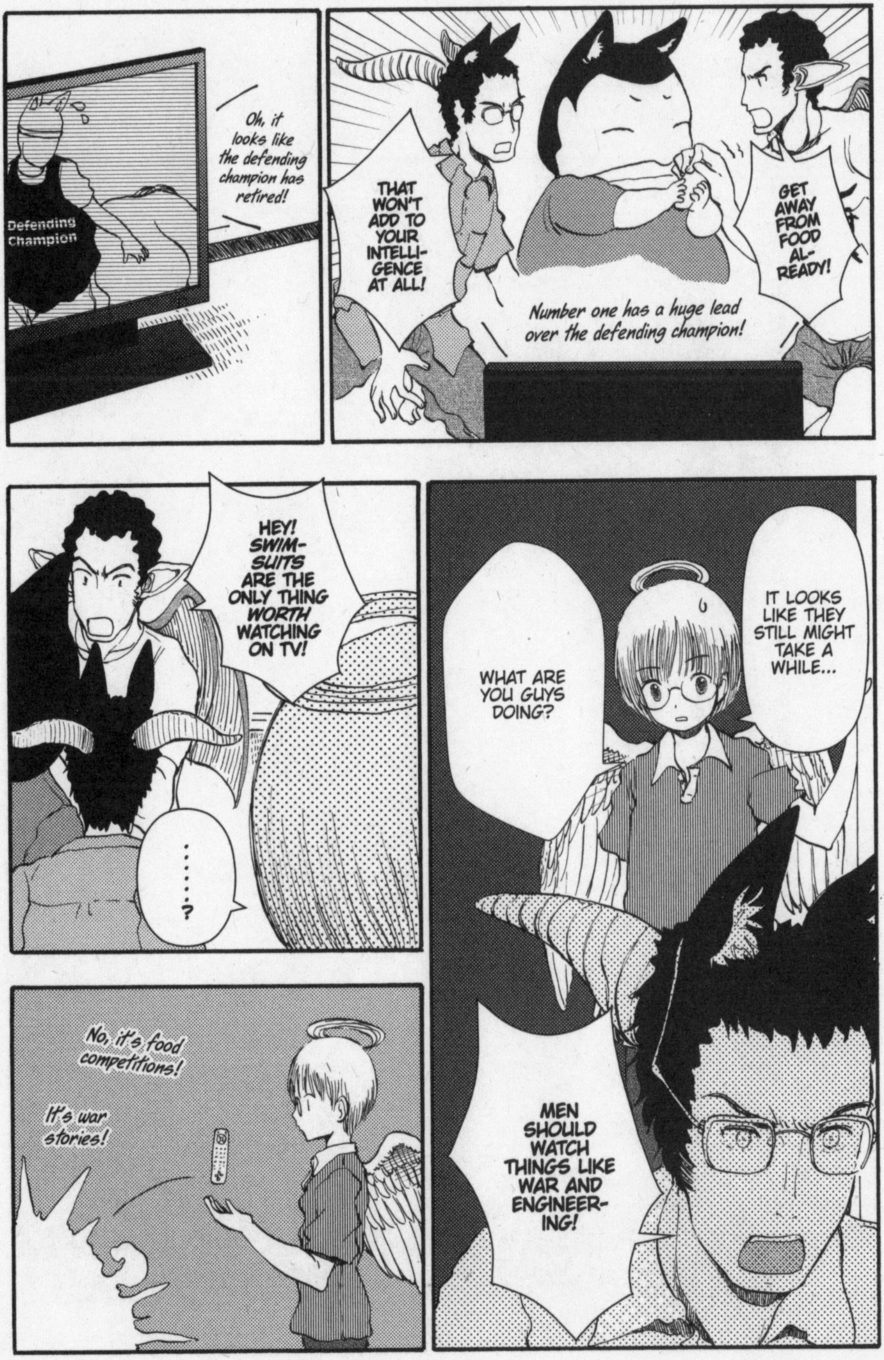
GET AWAY FROM FOOD AL-READY!
THAT WON'T ADD TO YOUR INTELLIGENCE AT ALL!
Number one has a huge lead over the defending champion!
Oh, it looks like the defending champion has retired!
Defending Champion
IT LOOKS LIKE THEY STILL MIGHT TAKE A WHILE...
WHAT ARE YOU GUYS DOING?
MEN SHOULD WATCH THINGS LIKE WAR AND ENGINEER-ING!
HEY! SWIM-SUITS ARE THE ONLY THING WORTH WATCHING ON TV!
......?
No, it's food competitions!
It's war stories!

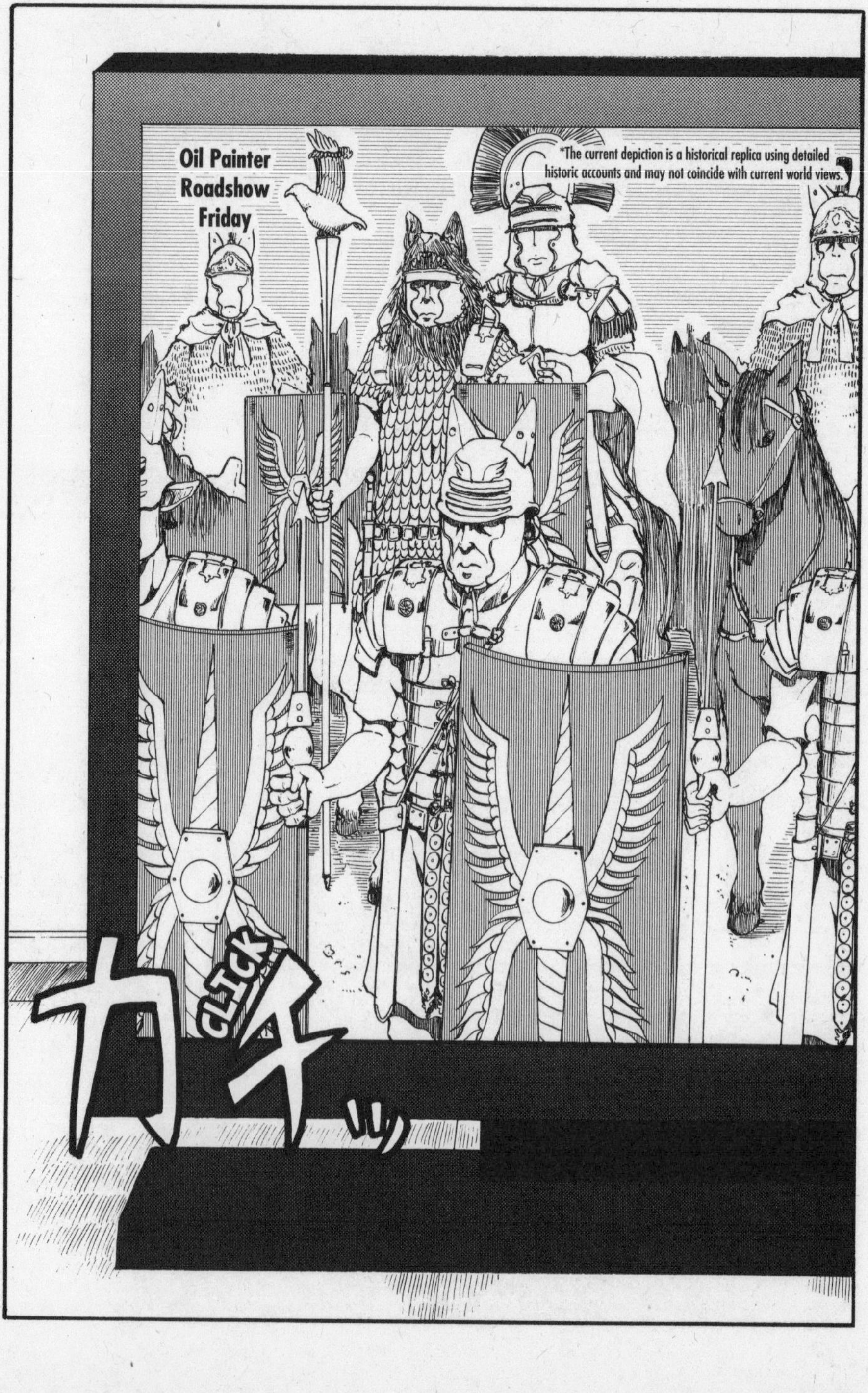

*The current depiction is a historical replica using detailed historic accounts and may not coincide with current world views.
Oil Painter Roadshow Friday
カチッ
CLICK

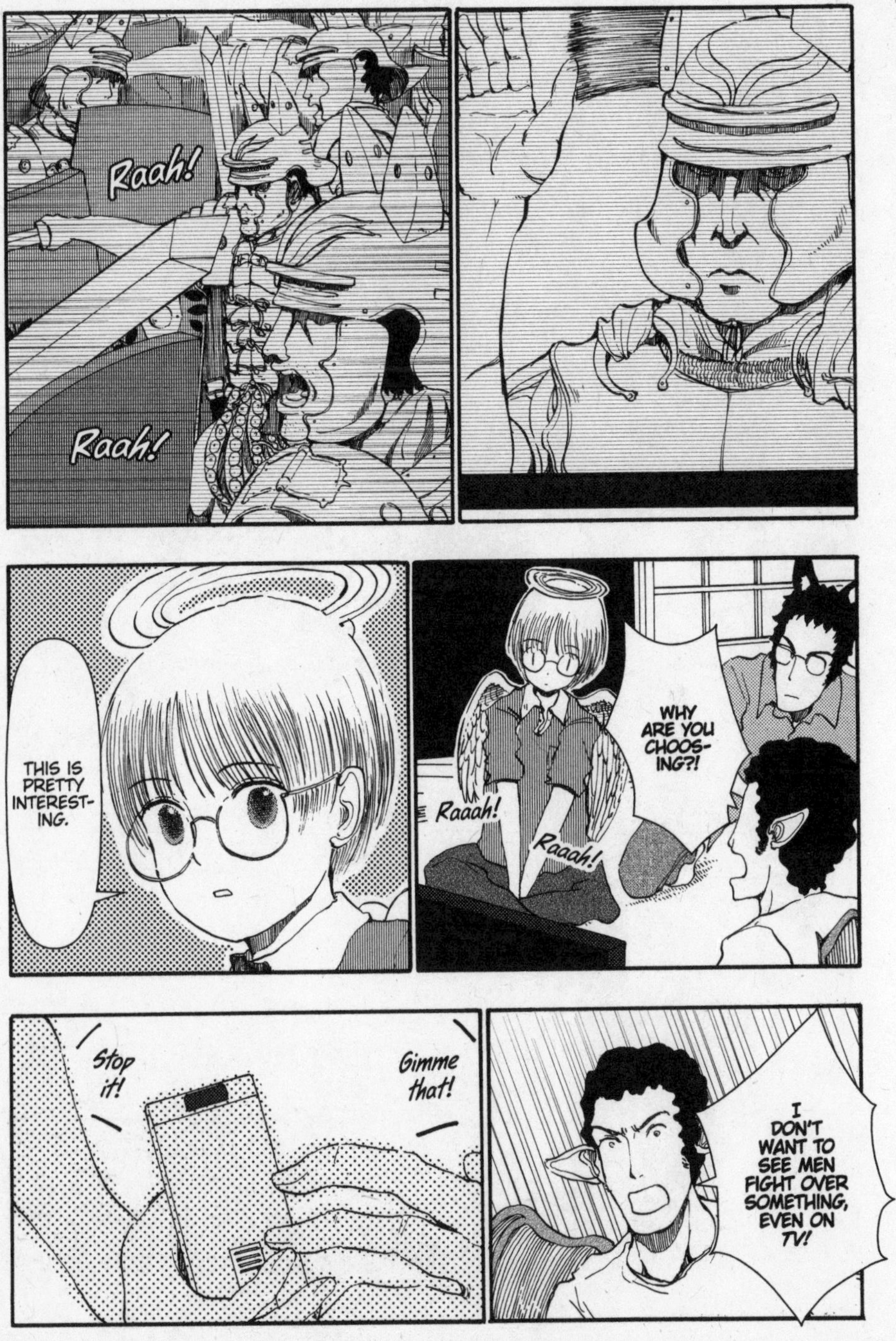
Raah!
Raah!
WHY ARE YOU CHOOSING?!
Raaah!
Raaah!
THIS IS PRETTY INTERESTING.
I DON'T WANT TO SEE MEN FIGHT OVER SOMETHING, EVEN ON TV!
Gimme that!
Stop it!

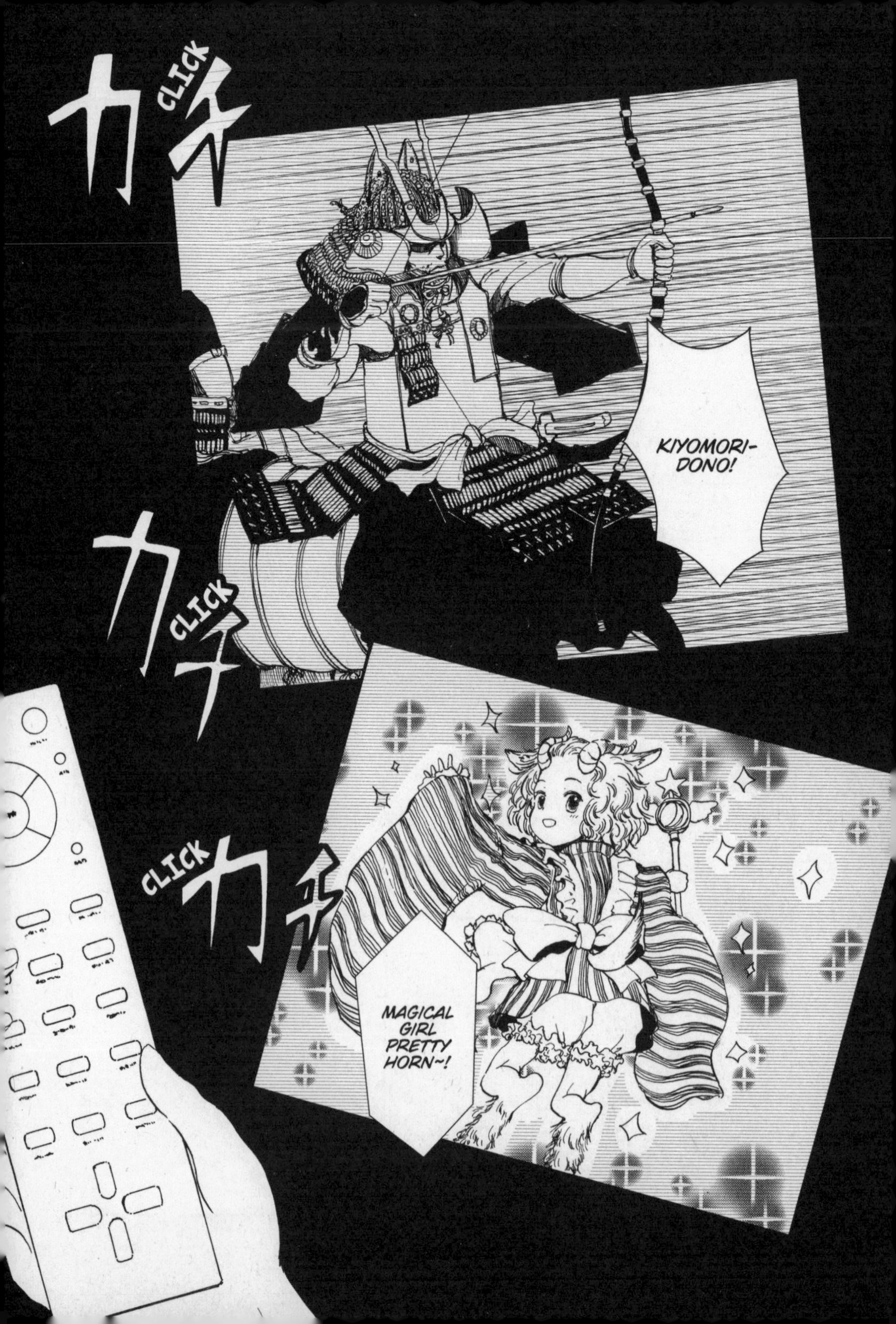
カチ
CLICK
KIYOMORI-DONO!
カチ
CLICK
カチ
CLICK
MAGICAL GIRL PRETTY HORN~!

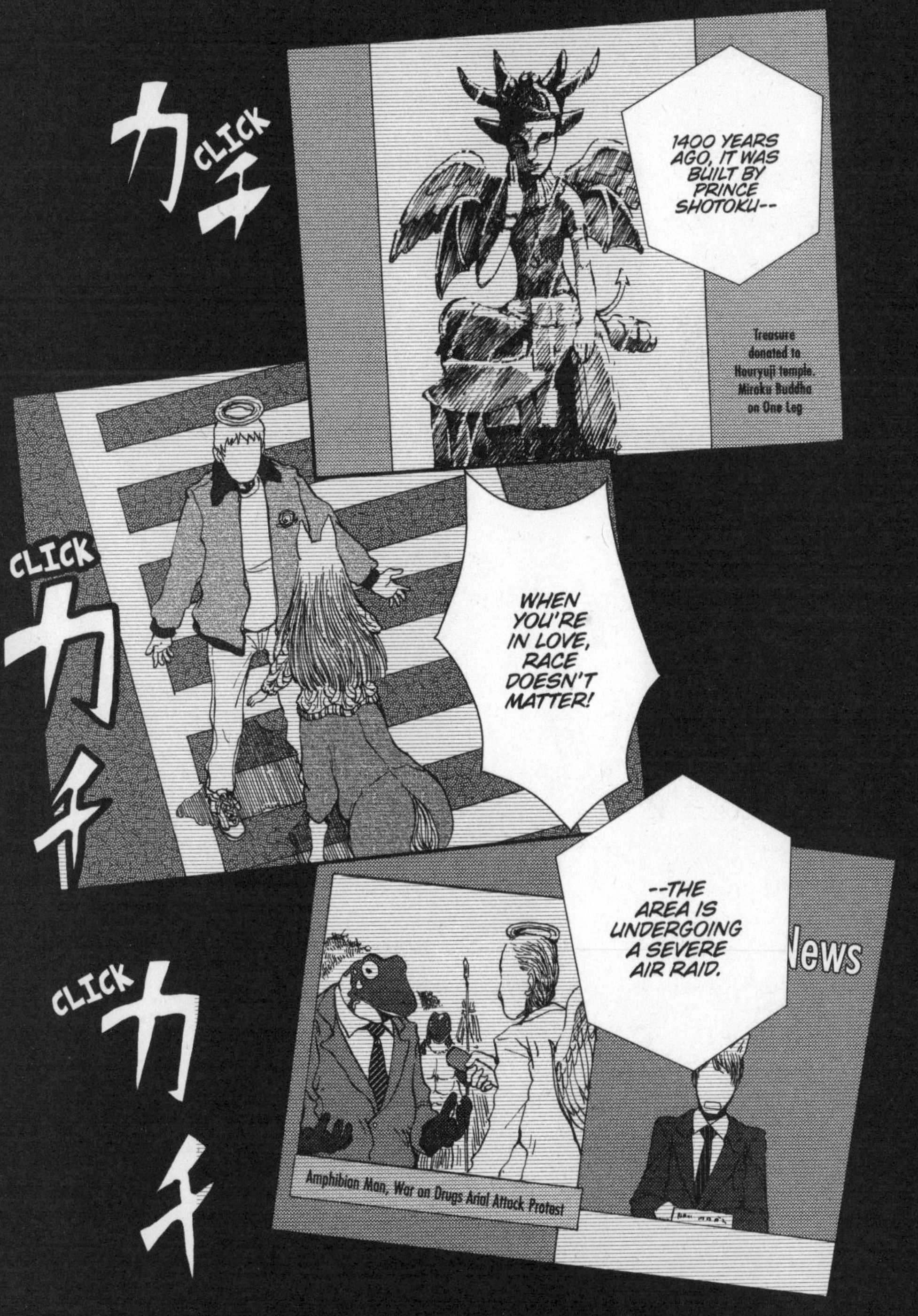
1400 YEARS AGO, IT WAS BUILT BY PRINCE SHOTOKU--
Treasure donated to Houryuji temple. Miroku Buddha on One Leg
カチ CLICK
WHEN YOU'RE IN LOVE, RACE DOESN'T MATTER!
CLICK カチ
--THE AREA IS UNDERGOING A SEVERE AIR RAID.
News
Amphibian Man, War on Drugs Arial Attack Protest
CLICK カチ

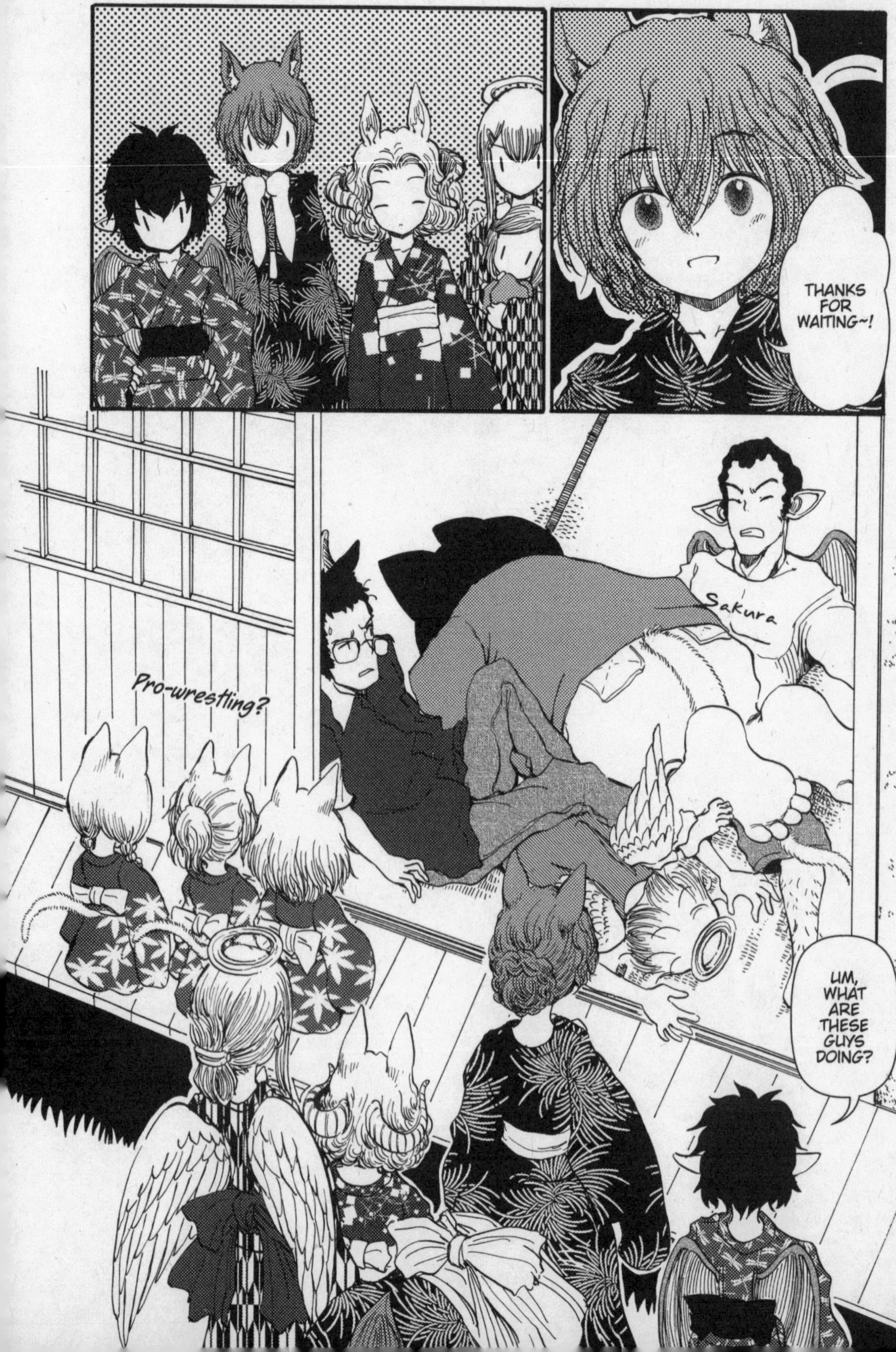
THANKS FOR WAITING~!
Sakura
Pro-wrestling?
UM, WHAT ARE THESE GUYS DOING?

A CentaUr's Life

SUPERNATURAL BEINGS: MAGICAL GIRLS

THIS IS ANOTHER SUPERNATURAL BEING THAT BEGAN IN MODERN TIMES. THERE ARE MANY LEGENDS OF MAGICAL FEMALES, BUT THOSE STORIES OFTEN DEPICT THEM AS DECREPIT WITCHES OR BEAUTIFUL WOMEN. MAGICAL GIRLS ARE GIRLS IN THE BLOSSOM OF YOUTH AND ARE OFTEN QUITE YOUNG. IT IS THOUGHT THAT THIS AGE RESTRICTION IS TO MAKE THEM CLOSER (AND THUS MORE APPEALING) TO THEIR TARGET AUDIENCE.

MAGICAL GIRLS COME IN MANY DIFFERENT SHAPES AND FORMS, PROBABLY BECAUSE THERE WAS NO ARCHETYPE (SUCH AS DRACULA FOR VAMPIRES) THAT DICTATED A SPECIFIC FORM. IN ORDER TO AVOID RACIAL FAVORITISM, TWO TYPES OF SHOWS ARE FORMULATED:

① A STORY WITH A TEAM OF MAGICAL GIRLS REPRESENTING ALL OF THE MAJOR RACES, OR

② A STORY IN WHICH THE MAIN MAGICAL GIRL CHARACTER CHANGES EVERY SEASON.

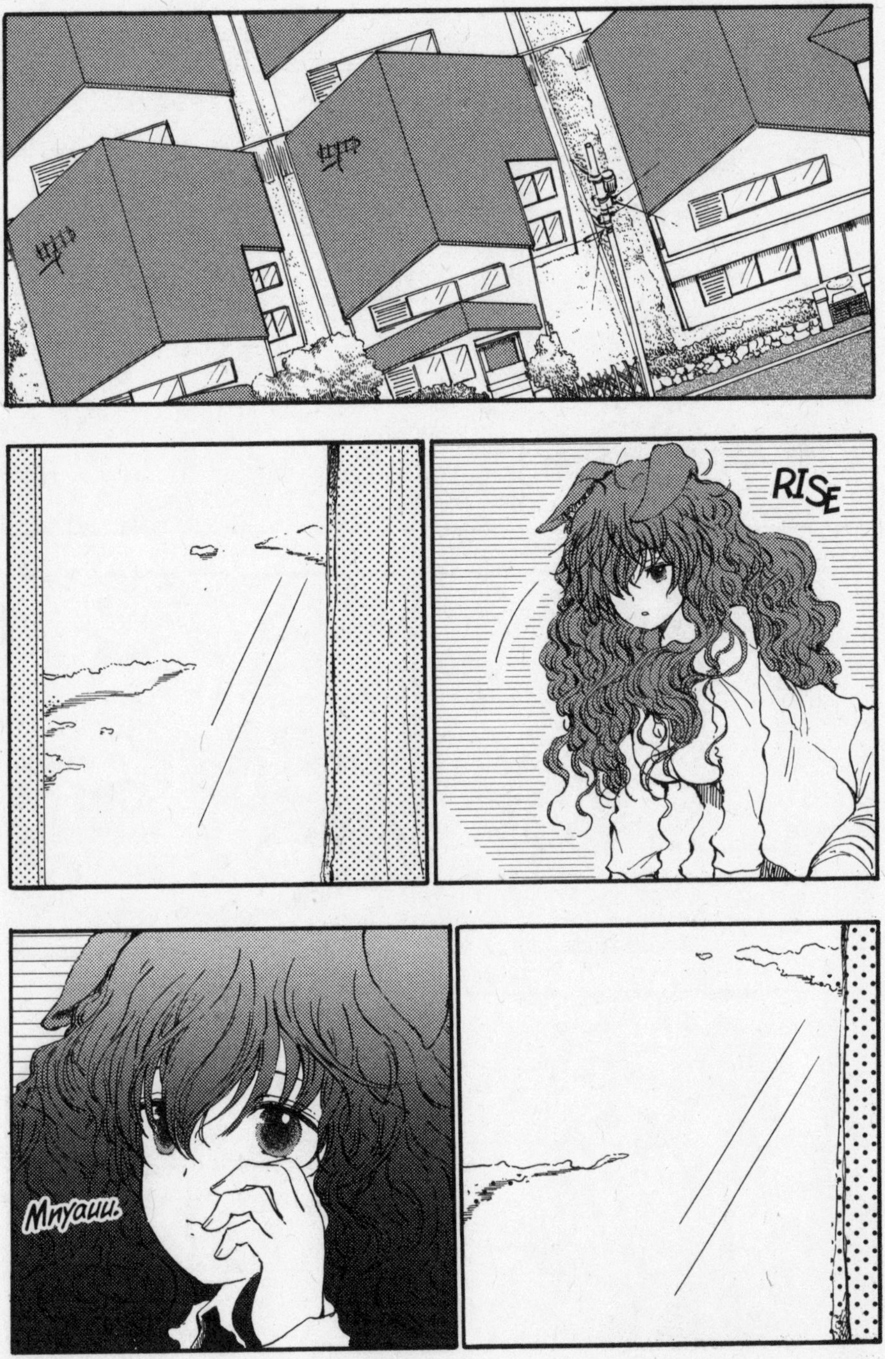
RISE
Mnyauu.

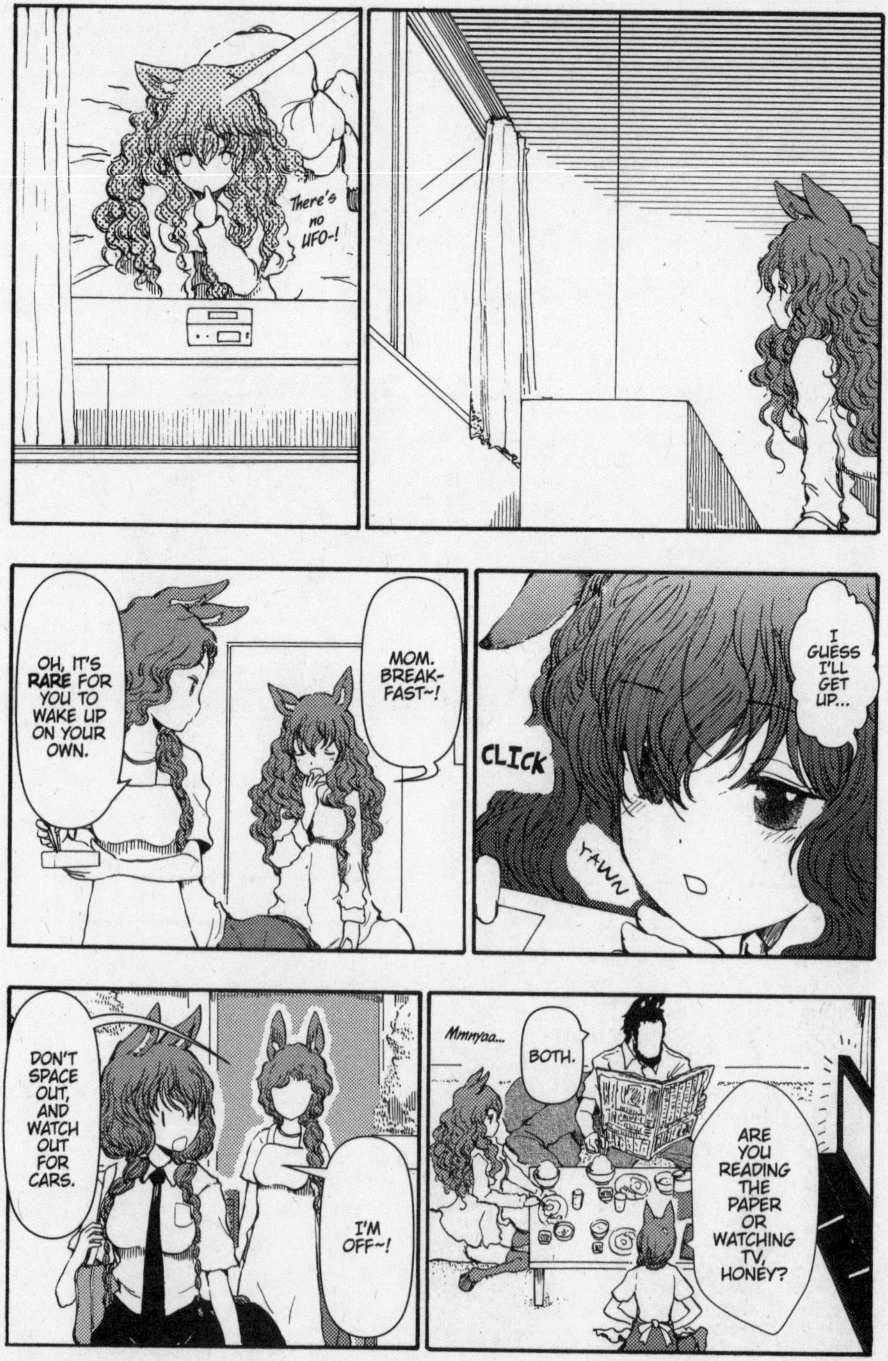
There's no UFO-!
I GUESS I'LL GET UP...
CLICK
YAWN
MOM. BREAK-FAST~!
OH, IT'S RARE FOR YOU TO WAKE UP ON YOUR OWN.
ARE YOU READING THE PAPER OR WATCHING TV, HONEY?
BOTH.
Mmnyaa...
I'M OFF~!
DON'T SPACE OUT, AND WATCH OUT FOR CARS.

CHAPTER 14

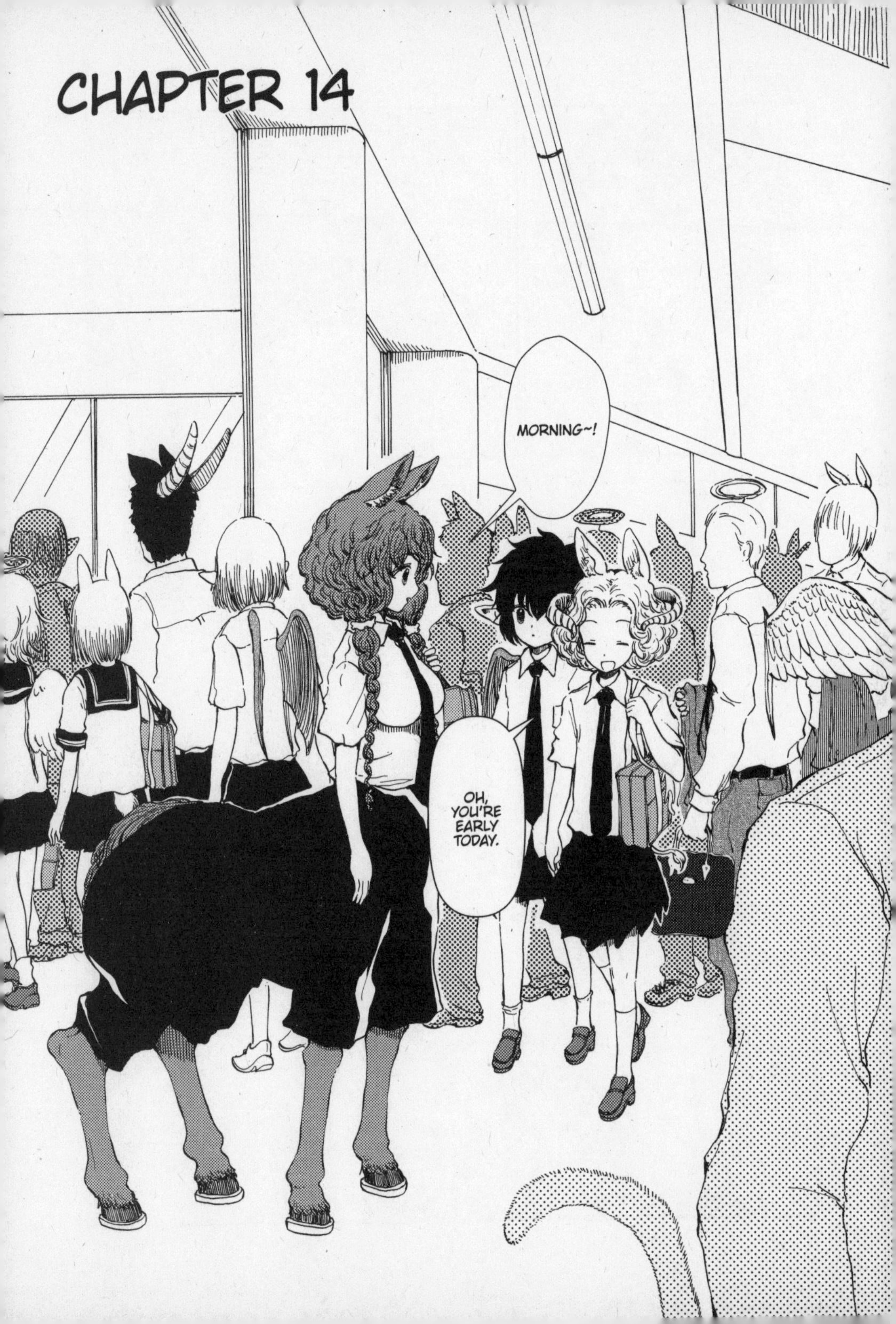
MORNING~!
OH, YOU'RE EARLY TODAY.

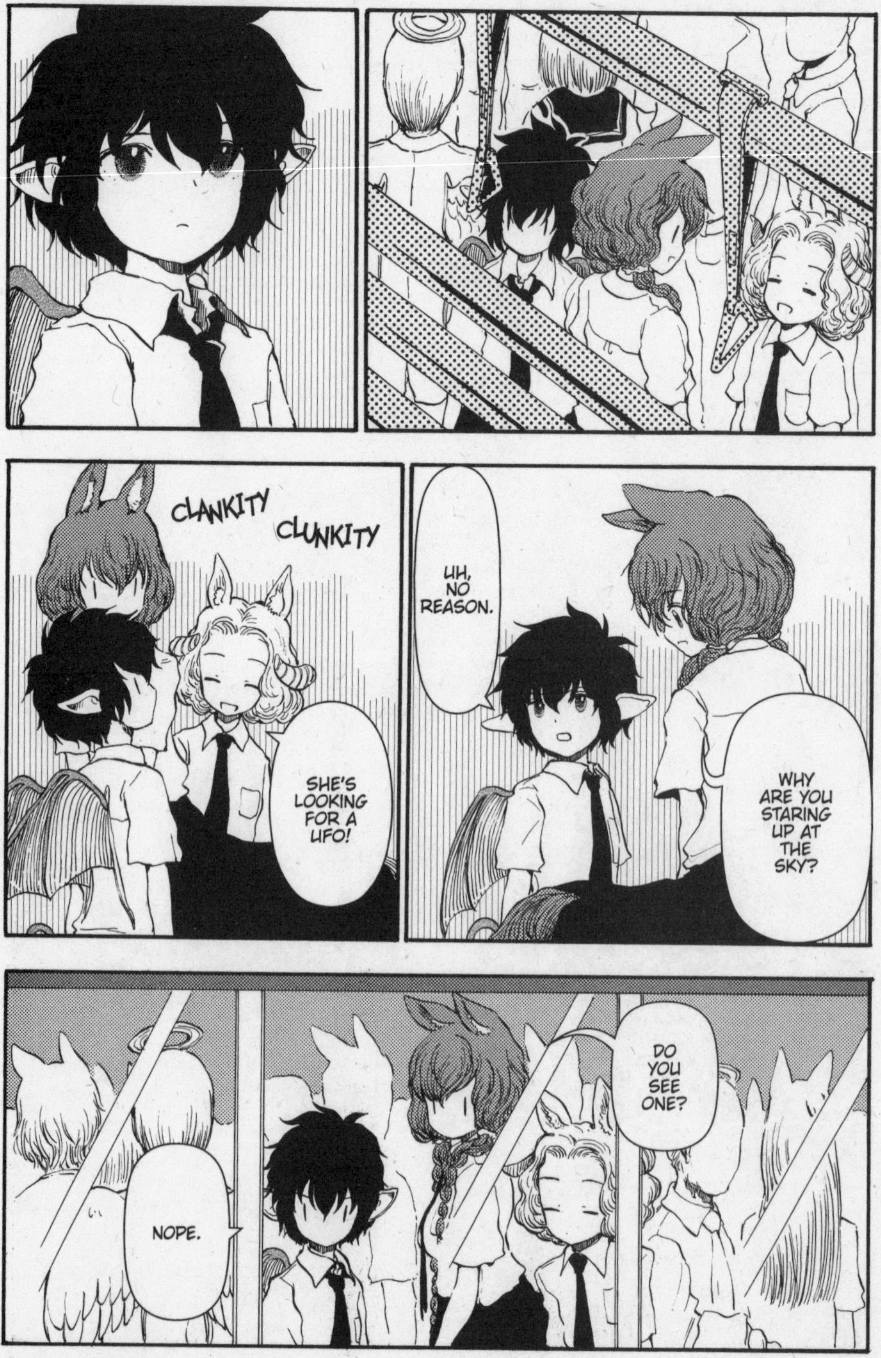
WHY ARE YOU STARING UP AT THE SKY?
UH, NO REASON.
CLANKITY CLUNKITY
SHE'S LOOKING FOR A UFO!
DO YOU SEE ONE?
NOPE.

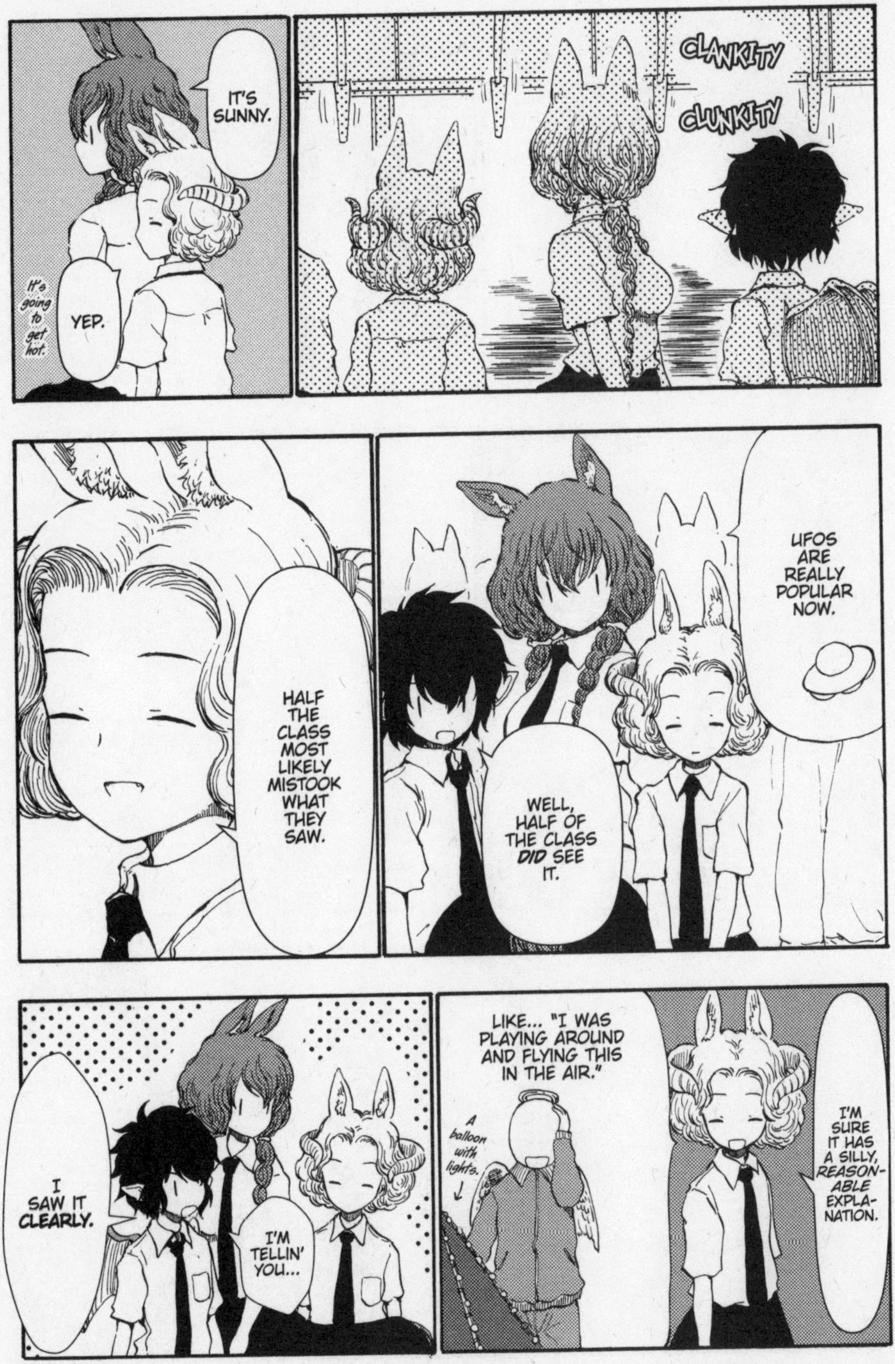
CLANKITY
CLUNKITY
IT'S SUNNY.
YEP.
It's going to get hot.
UFOS ARE REALLY POPULAR NOW.
WELL, HALF OF THE CLASS **DID** SEE IT.
HALF THE CLASS MOST LIKELY MISTOOK WHAT THEY SAW.
I'M SURE IT HAS A SILLY, *REASONABLE* EXPLANATION.
LIKE... "I WAS PLAYING AROUND AND FLYING THIS IN THE AIR."
A balloon with lights.
I'M TELLIN' YOU...
I SAW IT **CLEARLY.**

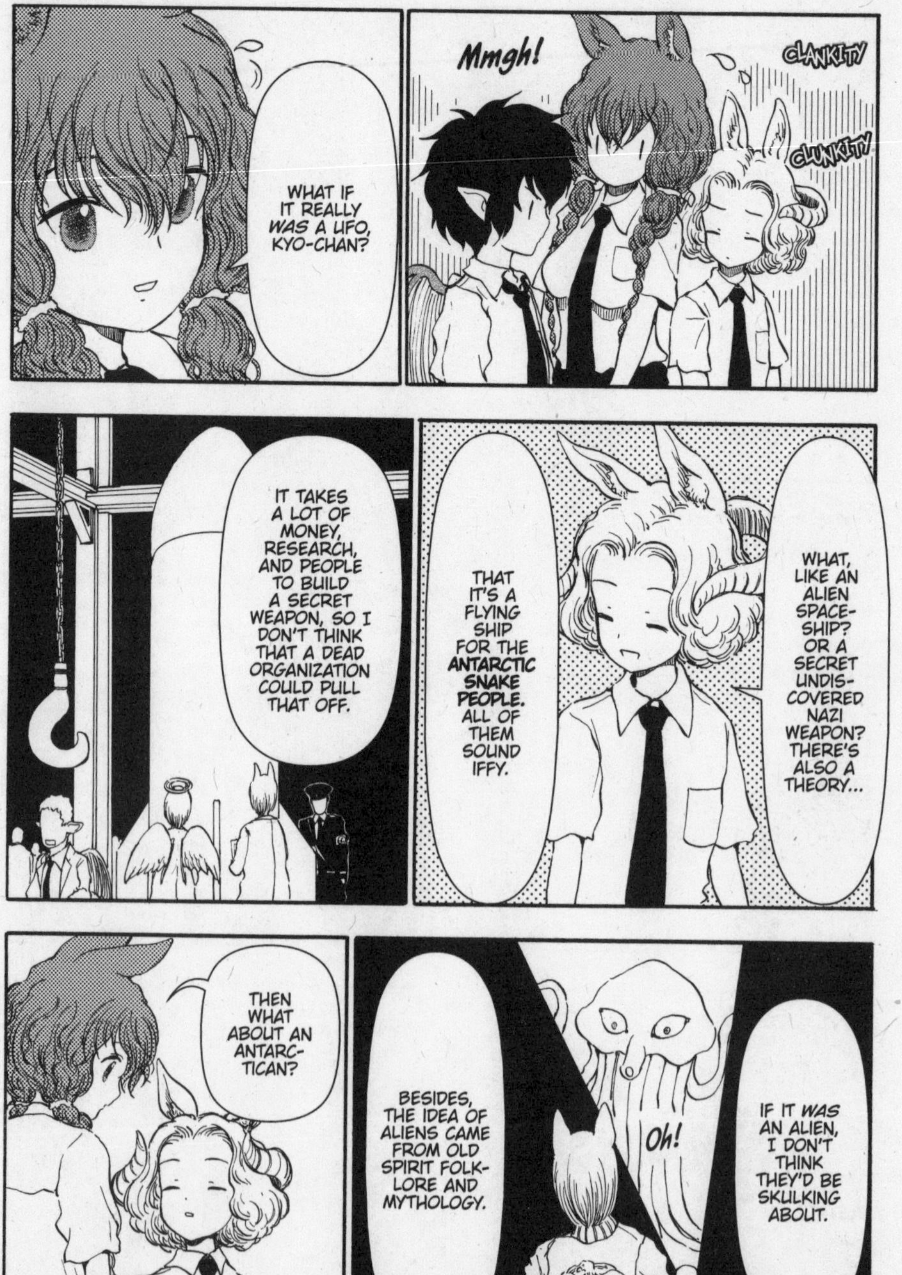
CLANKITY
CLUNKITY
Mmgh!
WHAT IF IT REALLY *WAS* A UFO, KYO-CHAN?
WHAT, LIKE AN ALIEN SPACE-SHIP? OR A SECRET UNDIS-COVERED NAZI WEAPON? THERE'S ALSO A THEORY...
THAT IT'S A FLYING SHIP FOR THE **ANTARCTIC SNAKE PEOPLE.** ALL OF THEM SOUND IFFY.
IT TAKES A LOT OF MONEY, RESEARCH, AND PEOPLE TO BUILD A SECRET WEAPON, SO I DON'T THINK THAT A DEAD ORGANIZATION COULD PULL THAT OFF.
IF IT *WAS* AN ALIEN, I DON'T THINK THEY'D BE SKULKING ABOUT.
Oh!
BESIDES, THE IDEA OF ALIENS CAME FROM OLD SPIRIT FOLK-LORE AND MYTHOLOGY.
THEN WHAT ABOUT AN ANTARC-TICAN?

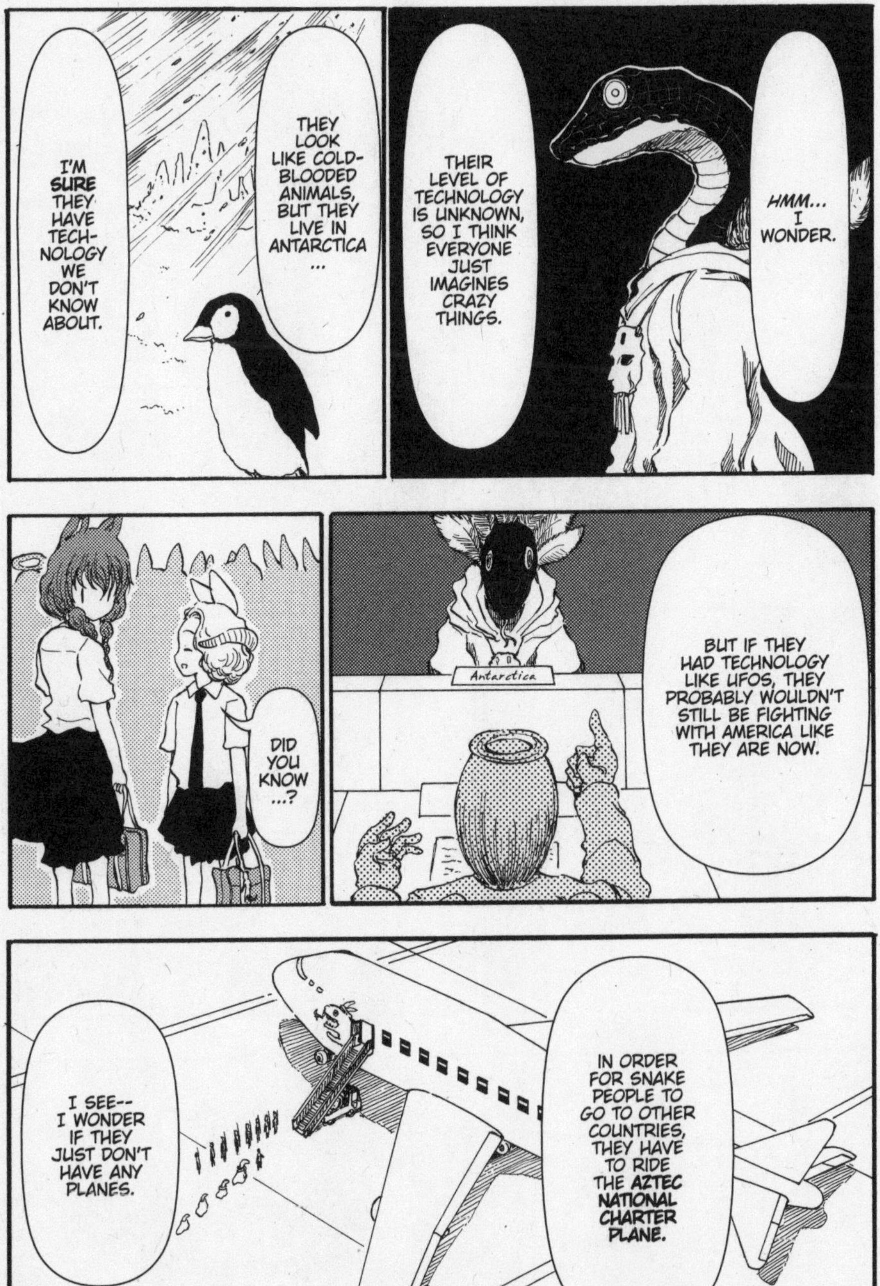
HMM... I WONDER.
THEIR LEVEL OF TECHNOLOGY IS UNKNOWN, SO I THINK EVERYONE JUST IMAGINES CRAZY THINGS.
THEY LOOK LIKE COLD-BLOODED ANIMALS, BUT THEY LIVE IN ANTARCTICA ...
I'M **SURE** THEY HAVE TECH-NOLOGY WE DON'T KNOW ABOUT.
Antarctica
BUT IF THEY HAD TECHNOLOGY LIKE UFOS, THEY PROBABLY WOULDN'T STILL BE FIGHTING WITH AMERICA LIKE THEY ARE NOW.
DID YOU KNOW ...?
IN ORDER FOR SNAKE PEOPLE TO GO TO OTHER COUNTRIES, THEY HAVE TO RIDE THE **AZTEC NATIONAL CHARTER PLANE.**
I SEE-- I WONDER IF THEY JUST DON'T HAVE ANY PLANES.

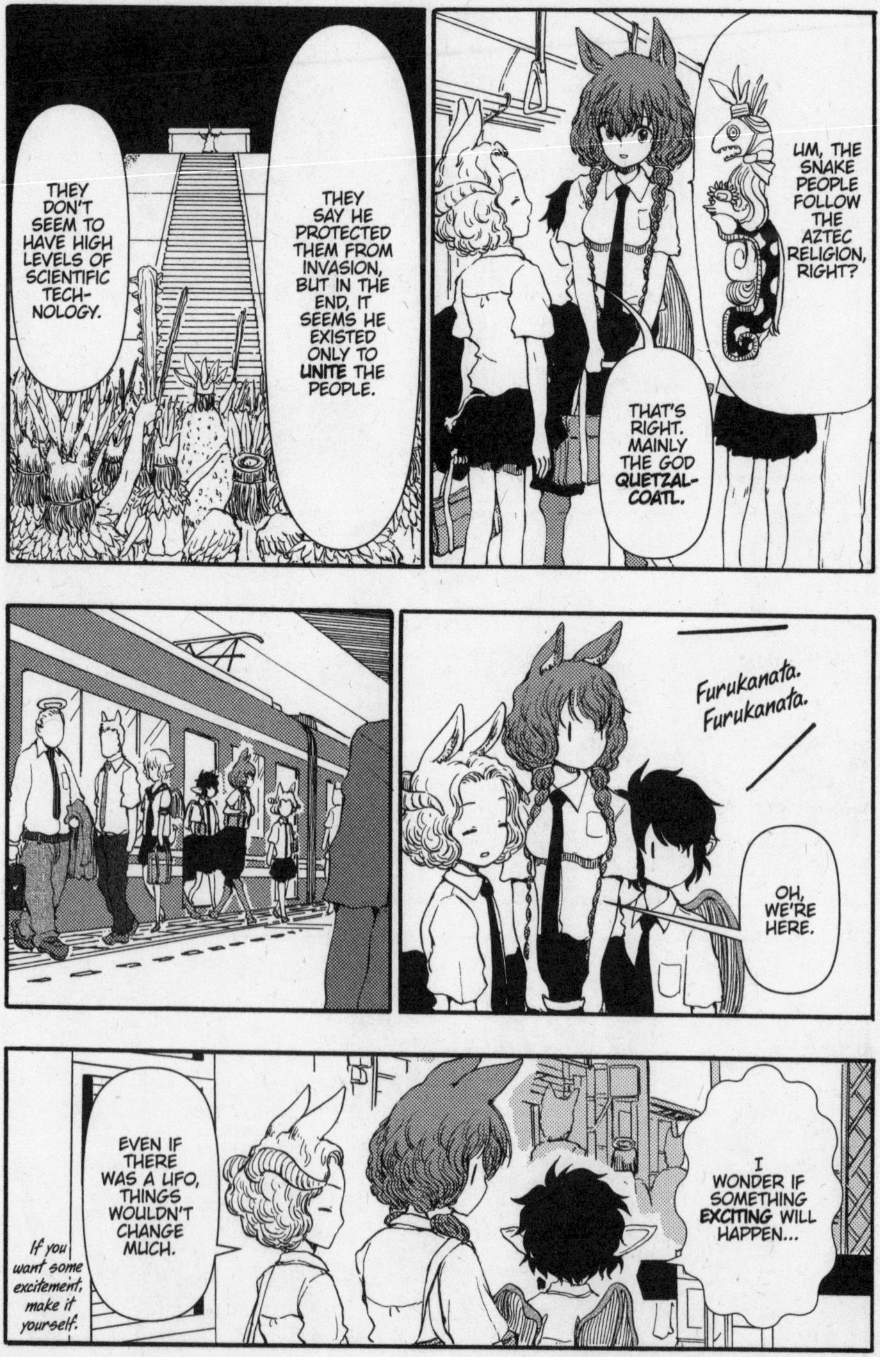
UM, THE SNAKE PEOPLE FOLLOW THE AZTEC RELIGION, RIGHT?
THAT'S RIGHT. MAINLY THE GOD QUETZAL-COATL.
THEY SAY HE PROTECTED THEM FROM INVASION, BUT IN THE END, IT SEEMS HE EXISTED ONLY TO UNITE THE PEOPLE.
THEY DON'T SEEM TO HAVE HIGH LEVELS OF SCIENTIFIC TECH-NOLOGY.
Furukanata. Furukanata.
OH, WE'RE HERE.
I WONDER IF SOMETHING EXCITING WILL HAPPEN...
EVEN IF THERE WAS A UFO, THINGS WOULDN'T CHANGE MUCH.
If you want some excitement, make it yourself.

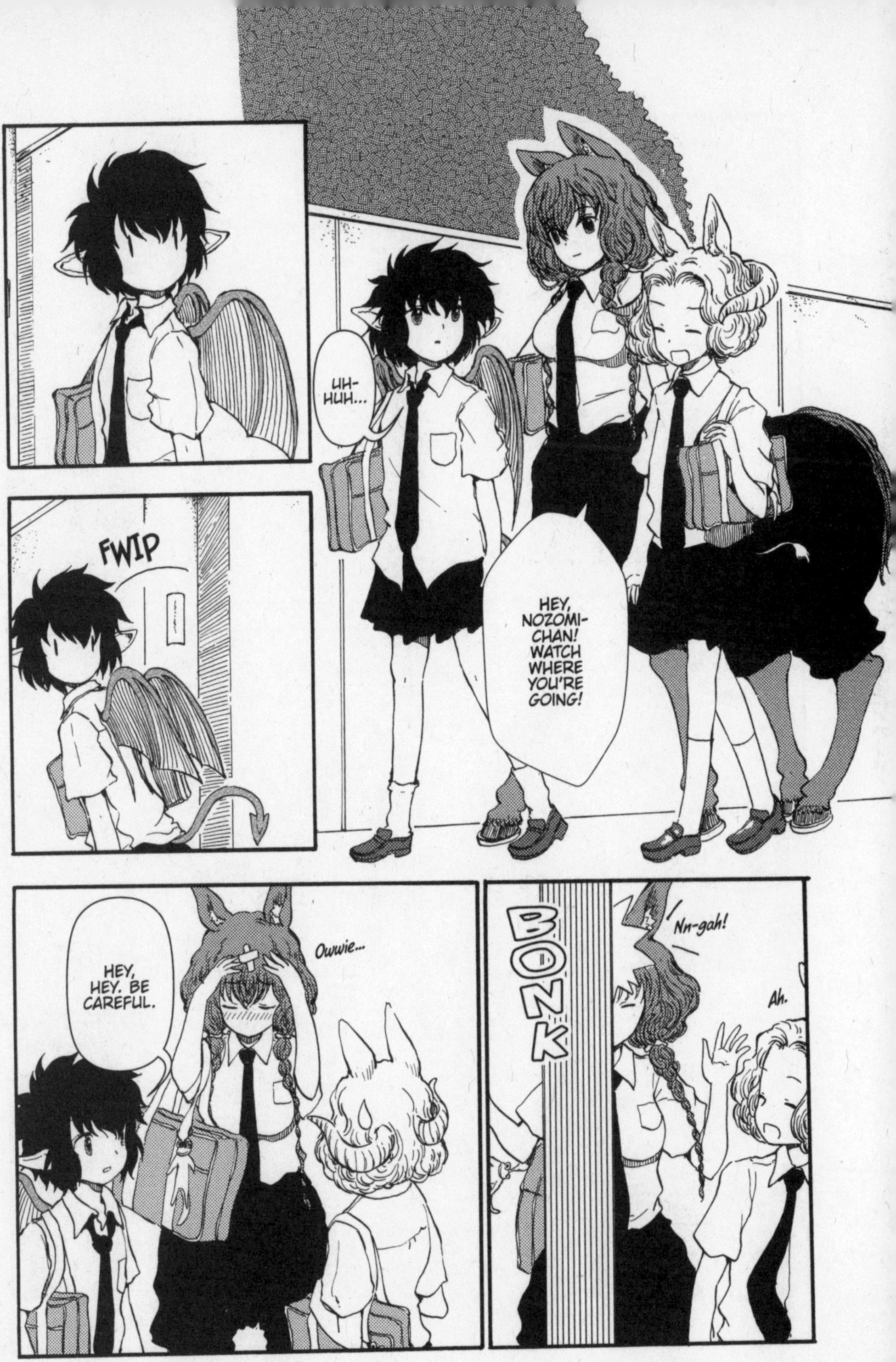
HEY, NOZOMI-CHAN! WATCH WHERE YOU'RE GOING!
UH-HUH...
FWIP
BONK
Nn-gah!
Ah.
Owwie...
HEY, HEY. BE CAREFUL.

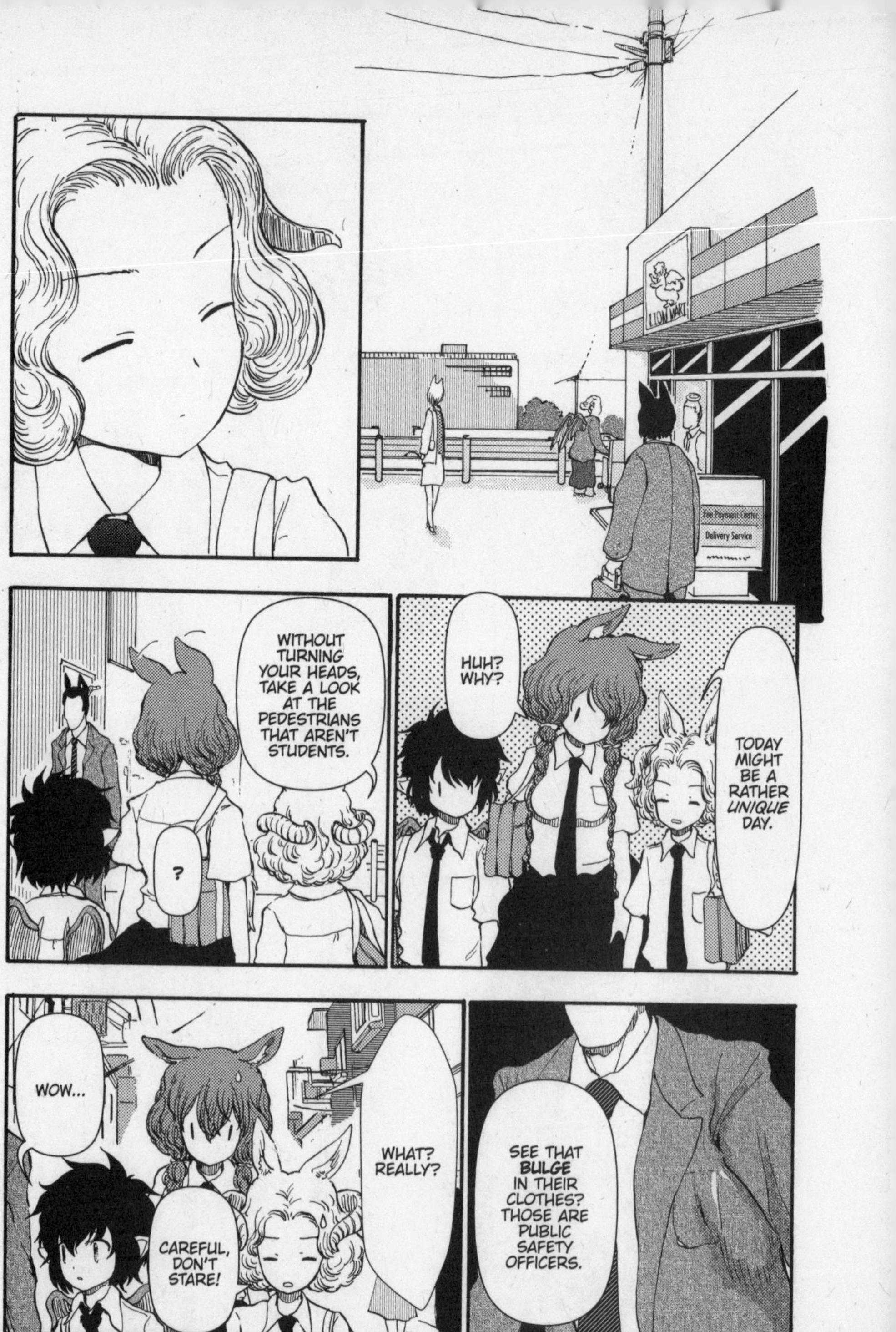
LION MART
Fee Payment Center
Delivery Service
TODAY MIGHT BE A RATHER *UNIQUE* DAY.
HUH? WHY?
WITHOUT TURNING YOUR HEADS, TAKE A LOOK AT THE PEDESTRIANS THAT AREN'T STUDENTS.
?
SEE THAT **BULGE** IN THEIR CLOTHES? THOSE ARE PUBLIC SAFETY OFFICERS.
WHAT? REALLY?
WOW...
CAREFUL, DON'T STARE!

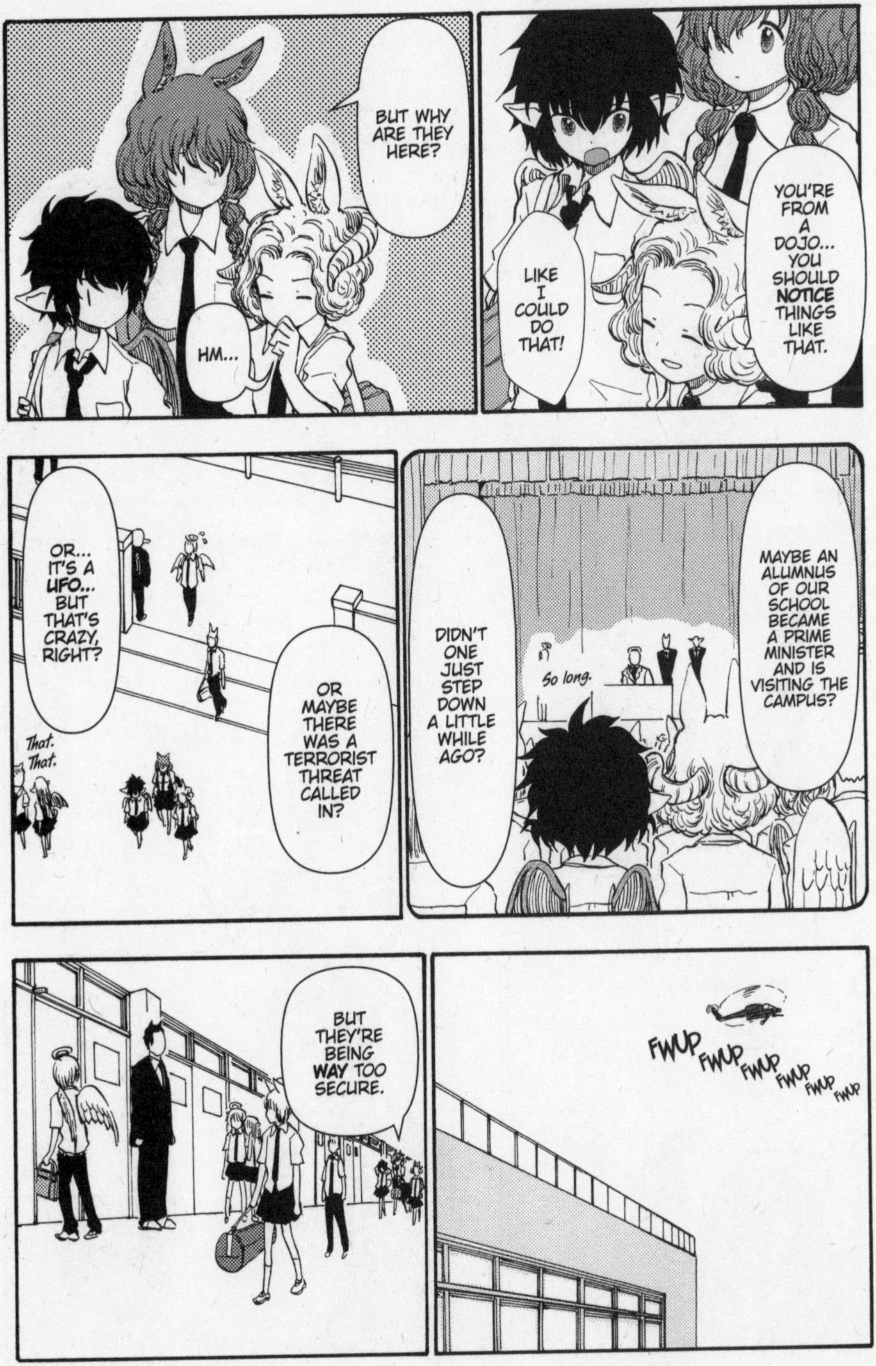
YOU'RE FROM A DOJO... YOU SHOULD **NOTICE** THINGS LIKE THAT.
LIKE I COULD DO THAT!
BUT WHY ARE THEY HERE?
HM...
MAYBE AN ALUMNUS OF OUR SCHOOL BECAME A PRIME MINISTER AND IS VISITING THE CAMPUS?
DIDN'T ONE JUST STEP DOWN A LITTLE WHILE AGO?
So long.
OR MAYBE THERE WAS A TERRORIST THREAT CALLED IN?
OR... IT'S A **UFO**... BUT THAT'S CRAZY, RIGHT?
That. That.
FWUP FWUP FWUP FWUP FWUP FWUP
BUT THEY'RE BEING **WAY** TOO SECURE.

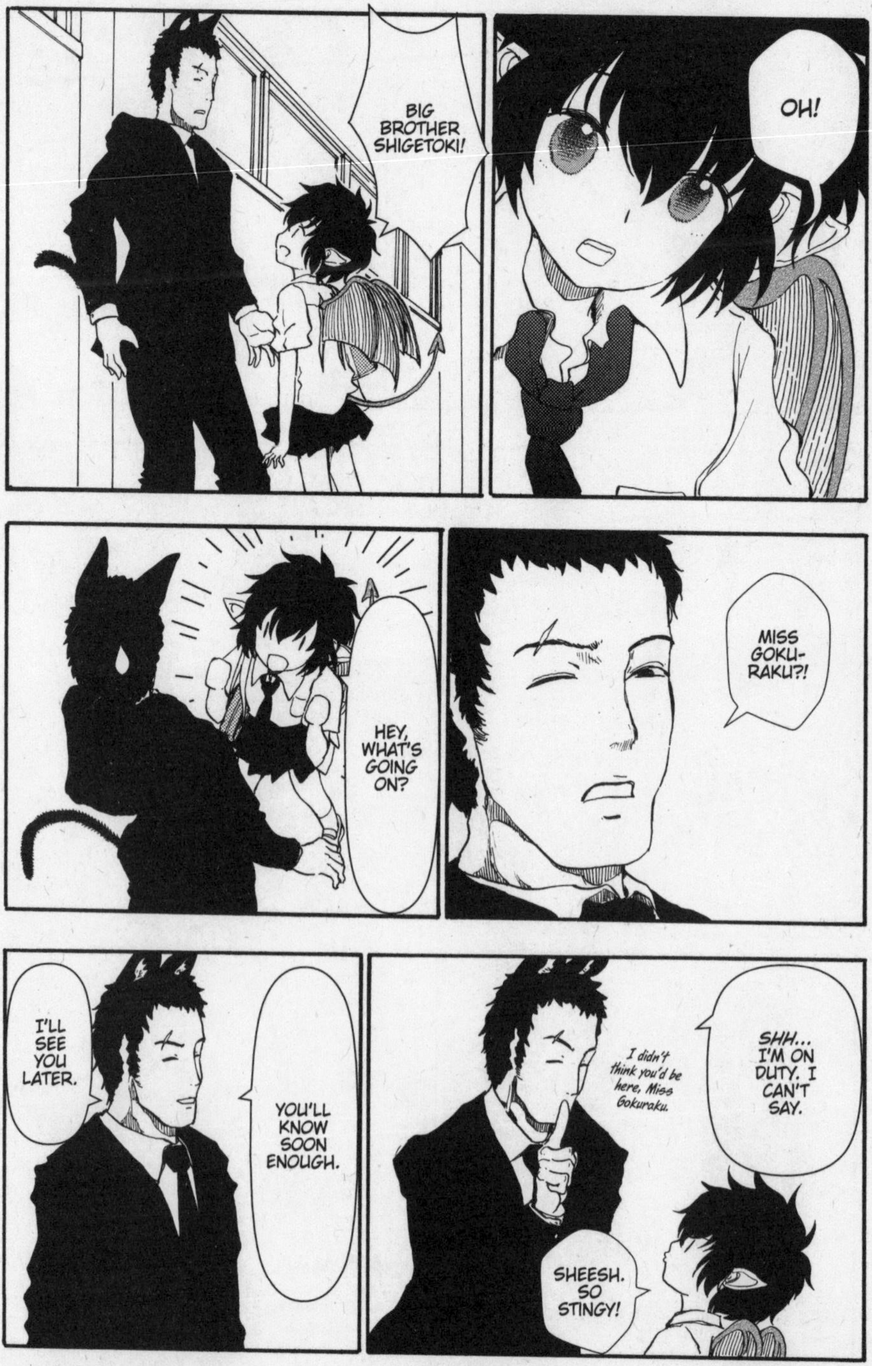
OH!
BIG BROTHER SHIGETOKI!
MISS GOKU-RAKU?!
HEY, WHAT'S GOING ON?
SHH... I'M ON DUTY. I CAN'T SAY.
I didn't think you'd be here, Miss Gokuraku.
SHEESH. SO STINGY!
YOU'LL KNOW SOON ENOUGH.
I'LL SEE YOU LATER.

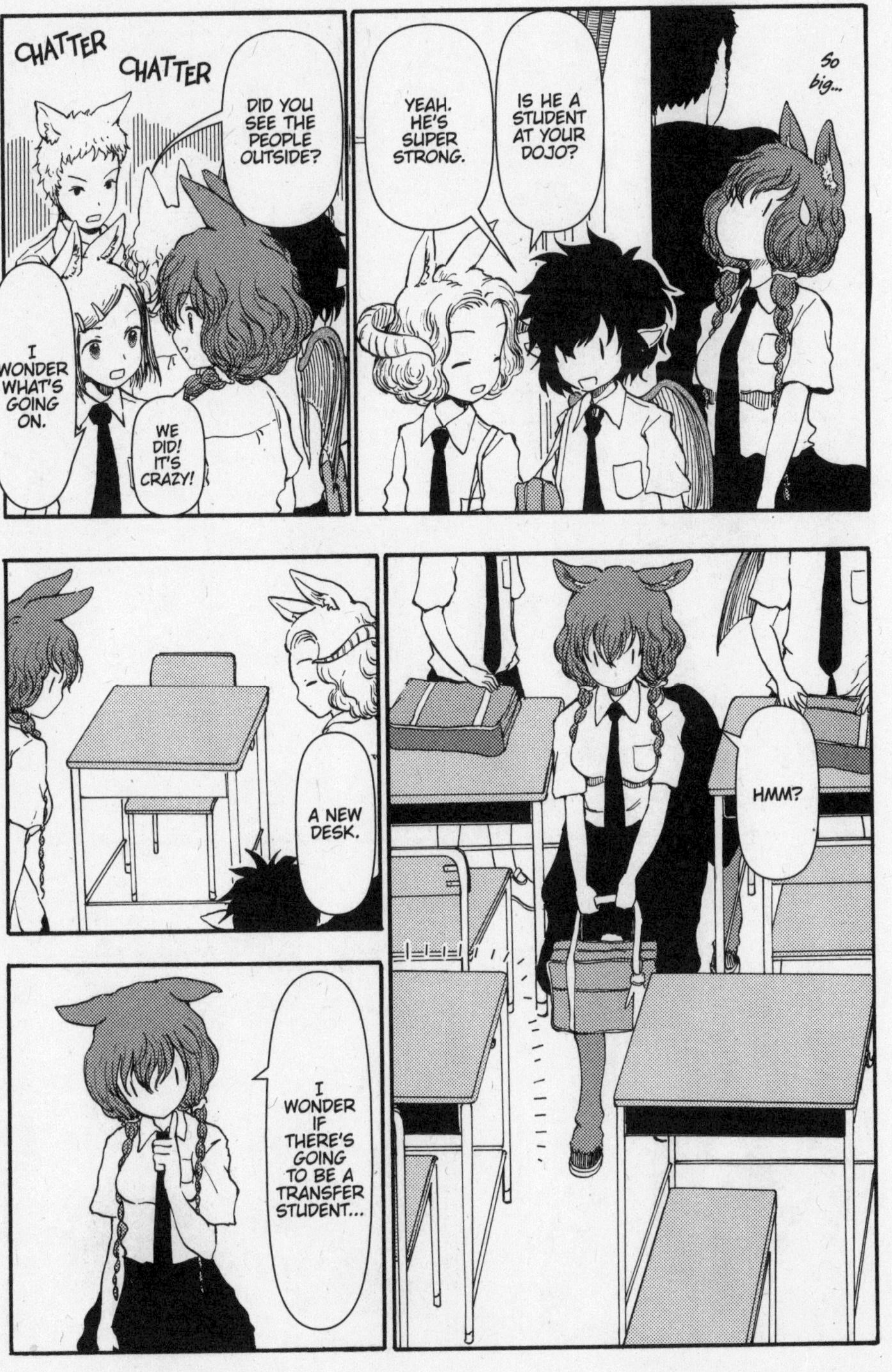
So big...
IS HE A STUDENT AT YOUR DOJO?
YEAH. HE'S SUPER STRONG.
DID YOU SEE THE PEOPLE OUTSIDE?
CHATTER CHATTER
WE DID! IT'S CRAZY!
I WONDER WHAT'S GOING ON.
HMM?
A NEW DESK.
I WONDER IF THERE'S GOING TO BE A TRANSFER STUDENT...

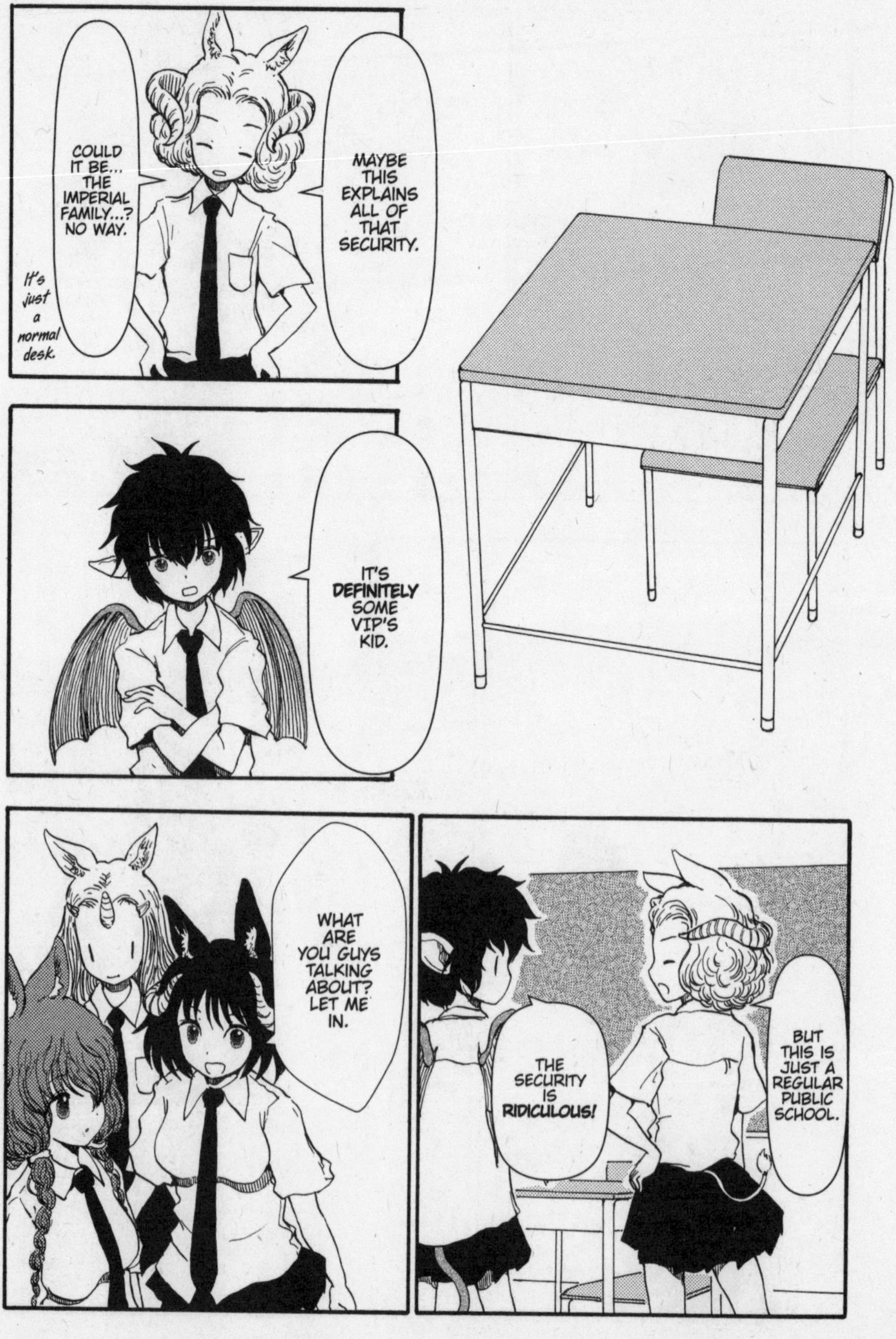
MAYBE THIS EXPLAINS ALL OF THAT SECURITY.
COULD IT BE... THE IMPERIAL FAMILY...? NO WAY.
It's just a normal desk.
IT'S DEFINITELY SOME VIP'S KID.
BUT THIS IS JUST A REGULAR PUBLIC SCHOOL.
THE SECURITY IS RIDICULOUS!
WHAT ARE YOU GUYS TALKING ABOUT? LET ME IN.

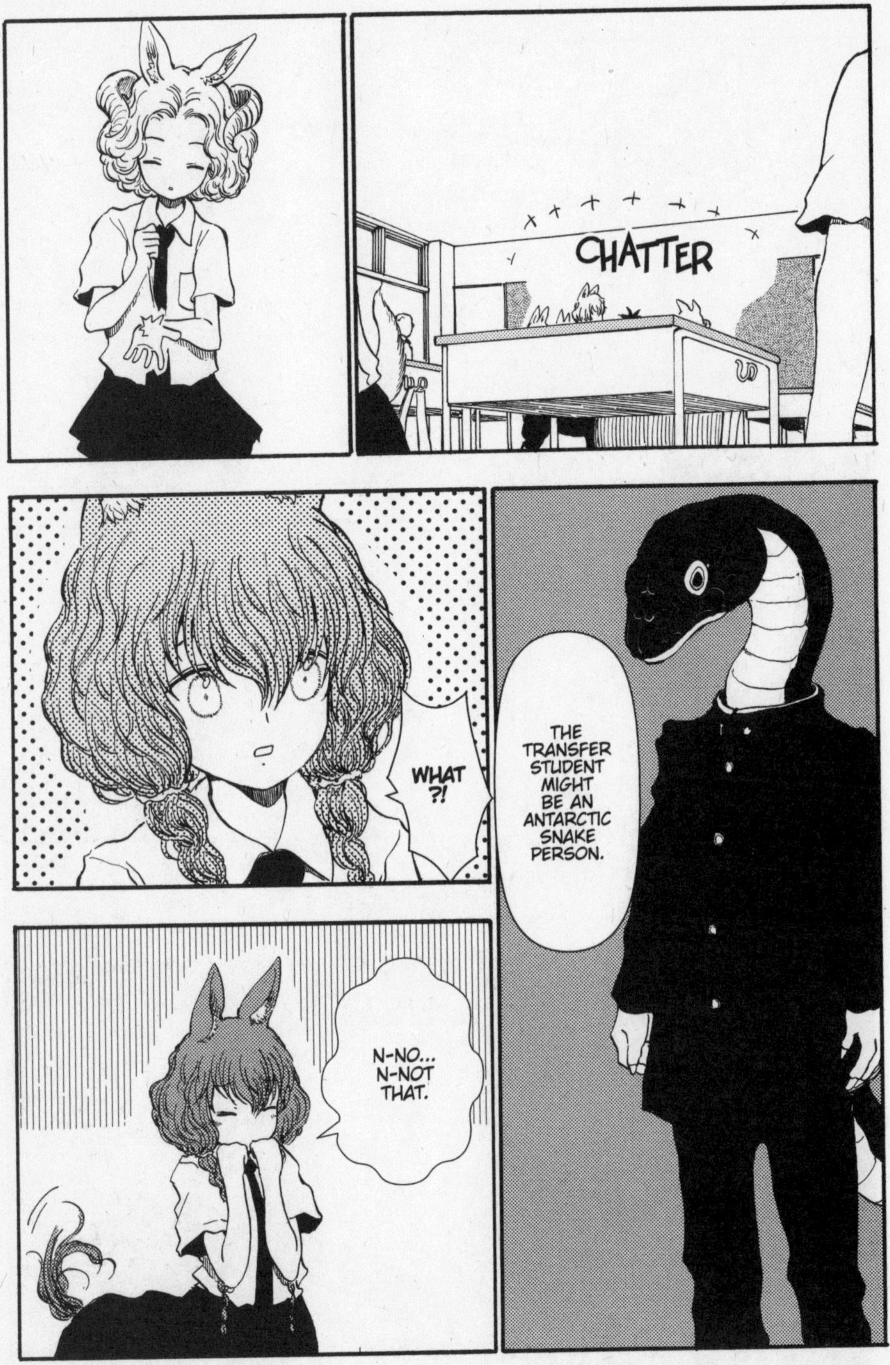
CHATTER
THE TRANSFER STUDENT MIGHT BE AN ANTARCTIC SNAKE PERSON.
WHAT ?!
N-NO... N-NOT THAT.

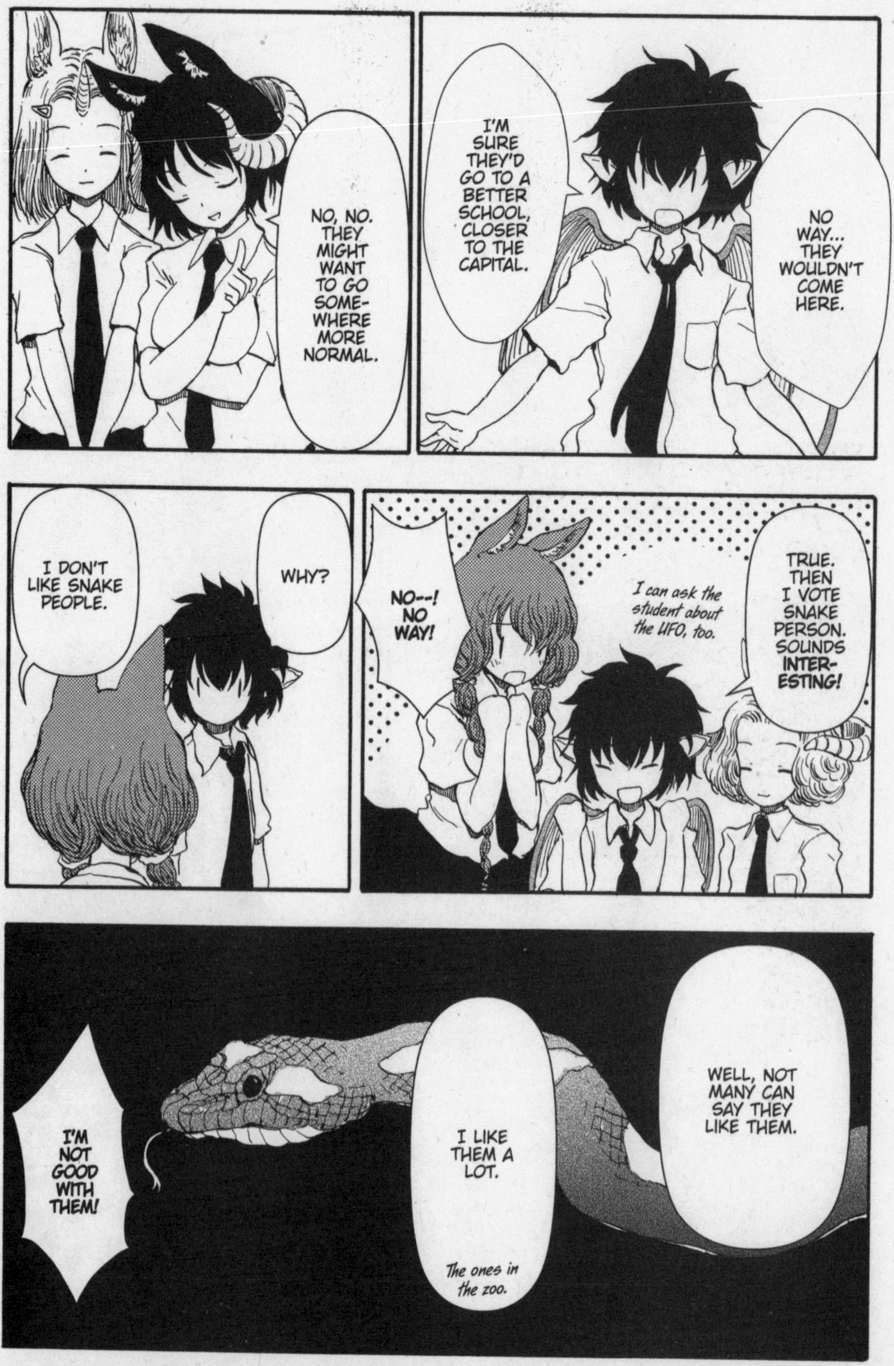
NO WAY... THEY WOULDN'T COME HERE.
I'M SURE THEY'D GO TO A BETTER SCHOOL, CLOSER TO THE CAPITAL.
NO, NO. THEY MIGHT WANT TO GO SOME-WHERE MORE NORMAL.
TRUE. THEN I VOTE SNAKE PERSON. SOUNDS INTER-ESTING!
I can ask the student about the UFO, too.
NO--! NO WAY!
WHY?
I DON'T LIKE SNAKE PEOPLE.
WELL, NOT MANY CAN SAY THEY LIKE THEM.
I LIKE THEM A LOT.
The ones in the zoo.
I'M NOT GOOD WITH THEM!

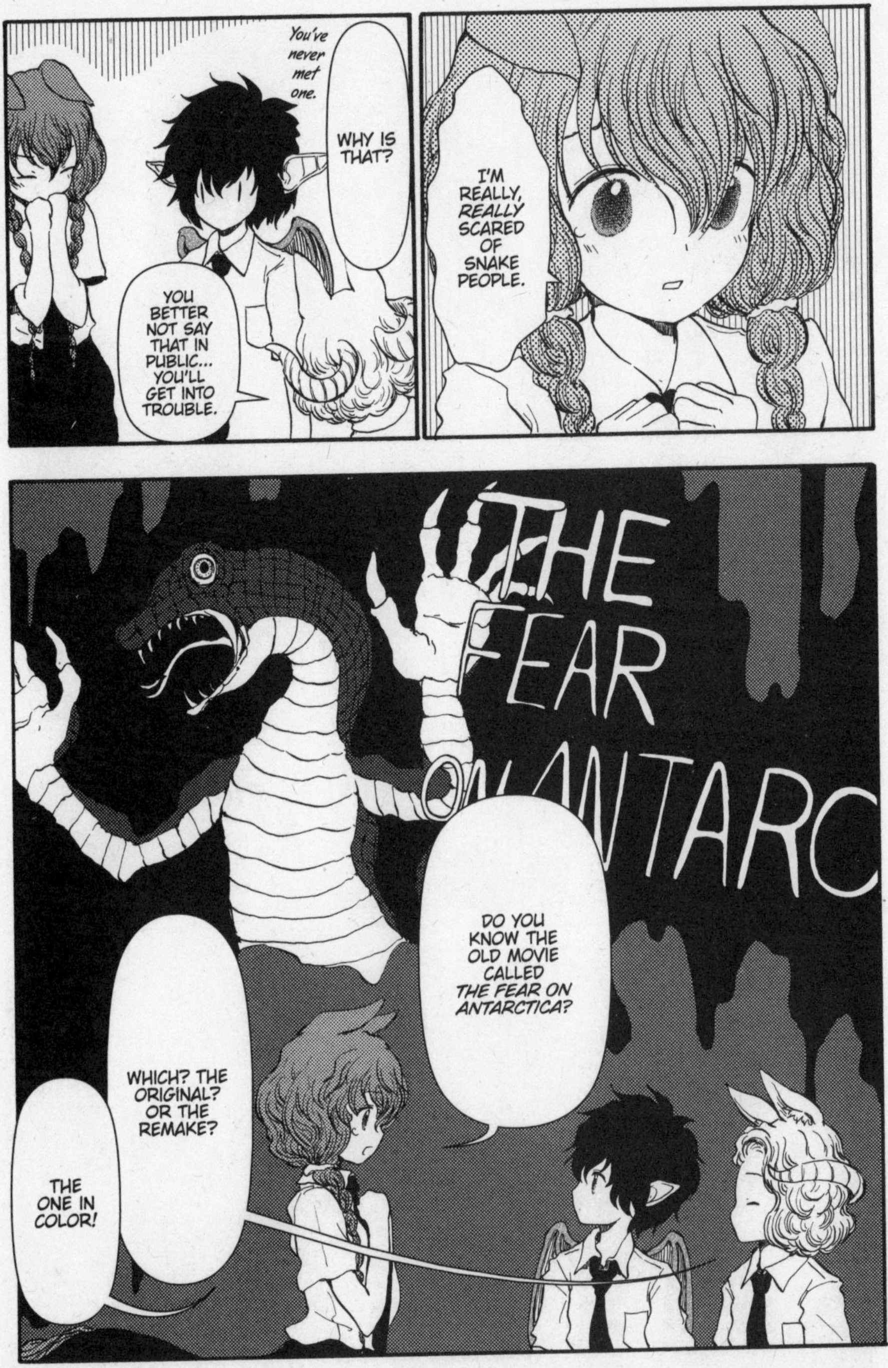
I'M REALLY, *REALLY* SCARED OF SNAKE PEOPLE.
WHY IS THAT?
You've never met one.
YOU BETTER NOT SAY THAT IN PUBLIC... YOU'LL GET INTO TROUBLE.
THE FEAR ON ANTARC
DO YOU KNOW THE OLD MOVIE CALLED *THE FEAR ON ANTARCTICA?*
WHICH? THE ORIGINAL? OR THE REMAKE?
THE ONE IN COLOR!

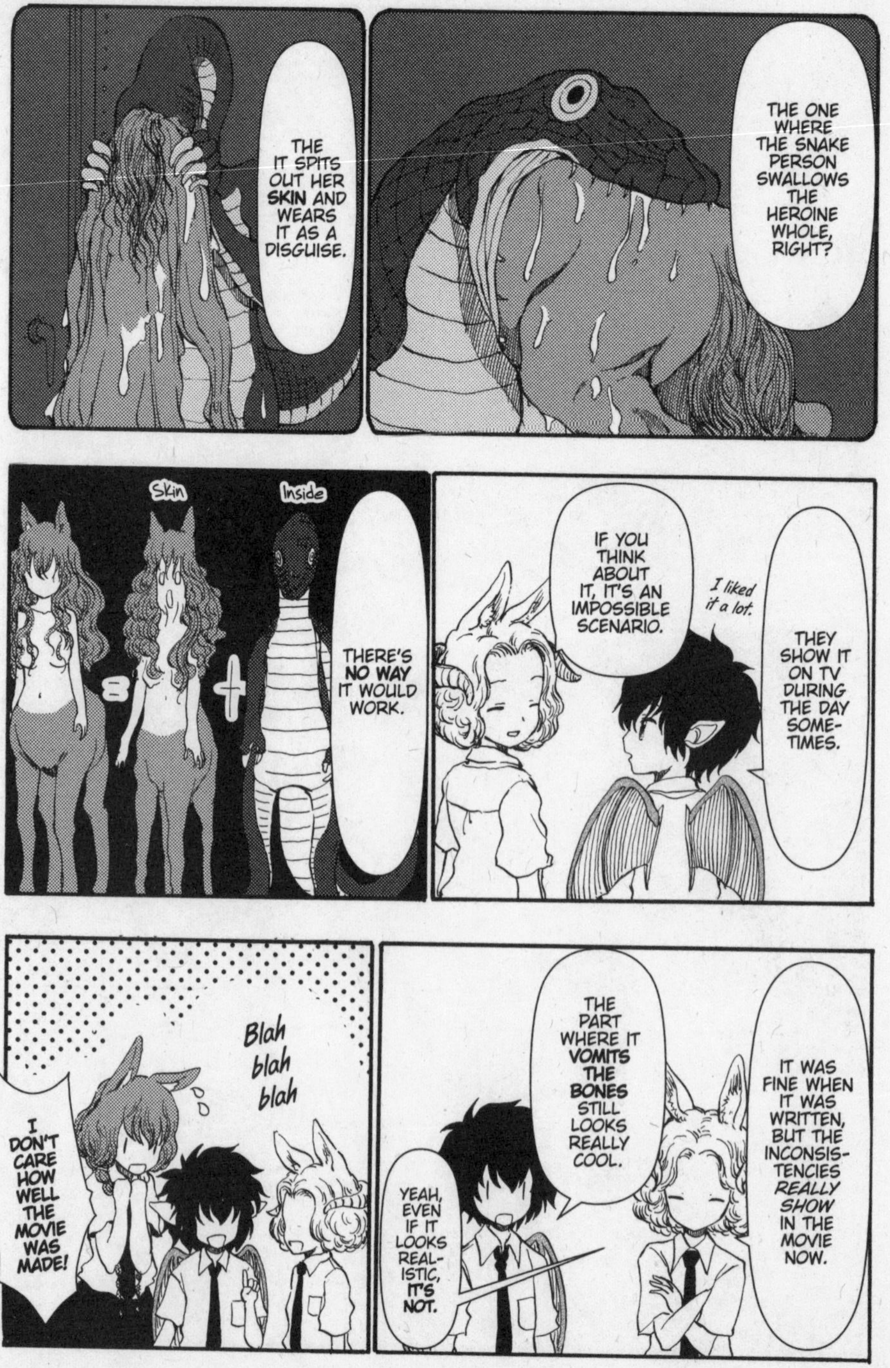
THE ONE WHERE THE SNAKE PERSON SWALLOWS THE HEROINE WHOLE, RIGHT?
THE IT SPITS OUT HER **SKIN** AND WEARS IT AS A DISGUISE.
THEY SHOW IT ON TV DURING THE DAY SOMETIMES.
I liked it a lot.
IF YOU THINK ABOUT IT, IT'S AN IMPOSSIBLE SCENARIO.
THERE'S **NO WAY** IT WOULD WORK.
Inside
Skin
IT WAS FINE WHEN IT WAS WRITTEN, BUT THE INCONSISTENCIES *REALLY SHOW* IN THE MOVIE NOW.
THE PART WHERE IT **VOMITS THE BONES** STILL LOOKS REALLY COOL.
YEAH, EVEN IF IT LOOKS REALISTIC, **IT'S NOT.**
Blah blah blah
I DON'T CARE HOW WELL THE MOVIE WAS MADE!

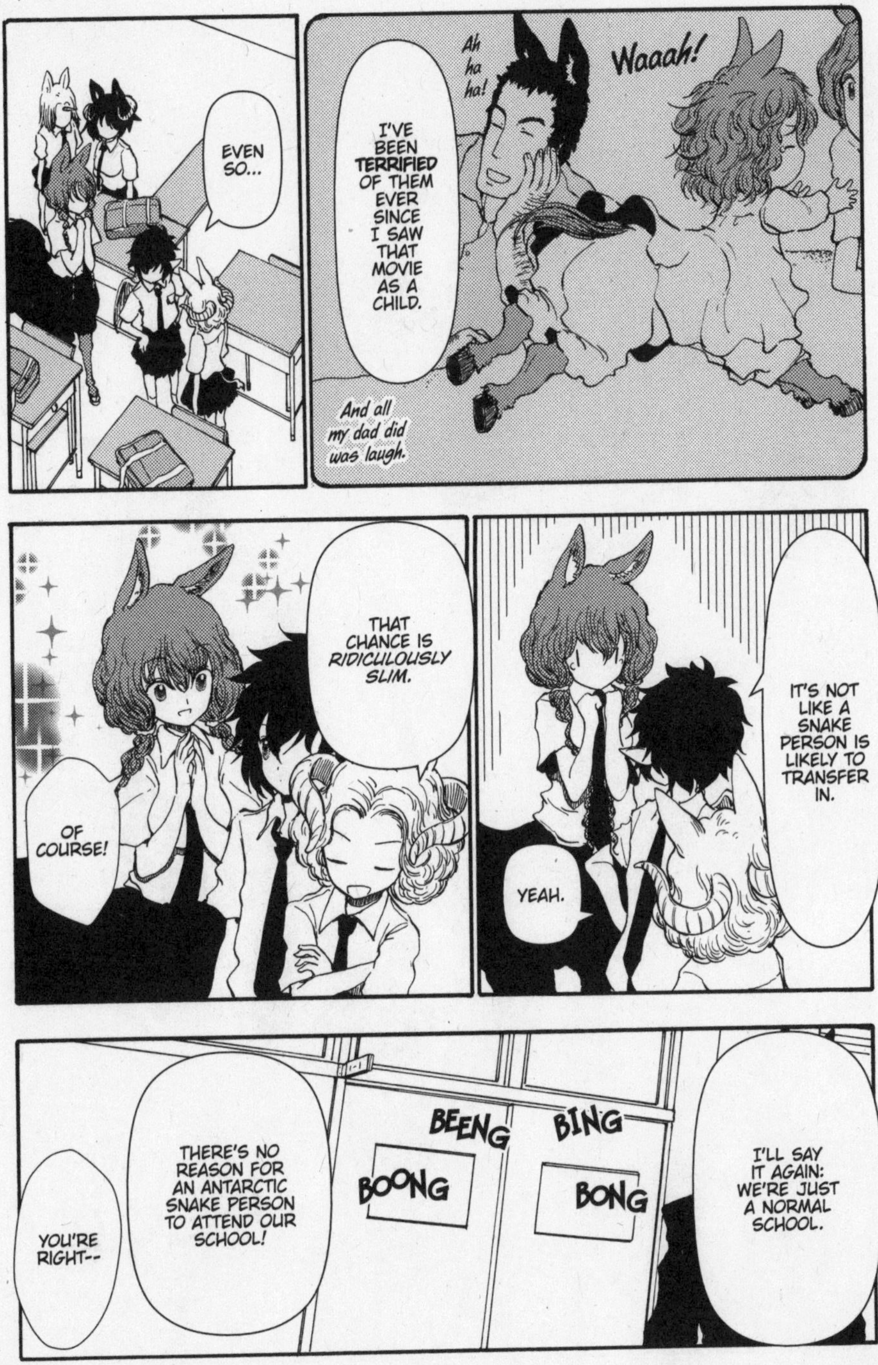
Waaah!
Ah ha ha!
I'VE BEEN TERRIFIED OF THEM EVER SINCE I SAW THAT MOVIE AS A CHILD.
And all my dad did was laugh.
EVEN SO...
IT'S NOT LIKE A SNAKE PERSON IS LIKELY TO TRANSFER IN.
YEAH.
THAT CHANCE IS RIDICULOUSLY SLIM.
OF COURSE!
I'LL SAY IT AGAIN: WE'RE JUST A NORMAL SCHOOL.
BING
BONG
BEENG
BOONG
THERE'S NO REASON FOR AN ANTARCTIC SNAKE PERSON TO ATTEND OUR SCHOOL!
YOU'RE RIGHT--

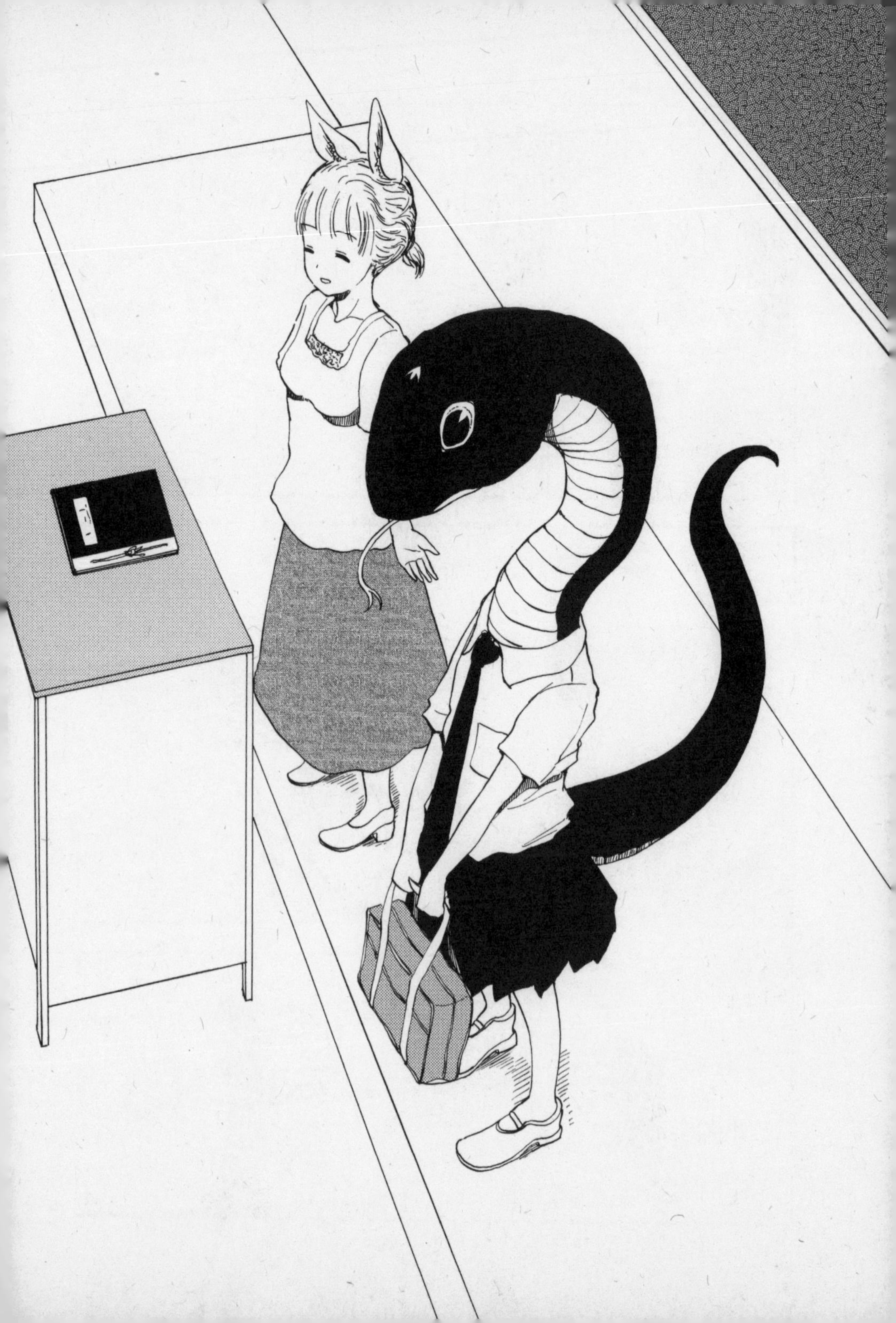

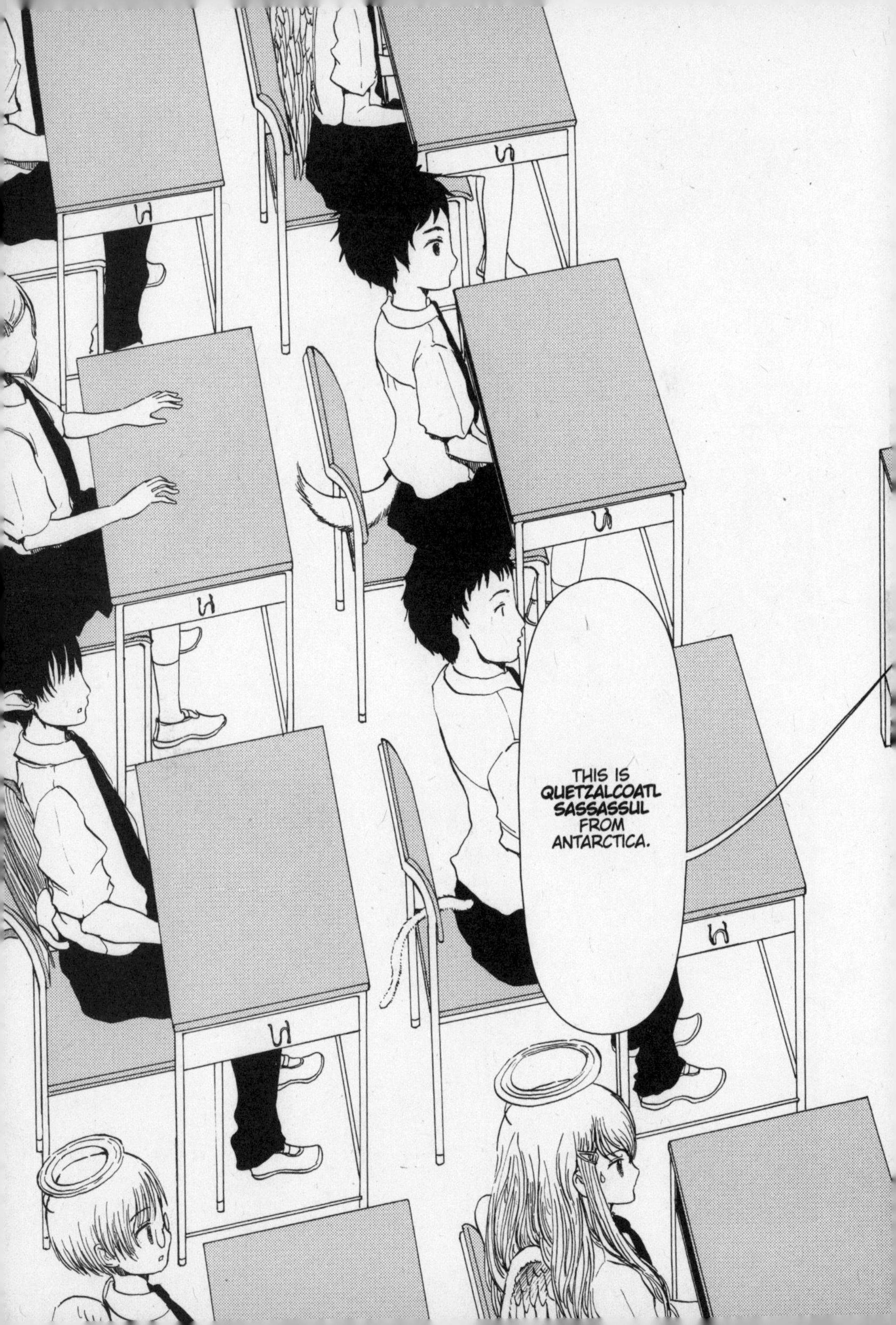
THIS IS QUETZALCOATL SASSASSUL FROM ANTARCTICA.

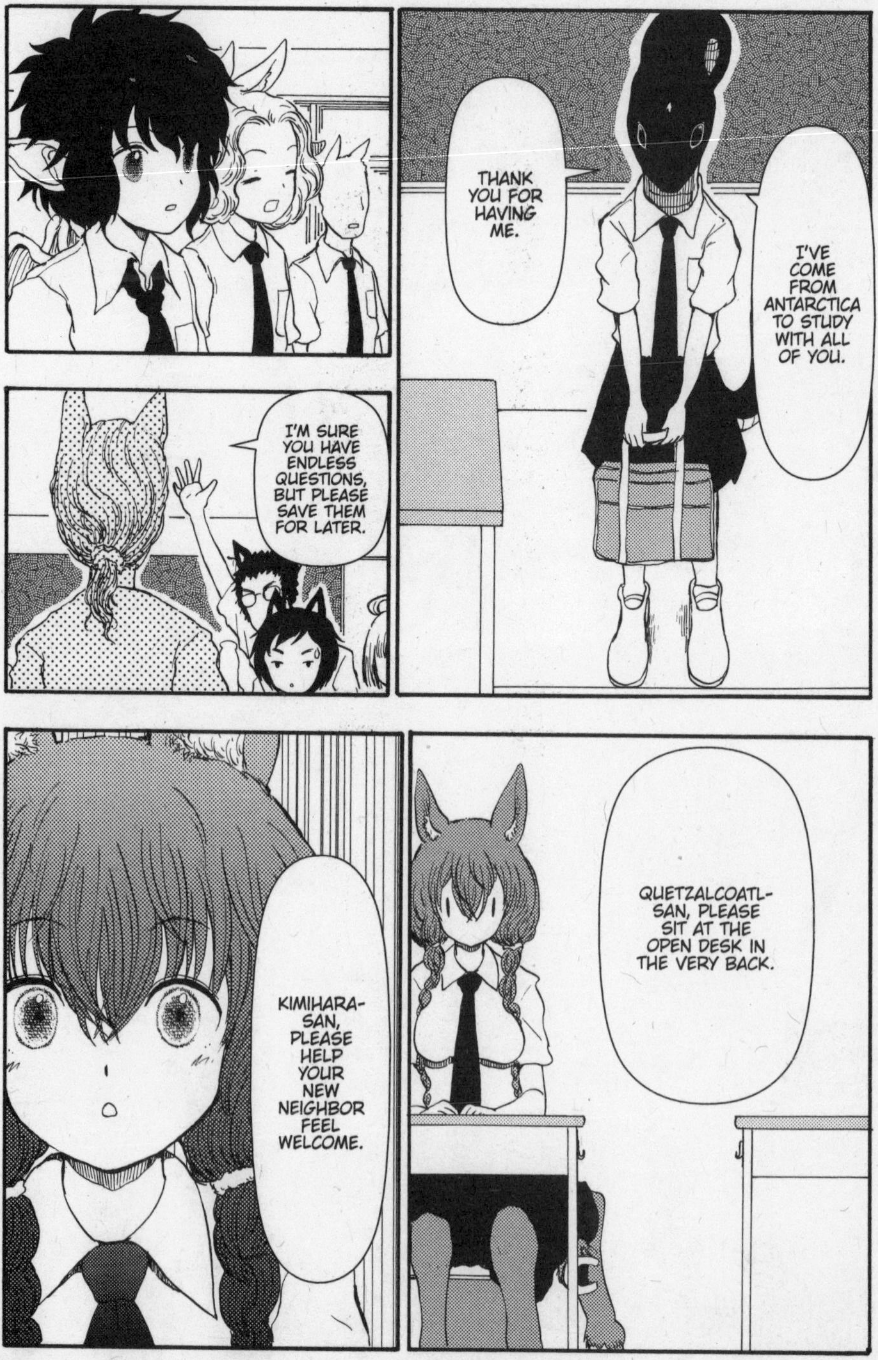
I'VE COME FROM ANTARCTICA TO STUDY WITH ALL OF YOU.
THANK YOU FOR HAVING ME.
I'M SURE YOU HAVE ENDLESS QUESTIONS, BUT PLEASE SAVE THEM FOR LATER.
QUETZALCOATL-SAN, PLEASE SIT AT THE OPEN DESK IN THE VERY BACK.
KIMIHARA-SAN, PLEASE HELP YOUR NEW NEIGHBOR FEEL WELCOME.

A Centaur's Life

AFTERWORD...

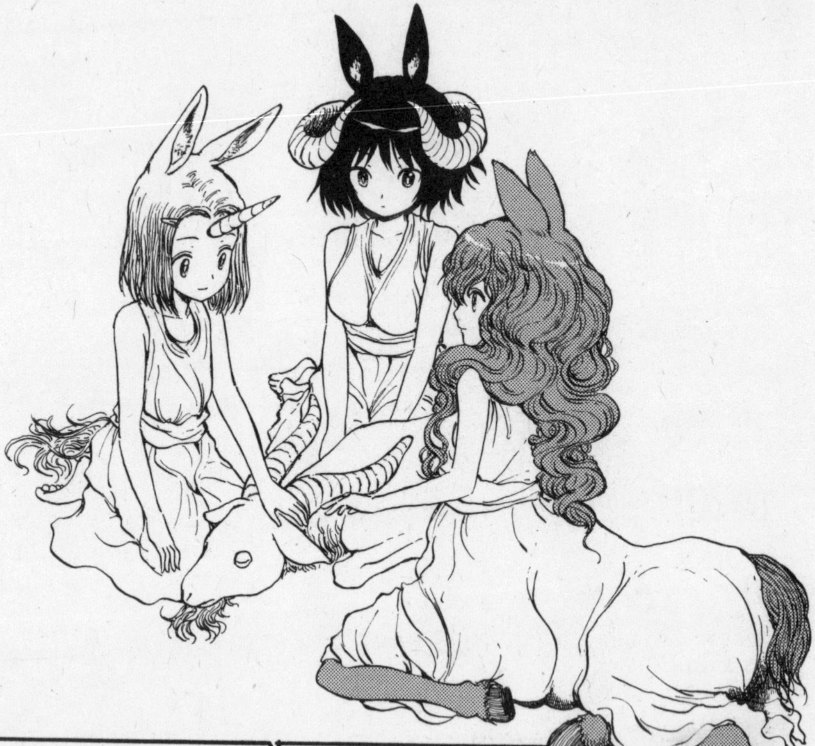

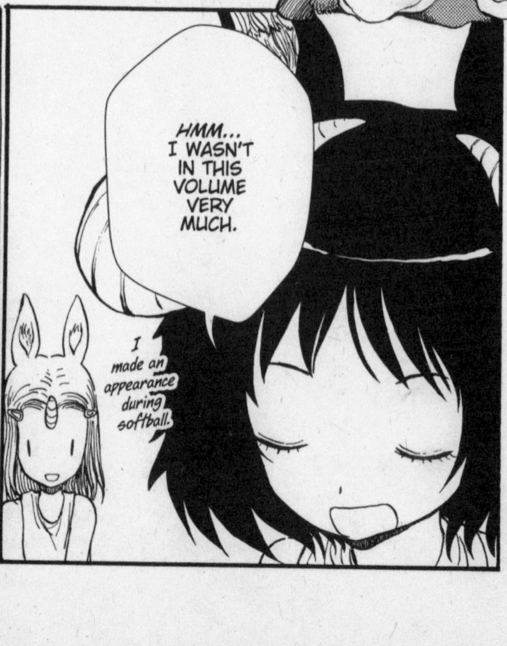
HMM... I WASN'T IN THIS VOLUME VERY MUCH.
I made an appearance during softball.

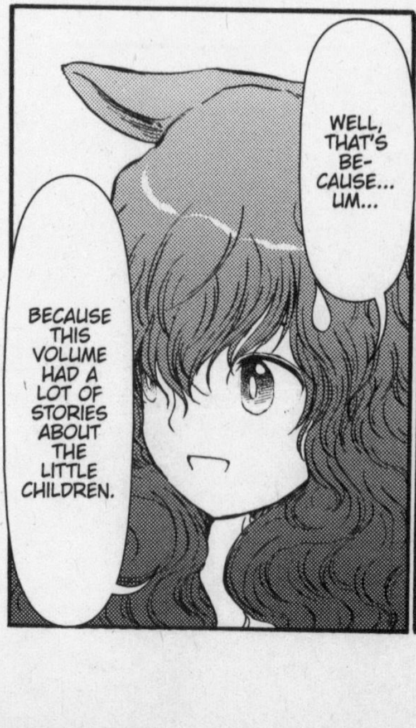
WELL, THAT'S BE-CAUSE... UM...
BECAUSE THIS VOLUME HAD A LOT OF STORIES ABOUT THE LITTLE CHILDREN.

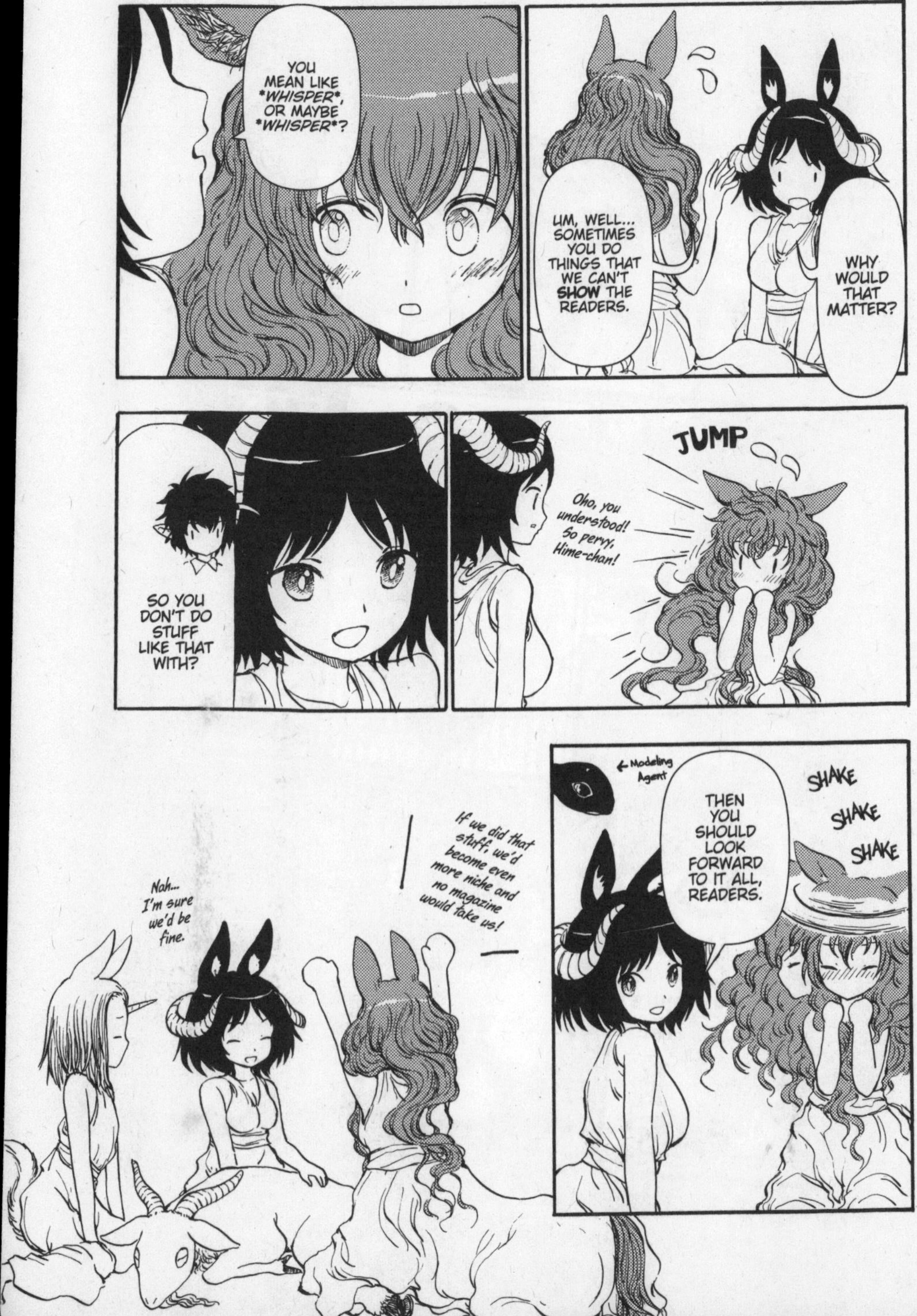
WHY WOULD THAT MATTER?
UM, WELL... SOMETIMES YOU DO THINGS THAT WE CAN'T SHOW THE READERS.
YOU MEAN LIKE *WHISPER*, OR MAYBE *WHISPER*?
JUMP
Oho, you understood! So pervy, Hime-chan!
SO YOU DON'T DO STUFF LIKE THAT WITH?
SHAKE
SHAKE
SHAKE
THEN YOU SHOULD LOOK FORWARD TO IT ALL, READERS.
← Modeling Agent
If we did that stuff, we'd become even more niche and no magazine would take us!
Nah... I'm sure we'd be fine.